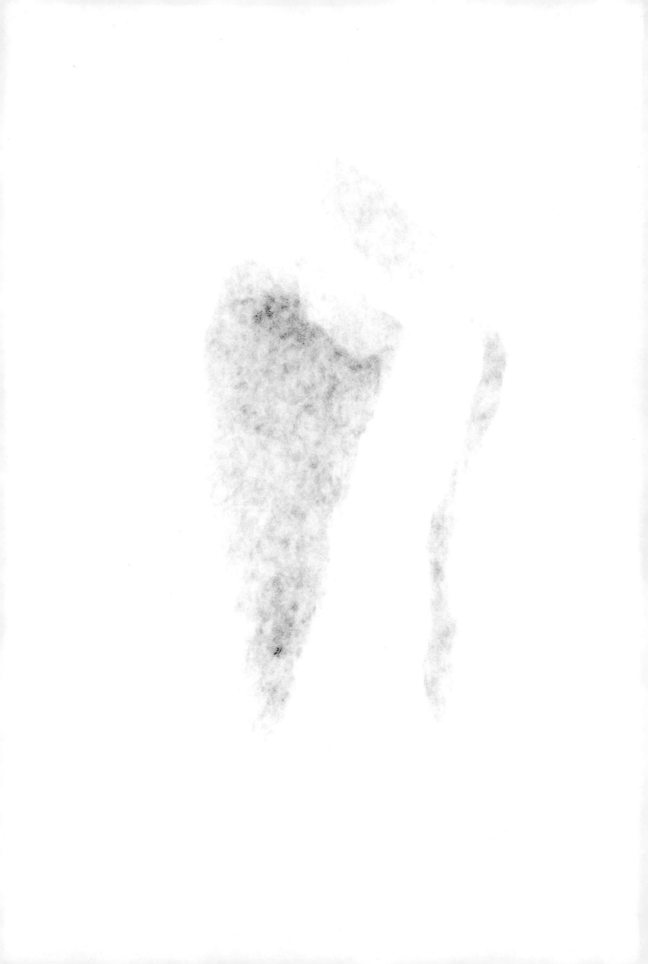

Evaluating Educational and Social Programs

Evaluation in Education and Human Services

Editors:

George F. Madaus, Boston College, Chestnut
  Hill, Massachusetts, U.S.A.
Daniel L. Stufflebeam, Western Michigan
  University, Kalamazoo, Michigan, U.S.A.

Previously published books in the series:

Evaluating Educational and Social Programs:

Guidelines for Proposal Review,
Onsite Evaluation, Evaluation Contracts,
and Technical Assistance

Blaine R. Worthen
Department of Psychology
Utah State University

Karl R. White
Departments of Special Education and Psychology
Utah State University

Kluwer-Nijhoff Publishing
a member of the Kluwer Academic Publishers Group

Boston/Dordrecht/Lancaster

Distributors for North America:
Kluwer Academic Publishers
101 Philip Drive
Assinippi Park
Norwell, MA 02061, USA

Distributors for the UK and Ireland:
Kluwer Academic Publishers
MTP Press Limited
Falcon House
Queen Square
Lancaster LA1 1RN, England

Distributors for all other countries:
Kluwer Academic Publishers Group
Distribution Centre
Post Office Box 322
3300 AH Dordrecht
The Netherlands

Library of Congress Cataloging-in-Publication Data

Worthen, Blaine R.
  Evaluating educational and social programs.

  (Evaluation in education and human services)
  Bibliography: p.
  Includes index.
  1. Education—United States—Evaluation—Methodology. 2. Educational
accountability—United States. 3. Educational surveys—United States. 4. Evaluation
research (Social action programs)—United States. I. White, Karl. II. Title. III. Series.
LB1028.W66 1987   379.1'54   86-20081
ISBN 0-89838-187-8

Printed in the United States of America

CONTENTS

Contents

PREFACE

During the past two decades, evaluation has come to play an increasingly important role in the operation of educational and social programs by national, state, and local agencies. Mandates by federal funding agencies that programs they sponsored be evaluated gave impetus to use of evaluation. Realization that evaluation plays a pivotal role in assuring program quality and effectiveness has maintained the use of evaluation even where mandates have been relaxed.

With increased use -- indeed institutionalization -- of evaluation in many community, state, and national agencies, evaluation has matured as a profession, and new evaluation approaches have been developed to aid in program planning, implementation, monitoring, and improvement. Much has been written about various philosophical and theoretical orientations to evaluation, its relationship to program management, appropriate roles evaluation might play, new and sometimes esoteric evaluation methods, and particular evaluation techniques. Useful as these writings are, relatively little has been written about simple but enormously important activities which comprise much of the day-to-day work of the program evaluator. This book is focused on some of these more practical aspects that largely determine the extent to which evaluation will prove helpful.

We deal in this volume with only four ways in which evaluation can be used to develop and maintain sound educational and social programs: (1) the use of evaluation to review and strengthen proposals for funding; (2) the use of onsite evaluation to strengthen and/or judge on-going programs; (3) procedures for establishing formal evaluation agreements or contracts; and (4) the provision of technical assistance to enable program administrators and staff members to improve both their program proposals and project operation. These four uses of evaluation are central to efforts of any agency or individual concerned with the administration or review of programs in education, health and human services, and other areas with high priority in a society's social agenda.

This book is unashamedly practical. We eschew here the theoretical discussions we may view as appropriate elsewhere. Instead, our intent has been (1) to provide straightforward discussion of how evaluation, applied to proposal reviews, onsite visits, and technical assistance, might serve to improve programs and projects, and (2) to provide guidelines for how to develop and use evaluation contracts that will assure that those evaluation activities will be effective. To make our discussions directly applicable, we provide specific guidelines, propose step-by-step procedures, and present many models and actual instruments that can be adapted by the reader.

This book is intended to serve two general audiences. First, it should be of great use for those persons responsible for the administration or operation of virtually any funded educational or social program or project. Second, it is aimed at the evaluation practitioners charged with reviewing and judging those programs. Within these broad audiences, this book should prove especially helpful to external proposal review panels, onsite evaluators, evaluation contractors and technical assistance providers and recipients. We hope this book proves as useful to these audiences as have the draft materials and training manuals from which we have drawn many of our examples and which have prompted colleagues to urge us to prepare this volume.

Blaine R. Worthen
Karl R. White

ACKNOWLEDGMENTS

We wish to acknowledge the contributions of the following individuals and agencies to our thinking and, in some cases, to instruments or other sample items contained in the appendices;

- Bill E. Cowan of the Utah State Office of Education, whose vision of what evaluation could do to improve proposal review and program and project operation prompted our initial design of many of the systems, procedures, and instruments used as samples herein;

- the Utah Council for Handicapped and Developmentally Disabled Persons, for permitting us to include examples of instruments and procedures developed for it by one of the authors and later refined by Richard Baer;

- our colleague Glenn I. Latham, who was responsible for revisions in some of the evaluation onsite system and instruments used as samples herein;

- David C. Lidstrom, who provided input into the design of some examples of onsite evaluation instruments and procedures presented in this book;

- the Wasatch Institute for Research and Evaluation and the Utah State Office of Education, for permitting us to incorporate herein portions of manuals prepared by those agencies to improve program and projects through better evaluation; we are grateful for their generosity to us and to the profession;

- The Association for Supervision and Curriculum Development, for their permission to include portions of materials to which they hold the rights; and

- the Colorado Department of Education, for allowing use of some guidelines developed for it by one of the authors.

Finally, we are indebted to Debra Peck, Sheree Winterbottom, and Sonja Nyman for their excellent technical assistance in producing this manuscript.

Blaine R. Worthen
Karl R. White

Evaluating Educational
and Social Programs

CHAPTER 1: INTRODUCTION

Many public and private educational and social service agencies distribute money to other public and private agencies or community groups to accomplish specific tasks. In almost all instances, funding agency officials and program administrators want to know whether the goals of the funded program or project were accomplished and whether the money was well spent. In those instances where program or project funding is determined by a competitive proposal process, administrators want to select those proposals which have the highest probability of success. In some cases they want to provide assistance and build capacity among applicants or project managers who might be less experienced.

Examples of such funding programs in the public sector include money distributed via the Developmental Disabilities Council in each state under Public Law 95-602, money distributed through State Education Agencies (SEAs) for innovation and development in local schools, money distributed through the Community Development Block Grant program, and money distributed through the Administration on Child, Youth, and Families to enable community agencies to operate Head Start programs. Indeed, the distribution of large blocks of money into smaller projects is one of the methods most frequently used by public and private agencies and organizations to address their objectives.

The purpose of such funding programs varies greatly. In some cases, there is a need to develop innovative and exemplary approaches to address widely recognized needs, such as reducing unemployment, enhancing the quality of life for the elderly, ameliorating the negative effects of teen-age pregnancies, or increasing reading comprehension among school children. In other cases, there is a need to contract for ongoing services, as is the case in establishing Head Start programs. And in still other cases, the purpose is to build capacity at the local level, as is the case with many of the Community Block Development Grants. In some cases, money is provided with a notion that it will serve as "seed" money in generating future support from other funding sources, and in other cases, there is the recognition that it is an ongoing service commitment.

Regardless of the specific purpose of the funding program, there is a need to evaluate how well the money is being spent and whether the purposes of the funding agency are being accomplished. Even though the process of distributing money from large blocks into smaller programs and projects has been going on for decades, there are remarkably few published guidelines about how it can be done most effectively. Consequently, program administrators approach the task very differently. In some instances the procedures they use are quite effective -- in other instances they are ineffective, or worse, just get in the way. Faced with the task of administering and evaluating such funding programs, many administrators find themselves somewhat confused because neither their training nor experience has prepared them for the task. Futhermore, there are remarkably few good examples of how to approach this task.

PURPOSE AND ORGANIZATION OF THIS BOOK

This book is intended to help fill the void. Based on field-based evaluations conducted over the last 15 years with several different types of programs and projects, guidelines and examples are offered which have broad applicability to a wide variety of educational and social services. Four general topics are covered, with a section of this book devoted to each:

- Proposal Solicitation and Review
- Onsite Evaluations
- Technical Assistance to Programs and Projects
- Evaluation Agreements and Contracts

Section I of this book is, appropriately, devoted to procedures and guidelines to improve the solicitation and review of competitive funding proposals. Most funded programs and projects have their genesis in such proposal review processes. Although not all money is distributed via such funding mechanisms, competitive proposal review is an increasingly popular method for funding social and educational programs and projects, particularly in the current era of shrinking financial resources. Given that bad proposals seldom lead to good programs or projects, it is patently clear that processes aimed at improving the quality of competitive proposals are important precursors to the establishment of effective educational and social programs. Similarly, procedures to select those proposals with highest potential from among the competitors is equally important. Inappropriately done, competitive proposal review is often little better than the non-competitive "good old boy" network, resulting in the selection of projects which may not have the capability to address the goals of the funding program. But appropriately conducted proposal reviews incorporate techniques that can be useful in assuring the success of the funding program, such as specifying the purposes of the funding program, training proposal reviewers, reporting the results of the review, and structuring the award of money. Unfortunately, there is virtually no place where these guidelines and techniques have been assembled for the use of those who are responsible for managing such programs.

Consequently, program managers are often left on their own in terms of how to structure the solicitation and review of proposals. Thus, they must frequently rely on trial and error or "learn as you go" procedures to decide how to solicit and review proposals. This is not only inefficient, but it usually results in a less than optimal product. The chapters in Section I are provided to help solve this problem.

Section II is devoted to procedures and guidelines for onsite evaluation, perhaps the most commonly used method for evaluating funded programs and projects. Virtually all administrators who are responsible for funding programs and projects of the type described above want to know if the money is being well spent and if the programs and projects are being successful in accomplishing their objectives. Relying only on self-report information is obviously inadequate, as dangerous as allowing banks to do their own financial audits. However, because financial resources are often limited, many people believe that effective external evaluations are impossible. Onsite evaluations provide an excellent and reasonably economical alternative to self-evaluation that, if properly structured, can provide reliable and valid information. Regardless of whether money for social or educational programs or projects has been distributed on a formula basis, through cooperative agreements, or on a competitive basis, appropriately conducted onsite evaluations can provide valuable information at very little cost. Unfortunately, without proper preparation and training, too many onsite evaluations are little more than a casual social visit among friends. Little value is derived from onsite evaluations when the purposes of the visit are not clearly structured, the evaluators are inadequately trained, the expectations are not established, and the expected products are not delineated. The chapters in Section II provide guidelines and examples of materials which can be used to increase the efficiency and products of such evaluation efforts.

Section III includes guidelines and examples of materials that can be used to provide technical assistance to agencies and groups who are well qualified in most areas, but may lack expertise in certain areas necessary to prepare competitive proposals or comply with specific requirements of the funding agency. For example, in selecting agencies to provide services to young handicapped children, reviewers need to identify those groups or agencies who are best able to provide high quality services. When selection is made on the basis of a competitive review, there is a danger that the decision will be influenced unduly by the applicant's ability to write a proposal, rather than their ability to provide high quality services. In such instances, it might be better to provide assistance to all prospective applicants so that the final decision is based more on capability as service providers, and less on capability as proposal writers. Similar examples of how technical assistance would be useful in accomplishing the goals of the funding agency could be given in the areas of program operation, accountability, and reporting. Based on the feedback of program managers, there is evidence that such an approach can substantially improve the operation of the funding program in accomplishing its goals. The guidelines and materials included in Section III chapters are based on the provision of such technical assistance to potential applicants and funding recipients.

Section IV is devoted to procedures and guidelines for establishing formal evaluation agreements and contracts, as well as for negotiating, monitoring, or terminating such agreements. Both evaluators and those who request their services are benefited if there is clarity about precisely what the evaluation study is expected to accomplish, and how, without clear agreements, otherwise good evaluations can be completely undermined by disputes and difficulties in client-evaluator relationships. The chapters in Section IV are provided to prevent such problems by showing how mutually shared understandings between evaluator and client can be achieved.

DESCRIPTION OF PROGRAMS UPON WHICH THIS BOOK IS BASED

This book contains practical guidelines and down-to-earth discussions of how to structure activities for onsite evaluations, proposal solicitation and review, and the provision of technical assistance. In addition, many concrete examples of both procedures and materials that have been used successfully are included. Most of the examples are drawn from actual experience with two funding programs -- one operated by a state education agency, the other operated by a state social services agency. Although a majority of the examples are drawn from these two funding programs, readers should note the applicability of these guidelines and materials to other educational and social programs. Readers are also encouraged to use the specific instruments and procedural guidelines contained at the end of each chapter, making appropriate modifications (and giving appropriate credit). Thus readers will have not only a general discussion of how to approach each task, but also step-by-step procedures and instruments they can modify to develop their own materials tailored to their own program.

In order to more fully understand the examples included in the remainder of this book, it is important to have a basic understanding of the objectives and organization of the two funding programs from which a majority of these examples are drawn.

A Program for Educational Innovation and Development

Under the Elementary and Secondary Education Act (ESEA) of 1965, state education agencies (SEAs) were provided with blocks of money to be used in developing innovative and exemplary programs. By the early 1980s approximately $180 million per year was distributed to SEAs, first under ESEA Title III, and later under the same authorization but relabeled as Title IV of the Education Consolidation Act. During President Reagan's first term, this money was combined with other monies to form the basis of the current Chapter 2 and Chapter 9 state block grants. Many states have continued to use a part of their state block grant money for innovative and developmental programs such as those long funded under Title IV.

Money distributed under the Title IV program was to fund efforts by Local Education Agencies (LEAs) who had identified serious gaps or weaknesses in their educational system, to enable them to develop new programs or adopt existing programs from elsewhere to respond to those areas of identified need. Funding of Title IV projects in Utah (the state in which the guidelines and materials included in this book were developed), was based on an annual competition in which each interested LEA submitted a proposal in competition with other LEAs of similar size and resources. Monies for the Title IV program were divided into two areas -- adoptable projects and developmental projects.

Adoptable projects were funded when an LEA identified a critical educational need within their system and was also able to identify an existing "validated" program which had a high probability of meeting this need. Information about the availability of such validated programs was obtained through the Department of Education's publication, **Educational Programs That Work** [1] and through the State Office of Education via various conferences, booklets, newsletters, and individual contacts. Only those programs that had demonstrated their effectiveness according to rigorous criteria established by either the state or federal government were available for adoption. In addition, staff from programs that wished to be on the adoptable list were required to be available to assist other local education agencies in adopting their particular programs. Adoptable programs were funded on a competitive basis usually for a one-year period. Funding of an adoptable project was based on the premises that (a) the LEA possessed or could obtain the expertise necessary to implement and test the effectiveness of the program; and (b) if the program proved to be effective in that particular application, the LEA was committed to continue the program after Title IV funding was expended.

Developmental projects were funded in those cases where an LEA identified a serious educational need within their system but was unable to locate an existing validated project which was appropriate for meeting this need. Proposals by LEAs to conduct a developmental project were required to demonstrate that the LEA had adequate resources and expertise to develop such a program and to evaluate the effectiveness of the program once it was developed. Funds for developmental projects were provided with the expectation that LEAs would continue, with their own resources, those programs which proved to be effective during the developmental period. Developmental projects were funded for up to five years but were typically funded for three years of developmental activities with a fourth and possibly fifth year of dissemination activity if the project proved to be effective.

The Title IV program from which the materials and procedures described in this book were drawn operated approximately 15 developmental and 20 adoptable projects each year. The funding level for each project ranged from $5,000 to $45,000 per year. By law, the state was required to conduct an evaluation of the Title IV funding program every three years for the federal government. In addition, however, state level program managers were anxious to operate the program in the most efficient manner possible so that the money would have maximum impact.

A Service Delivery Program for Handicapped Persons

The second program which provided examples used herein was operated by the Utah State Council for Handicapped and Developmentally Disabled Persons (hereafter referred to as the DD Council). Under Public Law 95-602, the governor of each state is required to establish a DD Council. One of the chief purposes of this council is to administer the state grant money which flows through from the federal government to each state. In Utah, as in most other states, one of the primary purposes of the state grant money is to enhance the delivery of services to handicapped and developmentally disabled persons.

Most states use this money for awarding project grants to public and private agencies and groups to (1) fill gaps in expanding service systems, (2) expand the reach of existing services to new groups of individuals, (3) foster the comprehensive planning of services and facilities to provide a more effective use of existing resources, (4) integrate services from various state, regional, and local agencies, or (5) develop innovative service systems and materials. Under the DD Act, each state must identify no more than two areas of priority service from among (a) case management services, (b) child development services, (c) alternative community living arrangement services, and (d) employment related activities. State grant money can then be spent to enhance the delivery of services in these priority areas. Nationwide, approximately $50 million was available in this funding program during fiscal year 1986.

DD projects in this particular state are funded on a competitive review basis, with all state, regional, and local public and private non-profit agencies and organizations eligible to apply. It is expected that the money for these projects will serve as "seed" money. In other words, this funding is not designed to relieve the state of support for existing services, and it is anticipated that those projects which are successful will be able to identify other sources of funding for ongoing operation. To underscore the "seed" nature of DD funds, applicants must provide during the first year of operation a 25% match for the federal money, which may be an in-kind contribution. During the second year, however, at least 10% of the total project funds must be a cash match and for the third year, the full 25% match must be cash. Grants are awarded on a yearly basis with renewal being on a competitive basis. No projects are funded for more than three years.

RELEVANCE OF THE EXAMPLES USED IN THIS BOOK TO OTHER PROGRAMS

The two funding programs described above are typical of literally hundreds of similar funding programs operated by state and federal agencies, as well as private foundations. The brief descriptions of those two particular programs should assist in interpreting relevant portions of the procedures and materials that are presented in the remainder of the book. The basic principles that will be demonstrated about conducting onsite evaluations, soliciting and reviewing proposals, establishing evaluation agreements, and providing technical assistance will, however, be applicable to a much broader range of projects.

The purpose underlying all of the procedures and guidelines presented in this book is that of program improvement. It is our belief that properly conducted evaluation can provide valid information about how well the project is accomplishing its objectives, while at the same time providing individual project managers with useful feedback and information for improving the quality of their program. The specific examples and procedures suggested have all been used in real-life situations and have resulted in demonstrable improvements in program operation and/or in the evaluations that serve those programs.

It should be noted at the outset that much of the material in this book consists of simple procedures and suggestions that represent little more than "common sense." Yet experience in educational and social service programs suggests that such common sense is too often lacking in many endeavors, with the result that inefficient and cumbersome systems are often developed, where simple and streamlined programs and procedures could have served as well. It is in the spirit of promoting simple and straightforward approaches to proposal solicitation and review, onsite evaluations, evaluation contracting, and technical assistance that the materials and procedures in this book are offered.

SECTION I: PROPOSAL REVIEW GUIDELINES AND INSTRUMENTS

Peer review of one sort or another is certainly the most frequently used method of judging the worth of a professional contribution in education and social sciences, as well as making decisions about the merit of proposed projects and programs and requests for funding.

During the past twenty years, there has been a great deal written about the peer review process. These writings have examined how the peer review process is used in refereed journals and/or funding programs, with respect to such issues as possible sources of bias [e.g., 2-5], reliability and validity of decisions [e.g., 6-8], and the utility of various approaches for operating such panels [e.g., 9-12]. (Bracketed numerals refer to reference list herein)

Although useful, this previous work is focused almost exclusively on the functioning of well-established peer review panels, which in most cases have been operating for a number of years. Such information is of relatively little use to someone faced with the responsibility of establishing a review process for the types of funding applications which are frequently sought by educational and social service agencies. In most cases, such a person has nowhere to turn for either guidelines or examples of materials used successfully in similar programs. This section is provided to serve as a source for those with such a need. Based on procedures for soliciting and reviewing funding proposals in education and social services agencies over multiple-year periods, the detailed procedures and examples of materials provided in the remainder of this section can be used by others in setting up a system of proposal solicitation and review for related types of programs.

VALUE OF SYSTEMATIC PROCEDURES

The value of **systematically** soliciting and reviewing proposals is emphasized by the results of a review done by the Utah State Office of Education three years following the implementation of a proposal solicitation, review, and selection system similar to that outlined in this section. The following conclusions were drawn from their review and analysis of that system.

1. The existence of a systematic process for soliciting, reviewing, and selecting competitive proposals is related to submission of better quality proposals. According to chairpersons and reviewers on teams who served during this period and in previous years, proposals submitted at the end of the three-year period (during which systematic proposal solicitation and review procedures were used) were generally of significantly higher quality than in the previous years. This observation was also borne out by an analysis in which proposals submitted during this period were compared with proposals submitted in prior years.

2. Local Education Agencies (LEAs) did not have difficulty following the format requested in the Request for Proposals (RFP) and outlined in sample "model" proposals which they were provided. In fact, most people appreciated knowing exactly what was expected and knowing on what basis proposals would be judged.

3. Ratings were generally higher on proposals which followed the format required in the RFP. As a result, the probability of funding was improved by adherence to proposal requirements specified in the RFP.

4. A small number of LEAs totally ignored the proposal specifications in the RFP. In general, such proposals tended to receive lower ratings. In other words, failure to include required information or sections in a proposal was generally a disadvantage to the applicant LEA.

5. There was substantial evidence that the system virtually eliminated from the award process the possibility of political considerations and individual influence (prevalent factors in far too many proposal review processes). The explicit criteria and procedures, the public nature of the review process, and the series of "checks and balances" which were built into the process by the Utah State Office of Education made such problems almost impossible.

6. Size and geographic location of the applicant agency did not seem to influence team ratings or recommendations for action in any particular manner, although receipt of technical assistance (as explained later) did seem to be related to proposal quality as judged by team ratings. It appeared that technical assistance in proposal preparation was particularly important to small districts without extensive previous experience in proposal preparation.

What was true for the review of Utah Title IV proposals is probably also true for review of proposals submitted to obtain funding for other educational and social service programs or projects, especially those operated under guidelines which are rigorous and/or technical in nature. In short, the better the quality and organization of submitted proposals, and the more fair, open, and objective the review received by those proposals, the better decisions will be about which programs to fund so that limited resources can have maximum impact to enhance the goals of the funding agency.

PURPOSE AND ORGANIZATION OF THIS SECTION

This section includes a summary of guidelines, steps, and procedures for a system of proposal solicitation and review. Although examples used in the section are drawn from materials developed in relation to the two specific funding programs described previously, they will have broad applicability to the review of virtually any type of educational or social services proposal. Foundations, universities, state and federal agencies, and any other agency which invites and reviews competitive proposals would be able to use these procedures, guidelines, and materials, with only minor adaptations.

The section is subdivided into three chapters, within which specific procedures and supporting materials relating to the following general topics are discussed:

- Chapter 2: Strategies for Eliciting High-Quality Proposals
- Chapter 3: Preparing for the Proposal Review Process
- Chapter 4: Conducting the Proposal Review Process and Presenting the Results

CHAPTER 2: STRATEGIES FOR ELICITING HIGH-QUALITY PROPOSALS

It is of little use to set up careful proposal review processes aimed at selecting for funding high-quality proposals if nothing has been done first to assure that there will be such high-quality proposals among those reviewed. Nothing is more frustrating (and futile) than to have to award earmarked funds to the "best" proposal(s) from a batch where none even rises to the level of mediocrity. It seems obvious, therefore, that the first concern of funding agencies should be to encourage and facilitate the submission of good proposals.

There are three general strategies for eliciting high-quality proposals: (1) providing technical assistance to those who, without it, would be less likely to submit competitive proposals; (2) developing and distributing a "proposal solicitation" which sets a high-quality standard for those who submit proposals in response to the solicitation; and (3) developing and disseminating "model" proposals that can be used as a guideline by those who wish to submit a proposal.

Providing technical assistance to potential applicants who have limited expertise in proposal writing is dealt with extensively in Section III and will not be discussed further here. The development of high-quality proposal solicitations and the use of model proposals are discussed and illustrated in the remainder of this chapter.

THE PROPOSAL SOLICITATION

Proposals submitted under any funding authorization will usually be no better than the announcement or solicitation used to elicit those proposals. We are concerned in this chapter with how potential applicants might best be encouraged to submit proposals and guided so that their proposals are of high quality and directly relevant to the funding agency's goals. There are two general ways that funding agencies typically use to solicit such proposals. The first is the development and dissemination of a Request for Proposals and the second is to invite prospective applicants to submit a concept paper or prospectus that might serve as the basis for later submission of a full-blown proposal. Each of these procedural options is considered in this section.

The Request for Proposals (RFP) Approach

In the RFP approach,[1] the funding agency or program sponsor who will award funds prepares and distributes a detailed, written request for proposals. This request, along with its appropriate cover letter or other transmission device, serves to (1) announce the availability of funds and the nature of the funding competition, and (2) outline the information potential applicants would need to know to enable them to submit a good proposal. The intent of the RFP is to solicit proposals from as many qualified applicants as possible and to cause those proposals to include the information necessary to enable the funding agency to make sound judgments about which proposal(s) should be funded.

Obviously, there are a variety of equally acceptable ways to structure an RFP; the important thing is to make certain that it communicates clearly the expectations of the funding agency and sets expectations and standards sufficiently high so that proposals which meet those standards will be of an acceptably high quality. Yet, far too frequently, the RFP will be so vague that it provides little direction or guidance to the potential applicant. Sometimes RFPs will be very specific on details to be included in the proposal but will fail to include important details, such as the activities' duration or deadlines, expected outcomes, or the resources available to conduct the activities.

Failure to include such important information is not necessarily carelessness; often it results from misguided ideas about what should and should not be included.

Before preparing a proposal the applicant is entitled to know what specific outcomes are expected by the funding sponsor. For example, if the sponsor wants quarterly reports, that constitutes more work than an annual report, and it will (and should) cost more. If, in addition to completing the particular project outlined, the applicant is expected to help demonstrate the products of the project to other potential users, the applicant has a right to know that so all expectations are clear before time and energy are invested in the preparation of a proposal.

Similarly, if constraints exist, the RFP should be candid. For example, if certain information will not be available to the applicant or if the project must be wholly completed in five months or if the applicant will be required to work with a specific subcontractor to accomplish certain project tasks, the applicant is entitled to know that before preparing a proposal.

---

[1] Variations of this approach such as the RFQ (Request for Quotations) are not dealt with separately here because the principles and considerations for their use are similar to those discussed here under the RFP approach.

An adequate RFP must include at least the following information:

- A cover letter to inform applicants of the RFP's purpose
- Description of the need addressed by the funding program and the context in which that need is to be met
- Clear statement of the goals of the funding program
- Constraints and conditions which would affect funded projects
- Specific outcomes and specifications expected of funded projects
- Resources available for project activities
- Criteria and processes to be used in reviewing submitted proposals.

The content which should generally be included in some form in each of these sections of an RFP for funding educational and social service programs is discussed below.

Cover letter. A cover letter which introduces the RFP to all eligible applicants should be written by someone with as much authority and "clout" as possible. In those cases where the funding program is a joint effort, it would be useful to have key people from each agency sign the cover letter. This letter should briefly summarize the purpose of the funding program and emphasize the deadline by which applications must be received. A contact person who can answer questions about the RFP should be named; and if technical assistance in writing the proposal is available, the cover letter should explain how such assistance can be obtained. It should be patently clear that it is of little use to expend energy developing a good RFP if every effort is not made to send that document to all qualified potential bidders and to generate as much interest in the application process as possible. Consequently, this cover letter should be short, attractive, and designed to arouse the interest of potential applicants. Consequently, this is not the appropriate place for detailed explanations of the nuances of the funding program. Such details can be explained in the actual RFP.

Need addressed by the funding program. Each funding program should be targeted to a particular need. Such a need may be quite broad, as was the case in the Title IV program (i.e., develop innovative and exemplary educational programs); somewhat more targeted, as was the case in the DD Council program (enhance the quality of services for developmentally disabled persons in the area of case management and alternative community living arrangements); or highly specific (e.g., develop and disseminate a handbook which will accompany an inservice training program for teaching social workers about the alternatives for treating chronic drug abusers). Regardless of the specificity of the funding program, this section of the RFP should outline the historical, contextual, empirical, and/or theoretical basis for the funding program. It should summarize briefly other work that has served as a precursor to the currently identified need, as well as discussing how needs in this area might affect other areas.

Goal of the funding program. As noted above, funding programs may address broad general needs or highly specific needs. In all cases, however, the RFP should make the goal of this particular funding program clear. In other words, there are a great many different types of goals which could be addressed by a funding program which has identified as a critical need the dramatic increase in teenage pregnancy and child bearing. The goal of such a funding program may be to reduce the incidence of teenage pregnancy and child bearing, or to better educate service providers about the increased incidence and associated problems, or to develop innovative programs to provide support for teenage mothers that will allow them to finish school and provide proper care to their child. In some cases, the agency will wish to leave the goal very broad. In other cases, it will be important to narrow down the type of proposals it wants to fund to address that particular need. Unless such specifications concerning goals are made, it should come as no surprise that many of the proposals will be "off target", regardless of how well the need has been defined.

Project constraints and conditions. Responding to an RFP requires attention to a great many details--the "nuts and bolts" of proposal development. A section of the RFP which is clearly set off from other parts of the document should specifically summarize information about who is eligible to apply (e.g., public and private non-profit agencies only, anybody, profit making agencies), how payment will be made (e.g., fixed price, cost reimbursement, cost plus), the timing of such payment, the duration of project funding that will be available, whether continuation applications will be required for multi-year projects, and whether there are certain requirements of grant acceptance (such as agreement to onsite evaluations, provision of reports and records, requirements for matching funds, or the maintenance of certain types of records). The exact details that will be contained in this section of the RFP will vary substantially depending on the administrative requirements of the funding agency, the type of program being funded, and the relationship of this funding program to other initiatives in which the funding agency is participating or sponsoring. The important point is that authors should not have to wade through a lot of irrelevant information to determine what sorts of constraints and requirements will be a part of the funding program. Consequently, it is important that this information be clearly set off and emphasized as a part of the RFP.

Project outcomes and proposal specifications. This section is related to the earlier sections on need and goals but provides substantial additional detail. The specific objectives of the funding program should be presented in detail. If the sponsoring agency has particular types of projects in mind, it is helpful if examples of those projects are provided. The target population to be benefited by the project or process should be specified. A summary of the type of information the sponsoring agency would like applicants to provide about their past history in doing similar kinds of work and details about how they propose to accomplish and evaluate the proposed work should be provided. One of the most helpful inclusions in an RFP is a section-by-section outline of what the funding agency wants included in the proposal. Such an outline should provide a brief summary of the contents of each section, as well as suggested page limits for each section. In some cases, it may be wise to be firm about the number of pages allowed so that all applicants compete on the same basis with respect to the amount of information they provide. This not only makes it easier for reviewers to judge the relative worth of various proposals, but also makes it more equitable for competing applicants.

Resources available for project activities. Some funding agencies make it a practice not to specify the amount of money available for the proposed activities, believing that if they do so every applicant will ask for the maximum amount and the agency may be cheated out of "bargain buys" they might otherwise obtain. More often than not, such a strategy is counter productive. The applicant needs to know what resources are available for the task(s) outlined in the RFP. If the sponsor can only commit $3,000 to the task, that information must be provided. Otherwise, the bidder is liable to waste time and money in the preparation of a proposal that calls for a $15,000 project. When applicants are left to play guessing games as to how completely they should approach outlined tasks, the resulting decisions about funding are often based more on the applicant's ability to guess how extensively the funding agency wishes each task to be pursued than on the qualifications of the applicant or the excellence of the proposal.

Proposal review criteria and processes. It is essential that applicants know on what basis their proposal will be evaluated. In most cases, it is best for reviewers to use some sort of point allocation system, as will be described later. If such a system is used, the criteria in the system and the points associated with each criterion should be included as a part of the RFP. Furthermore, it is useful to provide applicants with an example of the actual rating system that will be used by reviewers. Given that the purpose of the review process is to select those applicants who are best qualified to accomplish the goals of the funding program, there is no reason to play games with applicants by leaving them to guess what it is reviewers will value highly or the process they will use in judging proposals.

An example of an RFP used in the Title IV project appears, with an accompanying cover letter, at the end of this chapter in Exhibit 2.1. As can be seen from this sample RFP, the specific ways in which the sections outlined above are addressed will depend on agency requirements and the type of funding program being used. It is evident from this example that the requirements and purposes of the funding agency can be easily tailored to suit their own purposes within the guidelines offered above. For example, in the sample RFP, the State Education Office thought it would be more equitable if large school districts competed against other large school districts, instead of pitting them against smaller districts with less experience in obtaining external grants and contracts. Therefore, the total amount of money was allocated to four separate categories, depending on the size of the district. Furthermore, the goal of the Title IV RFP was very broad, therefore, little specific direction was given about the specific types of projects required.

In summary, it should be clear that the more specific and clear the RFP, the higher the probability that appropriate and relevant projects will be proposed and that the projects selected will be those most capable of accomplishing the goals of the sponsoring agency. One caution should be noted, however. There are two dangers in pre-specifying every detail that one wishes in a proposal. First, by requiring applicants to stipulate some details about the procedures they deem appropriate, the funding agency may have a greater variety of alternatives to select from. One of these alternatives may be both creative and uniquely responsive and thus, although unanticipated, the chosen option. Secondly, providing too much detailed substantive or procedural information invites proposals from those who have excellent verbal skills but little real substantive or procedural understanding. This kind of applicant, by writing a reflection of the RFP in the proposal response, may receive funding but be unable to perform the task. It is easier to identify applicants who lack genuine competence or sophistication when potential applicants are required to develop at least a reasonable part of the project plan on their own.

The Prospectus Approach

A useful technique for assisting applicants in preparing relevant proposals, as well as streamlining the review process, is to require all interested applicants to submit a brief prospectus prior to the deadline for receipt of full proposals. Potential applicants are contacted by letter, briefly describing the funding agency's need which exists. A brief statement, perhaps 500 to 1,000 words, is then submitted by interested applicants, outlining how they would approach the problem, along with a statement of their qualifications.

Requiring such a prospectus from interested applicants provides the sponsoring agency with an idea of how many proposals will be submitted (which can assist in planning for the review process), as well as providing an opportunity to give feedback to applicants who may be proposing irrelevant projects or processes. In such cases, corrective feedback can be given to assist applicants to better focus their proposal. Alternately, the sponsoring agency can review the prospectuses and select, on a competitive basis, those which seem to be most on target and most promising. Then, only those selected applicants can be invited to submit full proposals.

Another advantage of requiring a prospectus to be submitted by interested applicants is that some potential applicants may be willing to prepare a brief (1-3 page) prospectus, but would not be willing to prepare a full proposal unless they had some indication that their ideas and proposed activities would be positively viewed. In this way, the prospectus process can serve not only to encourage additional applications but also is often the only way to get the best qualified (who are often the most busy) individuals or agencies to apply.

An example of the materials used in inviting a prospectus for the DD Council project appears at the end of this chapter as Exhibit 2.2.

Choosing Between the RFP and Prospectus

Both the RFP and prospectus approach has strengths and limitations that should be considered in determining which is best suited to the particular situation.

Advantages of the RFP approach. There are three primary advantages to the RFP approach. First, it provides the funding agency a wide range of fully developed proposals from which to choose. Given more well-developed alternatives, one should be able to reach a better informed decision. The second major benefit of the RFP is the enhanced credibility of the funding decisions that can result from the rigorous and careful selection that use of an RFP can facilitate. Third, the RFP sometimes shows that there are possible gains from encouraging two or more applicants to combine their efforts in one funded project. Obviously, it is unethical for any funding agency to steal an idea from a rejected proposal and suggest that another selected applicant employ it. In many instances, the practice is illegal as well as unethical. However, if a client believes that two or more applicants acting collaboratively would be the best option, it is legitimate to explore that possibility with them.

Disadvantages of the RFP approach. There are disadvantages to the RFP route, as well. It is more costly for all parties. The funding agency must invest time and money in (a) preparing and distributing the RFP to prospective applicants and (b) judging the proposals received. The applicant must bear the costs of preparing a full proposal. Since these costs can be substantial, one may be restricting the award of project funds to those agents which have sufficiently large capital resources to permit them to speculate in the proposal preparation market. There is no evidence to suggest that capital reserves are necessarily related to quality of funded projects. Indeed, for many educational and social service projects, small-scale organizations or individuals often provide better and "more responsive" service.

Advantages of the prospectus approach. This approach is less costly for both parties than the RFP approach and therefore more feasible in many instances. Similar to the RFP approach, it serves to enhance the credibility of the evaluation and reduce charges of bias. It provides funding agencies with a preview of how many full-blown proposals might be submitted and an opportunity to limit that number if they wish, by selecting the best prospectuses and inviting only those applicants to submit full proposals. It provides funding agencies with an opportunity to provide feedback on the prospectus itself, thus redirecting applicants to develop a full proposal that is more on target than it otherwise might have been. It may attract busy, well-qualified applicants who might not respond to more demanding RFP requirements.

Disadvantages of the prospectus approach. This approach does not, however, permit applicants to develop ideas in sufficient detail to convey all the innovative strategies they might use if funded. Yet to require more would be to necessitate greater expenditure of the funding agency's resources to review longer, more complex plans. It might also draw unfairly on the applicant's resources, because if the funds are insufficient to support an RFP approach, the dollar amount of the project may be too small to warrant a heavy investment of the applicant's time and other resources in an effort to obtain project funding. Another caution is also in order. There are those who have mastered the terminology and semantics of education or social sciences without necessarily acquiring genuine expertise in these areas. A brief statement prepared by such an individual can be very persuasive in the absence of any requirement that the applicant demonstrate specific knowledge and expertise that is more apparent in a full-blown proposal. The rhetoric of a prospectus is obviously no substitute for a well-conducted project.

When to use the various approaches. Given the potential losses and benefits associated with each approach, how does one decide which to use? One thing is certain --

neither is appropriate unless the competition is truly open. If the award of funding is "wired," i.e., the most probable winner(s) identified prior to the receipt of proposals, or the solicitation aimed to favor a known applicant, disaster lurks. In the first place, the number of proposals one can expect to receive in response to future solicitations will drop substantially, for proposal writers in any field are a canny lot who soon learn which agencies pretend to use open competition to satisfy legal requirements, but really have the winner(s) picked in advance all along. Secondly, those who discover that they have wasted resources in a rigged competition are likely to make every effort to discredit the work that does go on. Finally, if it can be proved that the funding award was "wired," legal action might be instituted.

The financial resources available should be considered when one is reaching a decision on which option to choose. One can compute the costs associated with an RFP process -- staff salary and benefits, consultant fees, production and mailing costs, and so on. Comparing these costs to the dollars one is willing or able to commit to the funded project permits one to make a better judgment about whether the benefits of the RFP mechanism are worth the costs. Assume that the minimum expenditure for an RFP preparation and proposal review for a one-project competition is $500. It makes little sense to spend that amount of money if the total project funding will be $3,000 or less. Perhaps it is only worthwhile if the funding exceeds $5,000. Conversely, the cost of an RFP may be $10,000 and still be considered minuscule if it leads to better decisions about funding of 50 projects in a funding program which awards a total of $500,000 to those projects. In short, there is no single universal standard in either absolute or proportional terms. Perhaps the best advice one can offer is the old adage "you get what you pay for." The funding agency should decide what can be realistically afforded. The prospectus approach is the more economical option for soliciting proposals. Although initially expensive, use of the RFP approach (if it can be afforded) may lead to long-range savings by identifying qualified applicants with creative, inexpensive approaches to conducting the project.

Model Proposals

Proposal quality can often be enhanced by providing prospective applicants with a model of the type of proposal that is expected. These may be actual proposals selected during a previous review because of their quality, although it is generally more desirable to use fictitious model proposals which have been developed specifically to serve as examples. Such model proposals should follow the same format as the proposals to be submitted and should demonstrate how each expectation and specification in the RFP might be addressed. Such models might also be annotated, with accompanying instructional and explanatory comments added to help potential applicants see why each section of the model proposal was handled as it was. An example of a model proposal used in the Title IV project, with an appropriate cover letter, is shown at the end of this chapter in Exhibit 2.3 . Based on the experience of using this model proposal, it appears that the annotation is particularly useful.

EXHIBITS FOR CHAPTER 2: STRATEGIES FOR ELICITING HIGH QUALITY PROPOSALS

EXHIBIT 2.1: TITLE IV REQUEST FOR PROPOSALS

250 EAST 500 SOUTH STREET · SALT LAKE CITY, UTAH 84111 · TELEPHONE (801) 533-5431

UTAH STATE OFFICE OF EDUCATION

MEMORANDUM

TO: All Local District Superintendents

FROM: _____, Administrator
                Division of Program Administration

DATE: February 2, 1986

SUBJECT: Request for Title IV - Part C Proposals for FY XX

Enclosed are materials compiled by our Dissemination and Educational Development Staff which may be used to prepare applications for funding under **Title IV - Part C: Improvement in Local Education Practice**. Since guidelines for this project have been modified during the past year, **interested district personnel should read all of the enclosed materials and follow the instructions very carefully**. We also request that you distribute this information to others in your LEA who may have responsibility or interest in applying for Title IV - Part C funds.

Two primary sources of assistance are available to those Districts which complete an application. Attached are two "model" proposals for a hypothetical project. In addition to serving as an example, the model proposals include additional explanation and written instruction about the required format and content of proposals submitted by LEAs for Title IV - Part C funding. Secondly, the Utah State Office of Education (USOE) is prepared to assist those LEAs which have identified a serious educational need within their system, and want to apply for Title IV - Part C funds, but feel they lack sufficient in-house expertise to write a competitive proposal. LEA personnel who feel they may require assistance from USOE in completing their application should tear out, sign and return page one of the attached memorandum before 5:00 p.m., March 2, 1986 (or preferably much earlier to assure the LEA a choice in personnel who will provide such technical assistance).

Persons who have any other questions, should contact Mr. Bill Cowan as soon as possible.

REQUEST FOR ASSISTANCE IN PREPARING
TITLE IV - PART C PROPOSALS

(Mail to Mr. Bill Cowan, Utah State
Office of Education, 250 E. 5th South
Salt Lake City, Utah 84111)

DISTRICT: _____

GENERAL AREA OF PROPOSED PROJECT: _____
_____
_____
_____

GENERAL NATURE OF ASSISTANCE NEEDED (e.g., designing an evaluation; helping
focus the project objectives; writing the whole proposal):
_____
_____
_____
_____
_____
_____

District Official Authorizing the Request for Assistance:

_____
Signature

_____   _____
Date   Title

ESEA TITLE IV - PART C

Instructions for Completing Grant Application

Purpose

Under authority of P.L. 95-561 as amended, notice is hereby given of the opportunity to submit competitive proposals for the purpose of improving the quality of elementary and secondary educational practices.

Description of Title IV - Part C: Improvement in Local Education Practice

A total of approximately $500,000 will be available during FY 86 (July 1, 1986 - June 30, 1987) to fund Title IV - Part C projects in Utah LEAs. These monies will be awarded on a competitive basis to LEAs who have identified a significant need in their current educational system and propose to **continue** the development of new programs or **adopt** existing validated programs from elsewhere to respond to these areas of need. **(Please note that no new developmental projects will be funded during this year.)** Interested LEAs submit proposals in competition with other LEAs of similar size and resources. Projects funded by Part C fall into two areas: adoptable projects and developmental projects.

1. **Developmental projects** are funded when the LEA has identified a serious educational need within their system but is unable to locate other validated projects which are appropriate for meeting this need. Proposals by LEAs to conduct a developmental project must demonstrate that the LEA has adequate resources and expertise to develop a program, and evaluate the effectiveness of the program being developed over the three-year period. Funds for developmental projects are provided with the expectation that LEAs will continue, with their own resources, those programs which prove to be effective during the developmental period.

   Developmental projects can be funded up to five years but are typically funded for three years of developmental activities with a fourth and possibly fifth year of dissemination activities if the project proves effective. New developmental projects are only funded every three years. The most recent three-year cycle began in July of 1985. Consequently, **no new** developmental projects will be funded during this year. However, all LEAs who managed first-year developmental grants during last year will be required to submit a continuing developmental proposal if they wish to continue the project.

2. **Adoptable projects** are funded when a LEA identifies a critical educational need in their system and is also able to identify an existing validated program which has a high probability of meeting this need. Information about the availability of such

validated programs is disseminated by the U.S. Office of Education and the Utah State Office of Education through various conferences, booklets, newsletters, and individual contacts.   Those programs available for adoption have already demonstrated their effectiveness according to rigorous criteria set up by either the state or the federal government; and, staff from programs eligible for the adoption have demonstrated a willingness to assist other LEAs in adopting their program.

Adoptable projects are funded, on a competitive basis, every year and are typically funded for a one-year period, although adoptables may receive two years of funding if sufficient need is demonstrated. Funding of an adoptable project is based on the premises that: (1) the LEA possesses the expertise necessary to implement and test the effectiveness of such a program; (2) funds will be used only to test the effectiveness within the LEA of a project which has been validated elsewhere; and, (3) the LEA is committed to continue the program (if it proves effective) when Title IV funding is completed.

Introduction

Grants to LEAs under Title IV - Part C are based on competitive proposals submitted or post-marked by or before 5:00 p.m. March 27, 1986. A LEA may submit any number of proposals. However, if multiple applications are submitted for adoptable projects, the LEA is required to indicate the rank order of their preference for the applications.

Each project will compete for available funds with other project proposals from LEAs of similar size and resources as follows:

Category A	Category B	Category C	Category D
Alpine	Box Elder	Emery	Beaver
Davis	Cache	Grand	Daggett
Granite	Carbon	Millard	Garfield
Jordan	Duchesne	Morgan	Juab
Nebo	Iron	North Sanpete	Kane
Ogden	Logan	South Sanpete	North Summit
Salt Lake	Murray	Wasatch	Park City
Weber	Provo		Piute
	San Juan		Rich
	Sevier		South Summit
	Tooele		Tintic
	Uintah		Wayne
	Washington		

Funds Available

The approximate amount of funds available for adoptable projects from districts is as follows:

Category A	Category B	Category C	Category D
$ 152,000.00	$ 78,700.00	$ 28,800.00	$ 40,500.00

Funding Cycle

Requests for proposals are mailed to each LEA by February 2nd. If LEAs wish assistance in preparing applications, written requests for assistance must be received by Mr. Bill Cowan, Utah State Office of Education, before 5:00 p.m. on or before March 2, 1986. Assistance to LEAs desiring help in preparing applications for financial assistance is provided between March 3rd and March 26th. Applications for grant awards must be postmarked or received on or before 5:00 p.m. on March 27, 1986. Grant awards will be announced on or before May 15. Grant awards ordinarily become effective on July 1. The duration of the grant is for 12 months, ending on June 30, unless a request for an extension is made at least 60 days in advance. The maximum allowable extension is 90 days.

Proposal Review Procedures and Evaluation Criteria

Each proposal received before the specified deadline will be reviewed and evaluated by a panel of four people selected by the Title IV State Advisory Council and the Utah State Office of Education. Reviewers will be selected from among public school and higher education personnel who have demonstrated expertise and are familiar with the objectives and goals of Title IV - Part C. As noted previously each LEA will compete for available funds only with other LEAs of similar size and resources. Panel members will review each application according to the criteria specified below and will make funding recommendations to the Title IV State Advisory Council.

Criteria for Continuing Developmental Projects

Area*	Possible Points
1. Past Performance	30
2. Statement of Need	10
3. Quality of Objectives	10
4. Statement of Work	20
5. Qualifications of Personnel	20
6. Cost Effectiveness (Budget)	<u>10</u>
	100

Criteria for Adoptable Projects

Area	Possible Points
1. Statement of Need	35
2. Quality of Objectives	10
3. Statement of Work	25
4. Qualifications of Personnel	20
5. Cost Effectiveness (Budget)	<u>10</u>
	100

A Program Narrative written according to the format described below should be provided. Please note that the format of the Program Narrative will vary to some degree depending on whether the LEA is proposing an adoptable project or a continuing developmental project.

---

* Further elaboration on the elements which will be considered by reviewers in each section is included in the Program Narrative Section.

Instructions for Program Narrative

Contents of Program Narrative for Continuing Developmental Projects

The Program Narrative for Continuing Developmental Projects should be no longer than 25 pages and should include the following components:

1. **Abstract (1 page):** Provide a concise summary of the need to which the project is responding, a description of the project, the project's objectives, the proposed activities, and the anticipated outcomes and benefits of the project.

2. **Table of Contents (1 page):** A table of contents containing 2 or 3 levels of headings should be included to assist reviewers in locating specific sections of the application. Each page of the program narrative beginning with the Statement of Needs section should be consecutively paginated.

3. **Statement of Need (1-3 pages):** Discuss in detail the particular need to which the proposed project is responding. Evidence as to why the LEA views this as a critical need should be presented. Needs assessment data may, but need not necessarily include reference to test scores, survey data, or other statistical information. Of paramount importance is that the LEA demonstrate conclusively that the area to which this project is responding represents a top priority need in the LEA which has support of local administration and has been identified through a systematic and comprehensive process.

4. **Objectives (1-3 pages):** No more than six main project objectives should be listed. Although some process objectives are acceptable, most of the objectives should be outcome objectives. All objectives must be clearly stated in measurable terms. The relationship of the objectives to the need described in Section 3 must be clear. If desired, the applicant may want to group objectives under 1-3 project goals. For continuing projects it is permissable to revise the original objectives based on the previous year's experience.

5. **Accomplishments of Previous Year (5-8 pages):** Summarize the activities, accomplishments, and progress of the project during the previous year. Include any evidence regarding the effectiveness of the project and adherence to projected timelines. Any difficulties the project has encountered should be discussed along with the actual or proposed resolution.

6. **Statement of Work (5-8 pages):**

   a. **Program Development:** Describe the procedures and activities which will be necessary to conduct the project for the coming year. Activities for the coming year should be described in detail and activities for subsequent years (if any) should be described briefly.

b. **Evaluation of Project Effectiveness**: Describe in detail the evaluation activities which will be conducted to determine whether the project has been effective in responding to the critical area of need identified by the LEA. Evaluation activities should be structured so the LEA can make decisions about continuing the project after Title IV - Part C funding is completed, as well as providing information about the attainment of each of the objectives.

7. **Project Deliverables (1-2 pages)**: Summarize briefly the reports, instructional materials, handbooks, or other products that the project will produce. As a minimum this section should include reference to the interim and final reports of the project which will be submitted during the funding year.

8. **Qualifications of Proposed Staff (2-4 pages)**:

a. **Lea staff**: Describe the relevant training, experience, and expertise of involved LEA staff that will enable them to successfully implement and evaluate the project. The responsibilities of each staff member regarding the project should be discussed.

b. **Projected Technical Assistance**: Describe any additional technical assistance which will be required from non LEA staff in order to implement the project. The rationale for this assistance and the way in which assistance will be coordinated with LEA staff should be included.

9. **Budget**: Continuing Developmental Projects are funded to the degree necessary to develop, implement and test the effectiveness of a project which is responding to previously identified critical needs. Generally, it is anticipated that Title IV - Part C funding will be reduced during the 2nd and 3rd years of the project and LEA support and funding will be increased.

Each application for funding must be supported by a detailed budget adequate to establish the reasonableness of the proposed expenditures. The budget should contain two sections:

a. **Line item budget**: A line item budget should contain, as a minimum, projected expenditures in the following areas: (1) personnel, (b) employee benefits, (c) purchased services (e.g., capital expenditures), (f) total direct costs, (g) indirect costs, and (h) total costs.

b. **Budget narrative**: An attached budget narrative should show in detail how the line item total for each line was arrived at for all totals which are not readily apparent.

Contents of Program Narrative for Adoptable Projects

The Program Narrative for adoptable projects should be no longer than 25 pages and should include the following components:

1. **Abstract (1 page):** Provide a concise summary of the need to which the project is responding, a description of the project, the project's objectives, the proposed activities, and the anticipated outcomes and benefits of the project.

2. **Table of Contents (1 page):** A table of contents containing 2 or 3 levels of headings should be included to assist reviewers in locating specific sections of the application. Each page of the program narrative beginning with the Statement of Need section should be consecutively paginated.

3. **Statement of Need (1-3 pages):** Discuss in detail the particular need to which the proposed project will respond. Evidence as to why the LEA views this as a critical need should be presented. Needs assessment data may, but need not necessarily, include reference to test scores, survey data, or other statistical information. Of paramount importance is that the LEA demonstrates conclusively that the area to which this project is responding represents a top priority need in the LEA which has support of local administration and has been identified through a systematic and comprehensive process.

4. **Objectives (1-3 pages):** No more than six main project objectives should be listed. Although some process objectives are acceptable, most of the objectives for the proposed project will parallel closely those of the validated project which is being adopted. All objectives must be clearly stated in measurable terms. The relationship of the objectives to the need described in Section 3 must be clear. If desired, the applicant may want to group objectives under 1-3 project goals.

5. **Statement of Work (6-12 pages):**

   a. **Rationale for Selection:** Discuss the process and rationale used to select this particular adoptable project from among the available alternatives. What evidence exists that the project will meet the identified need, what alternative approaches were considered, and what advantages does this project have that led to its selection?

b. **Implementation**: Provide a brief description of the proposed project. Also describe in detail the activities and procedures which will be necessary to properly implement the proposed project. This discussion should provide evidence of the LEA's ability to conceptualize and carry out a project of this nature. A timeline showing the projected completion date of key project milestones should be included.

c. **Necessary Adaptation and Preservation of Key Elements**: Although some minor adaptation may be necessary by the adopting LEA, it is imperative that the "key elements" of the validated project be preserved during the adoption process if the identified needs are to be met. This section should describe the rationale and the extent of any adaptations which will be necessary for the LEA to adopt this project. Procedures for ensuring that the key elements of the validated project are preserved should be summarized.

d. **Projected Contact with Developer/Disseminator**: The adoption of most validated projects requires that the adopting LEA have contact with the original developer of the project or with trainers who have been certified by the original developer. The degree to which assistance from the original developer is planned and the procedures for obtaining and coordinating such assistance should be described. If no assistance or contact with the original developer is planned, the LEA's rationale should be given.

e. **Evaluation of Project Effectiveness**: Describe in detail the evaluation activities which will be conducted to determine whether the project has been effective in responding to the critical area of need identified by the LEA. Evaluation activities should be structured so the LEA can make decisions about continuing the project after Title IV - Part C funding is completed, as well as providing information about the attainment of each of the objectives. It is not the intent of this evaluation to revalidate the adopted project; such validation should already have taken place for any project judged ready for adoption.

6. **Project Deliverables (1-2 pages)**: Summarize briefly the reports, instructional materials, handbooks, or other projects that the project will produce. As a minimum this section should include reference to the interim and final reports of the project which will be submitted during the funding year.

7. **Qualifications of Proposed Staff (2-4 pages)**:

a. **LEA staff**: Describe the relevant training, experience, and expertise of involved LEA staff that will enable successful implementation and evaluation of the project. The responsibilities of each staff member regarding the project should be discussed.

b. **Projected Technical Assistance**: Describe any additional technical assistance which will be required from non-LEA staff in order to implement and evaluate the project. The rationale for this assistance and the way in which assistance will be coordinated with LEA staff should be included.

8. **Budget**: Adoptable projects will only be funded to the degree necessary to adequately implement and test the effectiveness of the program within the adopting LEA. Funds may not be used to disseminate a program throughout the LEA once effectiveness has been demonstrated. Furthermore, Title IV - Part C funds will not be approved to implement a program LEA-wide for purposes of testing the effectiveness of the program, if an adequate test could be conducted with implementation in only part of the LEA.

Each application for funding must be supported by a detailed budget adequate to establish the reasonableness of the proposed expenditures. The budget should contain two sections:

a. **Line item budget**: A line item budget should contain, as a minimum, projected expenditures in the following areas: (1) personnel, (b) employee benefits, (c) purchased services (e.g., consultants), (d) supplies and materials, (e) travel, (f) capital expenditures, (g) total direct costs, (h) indirect costs, and (i) total costs.

b. **Budget narrative**: An attached budget narrative should show in detail how the line item total for each line was arrived at for all totals which are not readily apparent.

EXHIBIT 2.2: DD COUNCIL PROSPECTUS GUIDELINES

UTAH COUNCIL for
HANDICAPPED and
DEVELOPMENTALLY
DISABLED PERSONS

Post Office Box 11356 / Salt Lake City, Utah 84147
Telephone (801) 533-6770

TO: Agencies and Organizations Serving the
       Developmentally Disabled in Utah
RE: Project Funds Available for FY 1987 under the DD Act

Applications for grants under the Developmental Disabilities Act (P.L. 95-602) are now being invited by the Utah Council for Handicapped and Developmentally Disabled Persons. Based on the level of federal funding last year, the Council anticipates that $195,000 will be available for grants. Applications will be considered in the two priority areas of service which have been adopted: (1) **case management**, and (2) **alternative community living arrangements**. These are defined in the attached guidelines.

As in the past, the first round of the application process will be submission of a one-page prospectus. A form for this purpose is enclosed. Ten copies must be received in the Council office by February 15, 1986. These will be screened, and selected applicants will then be invited to submit detailed proposals. Technical assistance will be offered to this group of applicants through a one-day proposal writing workshop conducted on March 1. Final applications will be due March 25; grant awards will be announced April 15, 1986.

In submitting an application, please review the attached guidelines carefully. The target group to be served must meet the definition of developmental disabilities and the services must fit the criteria for one of the two identified priority service areas.

If you decide to submit a one-page prospectus, please see that it reaches the Council office by **5:00 p.m. on February 15, 1986**. This is the **deadline**. Applications may be sent to the post office listed above, or delivered to the Council office which is located in Suite 234 of the State Department of Social Services, 150 West North Temple, Salt Lake City.

Should you have any questions, please feel free to call the Council executive director, Ms. Ineda H. Roe, at 533-6770.

Very sincerely yours,

Chairman

GENERAL GUIDELINES FOR PROJECT GRANTS
UNDER THE DEVELOPMENTAL DISABILITIES ACT

Utah Council for Handicapped
and Developmentally Disabled Persons

Target Group P.L. 95-602 defines "developmental disability" as a disability of a person which:

(A)   is attributable to a mental or physical impairment or combination of mental and physical impairments;

(B)   is manifested before the person attains age 22;

(C)   is likely to continue indefinitely;

(D)   results in substantial functional limitations in three or more of the following areas of major life activity: (i) self care, (ii) receptive and expressive language, (iii) learning, (iv) mobility, (v) self-direction, (vi) capacity for independent living, and (vii) economic self sufficiency; and

(E)   reflects the person's need for a combination and sequence of special, interdisciplinary, or generic care, treatment, or other services which are of lifelong or extended duration and are individually planned and coordinated.

Formula Grant Program. States are authorized to receive formula grants for planning, administration, and delivery of services to developmentally disabled persons. Funds may not be used for construction.

Prime concepts contained in the legislation are:

*   Federal support is provided for a wide range of diversified services in terms of lifetime human needs of persons with developmental disabilities. The Act provides for the co-mingling of funds under this program with those of other State programs. Co-mingling of funds reduces duplication and costs and enables the States to make use of diverse services such as health, welfare, education, and rehabilitation without imposing a set pattern of services on any one State.

*   Comprehensive planning of services and facilities provides for more effective use of existing resources at all levels.

- Programs are developed to fill gaps in existing service systems and to expand the reach of existing services to new groups of individuals.

- Services and resources are integrated in all State, regional and local agencies assisting the developmentally disabled.

- Use of Federal funds must not result in a decrease in the level of effort by States and localities in providing services to persons with developmental disabilities. This program should stimulate an increase in effort.

To implement these concepts, the Act:

(1) emphasizes development of community based services and expansion of programs for those individuals with substantial handicaps;

(2) brings together the major State agencies, nonprofit groups and consumers to plan for the developmentally disabled and establishes a State Planning Council to provide leadership in advocacy, planning and evaluation activities through its responsibilities and membership, while designated State agencies administer or supervise the administration of the programs;

(3) gives priority to those persons whose needs cannot be covered or otherwise met under the Education for All Handicapped Children Act, the Rehabilitation Act, or other education, health or human service programs;

(4) encourages the States to concentrate on planning and programming for the more severely handicapped among the developmentally disabled and emphasizes coordination with other Federally assisted programs to serve these persons (maximum flexibility is permitted each State to determine its priorities, to decide which services and projects are funded, and to focus on developing new or innovative programs to fill gaps in existing services); and

(5) provides for awarding "seed" grants from the formula grant funds which are received by each State. In Utah, this amount was approximately $195,000 during the last fiscal year. The formula grant for 1987 is still uncertain, but it should be approximately the same.

Project Grants. These "seed" grants are designed to fill gaps in the existing service structure in the State and to expand services to groups of developmentally disabled persons not now receiving services. They are not designed to relieve the State of support for existing services.

The DD Act identifies four areas of priority services: (1) case management, (2) child development, (3) alternative community living arrangements, and (4) non-vocational social development services. It further requires that 65% of the State's DD allocation must be spent in at least one and not more than two of these service areas.

As its two priority service areas for FY 87 funding, Utah has selected:

- Case Management
- Alternative Community Living Arrangements

Case Management is defined as services which (1) assist DD persons to gain access to needed social, health, education and other services, (2) assist providers of services to adapt methods of service delivery to meet the highly individualized needs of DD persons, and (3) enable administrators to share responsibility for negotiating, coordinating and obtaining the appropriate mix of needed services.

The Utah Council has identified eleven "pathway functions" which in combination make up the total process of case management. These components are:

(1) Outreach/Identification	(7) Service Plan
(2) Intake	(8) Corrective Services
(3) Emergency Services	(9) Maintenance
(4) Information & Referral	(10) Follow-up
(5) Problem Assessment	(11) Follow Along
(6) Diagnosis & Evaluation	

Any proposal which promises to have progressive impact on the problem (i.e., the need for an effective statewide system of case management) will be considered. The Council does not intend to fund provision of direct service under this category; rather it will consider projects designed to coordinate and provide for smooth transition between direct services.

Projects could focus on one of these components, or a creative mix of elements which would enable the highly individualized special needs of severely impaired persons to be met and which would insure transition from one program phase to the next. Proposals which demonstrate such a creative mix, with ongoing tracking and documentation of the process, will receive more favorable consideration.

Alternative Community Living Arrangements is defined as services which assist DD persons in maintaining suitable residential arrangements in the community, including in-house services (such as personal aides and attendants and other domestic and supportive services), family support services, foster care services, group living services, respite care, and staff training, placement and maintenance services.

Proposals in this category should focus on the services described in the definition and should relate to the development of a system which enables a handicapped person to achieve the most normal and least restrictive environment possible within the context of that person's disability. The Council will consider any project showing innovative and progressive impact to this end.

This year the Council has particular interest in a proposal which would address gaps in the continuum of residential services in the state. Although this is a priority, all proposals will be judged on a competitive basis and the Council will fund those which, in its estimation, have the greatest potential for improving the lives of DD people.

Eligible Applicants. State, regional and local public and private nonprofit agencies and organizations are eligible to apply for grants under the DD Act.

Federal Share and Non-Federal Matching. The Federal share of support under a DD grant may not exceed 75%. The regulations also provide that if a service project can be identified as serving an urban or rural poverty area, the Federal share may be up to 90%. However, it has been the policy of the Council, in the past, to adhere to the 75-25 formula in order to maximize the Federal dollars.

The non-Federal share of at least 25% may be "in kind" matching, as defined in Federal Register, Vol. 38, No. 181, Part 2 (Sept. 19, 1973).

In order to underscore the "seed" grant nature of DD funds, the Council has adopted a policy that grants renewed for a second year must provide 10% cash match, and for a third year, the full 25% match must be cash.

Length of Project Grant. Grants are awarded on a yearly basis and a contract is drawn between the grantee and the Council and the State Department of Social Services, the designated administering state agency. Funds are disbursed on a reimbursement basis. Renewal of grants may be sought, but the Council has adopted the rule of funding for not more than three years. Applicants for refunding will be subject to critical evaluation of the achievement of specific objectives.

Further Information. Please direct inquiries to the Utah Council for Handicapped & Developmentally Disabled Persons, P. O. Box 11356, Salt Lake City, Utah 84147, or telephone the Council's executive director, Ms. Ineda H. Roe, at 533-6770.

UTAH D.D. PROJECT GRANT

(Due Date):   March   (one-page prospectus)   (Submit 10 Copies)

Applicant Agency/Organization:

Contact Person:

Address:

Telephone:

I.   **Project Title:**

II.   **Area of Priority Service:** __ Case Management __ Alternative Community
        (See definition in Guidelines, P. 2)   Living Arrangement

III.   **Problem Statement:**

IV.   **Objectives:**

V.   **Methods:**

VI.   **Evaluation:**

VII.   **Funding:** Estimated amount of DD funds needed $_____
                     Source and amount of non-Federal match $_____ _____
                                                                        (source)
VIII.   **Future Funding Plans:** (Beyond DD Grant)

EXHIBIT 2.3: TITLE IV MODEL PROPOSAL

250 EAST 500 SOUTH STREET · SALT LAKE CITY, UTAH 84111 · TELEPHONE (801) 533-5431

UTAH STATE OFFICE OF EDUCATION

TO: All Local Education Agencies

FROM: Bill E. Cowan, Specialist
     Title IV - Part C

SUBJECT: Model Proposals for Title IV - Part C Grant
     Applications for 1986 - 1987 school year

The enclosed proposal is an example of a **continuing developmental** Title IV grant application. The format of the application follows the guidelines recently distributed in the call for proposals. As you prepare your own proposals, you should use this model proposal as a guide.

You should note that the enclosed proposal is single spaced with double columns. Two columns were used in order to provide you with explanation and suggestions. Your proposal should be **double** spaced and fill the entire page (except for the ABSTRACT, which should be single spaced). The length suggestions in the Call for Proposals refer to double spaced pages. If you have any questions about the model proposal or about the requirements for Title IV - Part C funds, contact Bill Cowan at the Utah State Office of Education.

SAMPLE PROPOSAL

Model Proposal
**Notetaking and Tutoring for Mainstreamed Hearing Impaired
Students**

TABLE OF CONTENTS

NOTETAKING AND TUTORING FOR
MAINSTREAMED HEARING IMPAIRED
STUDENTS

ABSTRACT

The enrollment of hearing impaired students in the Lake Valley School District has increased dramatically over the past ten years. In 1975 there were two secondary aged hearing impaired students and in 1985 this number increased to 32. A needs assessment conducted in the district in 1985 indicated that these newly enrolled hearing impaired students needed more than the traditional support service of interpreting. The data demonstrated that notetaking and tutoring services were also critically needed by the hearing impaired students. As a result of the needs assessment, the district began to develop a program to train normally hearing peers and paraprofessional adults as tutors and notetakers. The primary goals of the program are to help hearing impaired students succeed in the regular classroom and to improve the social contact between hearing impaired and normally hearing students. During the first year of the project, the district: 1) conducted a materials search, 2) completed content and task analyses on both tutoring and notetaking, 3) produced a prototype copy of the notetaking training materials, and 4) conducted a small pilot test with the notetaking training program. During the coming year the district will: 1) revise the notetaking materials, 2) design a handbook for tutors, 3) design workshops to train tutors and notetakers, and 4) implement the entire instructional system with normally hearing peers and paraprofessional adults. In order to evaluate the effectiveness of the program the district will: 1) have the materials critically reviewed, 2) videotape tutoring sessions and rate the quality of these sessions, and 3) survey teachers, students, and tutor/notetakers. In each of these evaluation activities data will focus on two questions: 1) should the program be continued? and 2) if the program is continued, how could it be improved? If the data indicate that the program is perceived positively, the district will propose a continuation of its development for the third year of the project. During this final year, summative data will be gathered on the entire instructional system.

SUGGESTIONS TO APPLICANTS

The abstract is a brief condensation of the larger proposal. It should contain each of the major parts of the proposal you see bracketed in this example. The abstract should not contain any information on the qualifications of proposed staff or budget figures.

The statement of work section is the heart of the abstract. It should contain a concise description of the major development and evaluation tasks you expect to accomplish during the coming year.

If appropriate, include a brief description of your project plans for the following year.

NOTETAKING AND TUTORING FOR MAINSTREAMED HEARING IMPAIRED STUDENTS

STATEMENT OF NEED

In 1980, the Lake Valley School District was selected as one of two target school districts in the state to accept mainstreamed hearing impaired students. As enrollment data were analyzed in the school district, a distinct increase of hearing impaired student enrollment was noted. In 1975, the school district enrolled only two secondary aged hearing impaired students. In 1980 there were ten hearing impaired students enrolled and by 1985 the enrollment increased to 32 hearing impaired students.

As more hearing impaired students enrolled in secondary programs, the district began to examine the types of support services needed by these students. During intake interviews, parents usually requested three types of services for their hearing impaired children: (1) interpreting services, (2) note-taking services, (3) tutoring services. While some parents felt that their child did not need all three services, all parents requested at least two of the services. When the initial Title IV developmental proposal was submitted last year, the district had no means of providing these critical support services to hearing impaired students.

As part of the initial developmental proposal submitted last year, the district conducted a needs assessment with hearing impaired students, specialists in deaf education, teachers, and parents. The results of that needs assessment indicated that students viewed interpreting and notetaking as extremely important and equally valued support services. When academic performance of hearing impaired students was examined, however, it was found that notetaking alone did not ensure academic success. Even for students who had both interpreting and notetaking services, teachers still felt a need for additional remedial instruction. Another important finding in the needs assessment indicated that almost none of the hearing impaired students had developed a healthy social relationship with normally-hearing students.

SUGGESTIONS TO APPLICANTS

The Statement of Need section in a continuing developmental proposal should briefly summarize the need statement of your new developmental proposal written the previous year.

The need statement should also include any new data gathered during the first year of the project. As you move through a development project, your needs often change or become more focused. Describe any "new" needs which have surfaced and describe evidence for these needs.

OBJECTIVES

First goal: To help hearing impaired students succeed in the regular classroom.

1. To improve the academic performance of hearing impaired students as measured by criterion referenced tests administered by the teacher and norm referenced tests administered by the school district.

2. To improve hearing impaired students' personal study habits as measured by students' and tutors' perceptions.

3. To increase hearing impaired students' independent study time.

Second goal: To improve the social contact between hearing impaired and normally-hearing students.

1. To increase the attendance of hearing impaired students at school social functions.

2. To increase the amount of personal contact and communication between hearing impaired and normally-hearing students.

3. To provide more opportunities for hearing impaired students to act as tutors for normally-hearing students.

ACCOMPLISHMENTS OF PREVIOUS YEAR

One of the most important accomplishments of the first year of the funding was the completion of a more thorough needs assessment. Several important conclusions resulted from the needs assessment efforts of the district. First, hearing impaired students had difficulty reading the notes taken by volunteers. Second, it was often difficult to find interested volunteers who were willing to commit themselves to the task. Third, the needs assessment demonstrated that even when adequate notes were provided to students, comprehension of course content still suffered. These data indicated that hearing impaired students in a

Make the objectives short and pointed. In this proposal each objective fits under a broader goal. The goal need not be "tight". But the objectives should be discrete and measurable.

Some of these objectives are not designed to be measured with paper/pencil tests--but each objective is stated so that the proposal reviewer can see how you intend to measure it.

In a continuing developmental proposal it is important to state clearly the accomplishments of the previous year. You should feel free to describe your "real" accomplishments, even if they differ from what you expected to do.

mainstreamed setting needed more than the interpreting and notetaking support services provided. Fourth, of the ten hearing impaired students that were tracked during the needs assessment, only two students had developed meaningful friendships with normally-hearing students. The remaining eight hearing impaired students had almost no social contact outside of school with either hearing impaired or normally-hearing students. As the family members of these eight socially isolated students were interviewed, it was determined that the students' socialization in the School for the Deaf had been more healthy than it was in the mainstreamed setting. In other words, these eight students had previously felt comfortable with certain other hearing impaired friends and now had been unsuccessful at making any hearing impaired or normally-hearing students friends.

Materials Search

Following the needs assessment, a thorough materials search was conducted to identify strategies and/or programs that would aid the district in developing a new notetaking and tutoring instructional system. As part of the materials search, written and telephone contacts were made with six major institutions in the country involved in educating hearing impaired students: 1) The National Technical Institute for the Deaf in Rochester, New York; 2) Gallaudet College in Washington, D.C.; 3) the California State University at Northridge; 4) the Seattle Community College; 5) the Technical Vocational Institute in Minnesota; and 6) the Texas School for the Deaf at Austin. Each institution was asked to provide information regarding notetaking and tutoring strategies for mainstreamed deaf students. Publishers such as the Alexander Graham Bell Association of the Deaf and the Conference of American Instructors of the Deaf were contacted concerning published programs on notetaking and tutoring.

Most new developmental projects should include a materials search. If you did not conduct a formal search, describe how you determined that a new program needed to be developed. (For example, you may have contacted experts who assured you that such programs were not available).

The results of the materials search indicated that institutions involved in deaf education were just beginning to consider the support services of tutoring and notetaking. While most institutions had elaborate training programs for interpreters, none of the institutions had a viable program for training notetakers or tutors. Certain of the institutions had begun, but not yet completed, the development of such

Usually, a materials search results in the identification of some programs that are close to your project. You should summarize the ideas you have borrowed from such programs.

programs. Telephone contacts were made with the developers at those institutions responsible for creating a training model for the notetaking and tutoring services. These contacts, however, showed that the institutions were in the preliminary stages and had not yet finalized any training programs or models. While the materials search did not identify any validated training procedures for notetakers, training programs for tutors were found. None of the tutoring models identified had been validated with hearing impaired students, but two of the models did seem to have potential for such. These two models were entitled **The Programmed Tutorial Model** and the **Structured Tutoring Model**. After careful review by administrators, special educators, and deaf education specialists on the selection committee, it was determined that the structured tutoring model would provide the district with the best pattern for developing its own tutoring program for hearing impaired students.

It is important to summarize how your program will differ from what is already available.

Content and Task Analyses

During the first year of funding, the project team conducted independent content and task analyses for both notetaking and tutoring. In the task analyses, each team member independently listed all of the tasks and subtasks that would be necessary to be a proficient notetaker and a proficient tutor. These individual analyses were compared for consistency. Final lists were then prepared by the committee and reviewed by experts involved with deaf education support services. The final lists contained major skills necessary for notetaking and separate skills necessary for tutoring. Underneath each major skill, subskills were listed and content specifications suggested for organizing the skills and subskills into an appropriate format for instructional presentation.

In most developmental projects you will conduct some kind of content and/or task analysis so that you can identify the precise components of what you want to teach.

The major skills identified for notetaking were as follows: 1) ability to modify language so that hearing impaired students can comprehend it, 2) ability to organize classroom lecture material that is presented haphazardly, 3) ability to use effective instructional techniques when taking notes (generate additional examples and modify teacher generated definitions), and 4) awareness of common experiential deficits of hearing impaired students.

If you are unfamiliar with procedures for conducting task or content analysis, you can involve a professional program developer as a technical consultant.

The major skills identified in the content and task analyses on tutoring indicated that proficient notetaking skills would be easier to acquire than would proficient tutoring skills. The major skills identified for tutoring were as follows: 1) basic skills in manual/simultaneous communications, 2) general skills in communicating with hearing-impaired students (techniques for communicating with both oral and simultaneous communications students), 3) skills in general tutoring techniques (e.g., being supportive of the student, providing structure in tutoring sessions, and increasing student independence), 4) expertise in the content being taught.

Based on the task and content analysis, it was determined that student peers would be trained as notetakers and paraprofessional adult aides would be trained as tutors for the mainstreamed hearing impaired students in the district. It was argued that student peers would not be able to become effective tutors because of the difficulty in acquiring communications skills. The committee agreed that paraprofessional adult aides would be more appropriate as tutors because they would be able to participate in communications training. It was also argued that another advantage of using paraprofessional adults as tutors would be the tighter control made possible because they would be employees of the district.

Your accomplishments may differ greatly from the accomplishments described in this proposal, but the section is important and should be given careful thought.

Notetaking Training Materials Produced

During the first year of the project, a 50 page manual was drafted as a notetaking training aide. The manual contains three major sections. The first section describes appropriate procedures for interacting with the hearing impaired student and the classroom teachers. Notetakers are encouraged to provide teachers with examples of their notes and to encourage hearing impaired students to provide critical feedback on the notes, so that notetakers can improve their skills. The second section of the manual focuses on the mechanics of notetaking, including: organization techniques, using white space, making copies of notes, identification and pagination. The third section of the manual provides examples and directions for making instructional modifications in the classroom lecture as the

One of the most important parts of last year's accomplishments is a description of the products you produced. If you did not complete any final instructional products, you should describe how much of the product you have completed.

notes are taken. Notetakers are encouraged to increase the number of examples given to explain concepts, use visual diagrams wherever possible, and modify difficult concept definitions.

Notetaking Pilot Test

During the first year, ten notetakers were trained in one high school to serve 15 hearing impaired students. The basic conclusions of the notetaking pilot test indicated that the training given to student peers was effective. Through a notetaking simulation study, hearing impaired students were asked to rate the quality of notes taken by trained notetakers and notes taken by untrained notetakers. The results of the study indicated that hearing impaired students consistently preferred notes taken by trained notetakers. Teachers who reviewed the notes taken by trained and untrained notetakers also agreed consistently that the training was producing an important and positive effect.

A developmental project should include some form of a pilot test. You may describe here any attempt you have made to try out your ideas. You may not have conducted a formal pilot test during the first year, but even if you only have preliminary feedback from a small sample of students or teachers, describe the results in this section.

One of the surprising findings during the first years' pilot study concerned the increased interest level of normally hearing students in the hearing impaired program. Because of the interests that have been generated by the notetaking pilot test, the special education director in the district proposed that a course in sign language be offered in the foreign language department of the high school. Although the course was not heavily advertised, 40 students (38 normally-hearing students and 2 orally trained hearing impaired students) registered for the course. At the completion of the term, the sign language instructor asked the students in the class if any of them would be interested in participating as tutors the following year in the notetaking and tutoring project. Twelve of the students indicated such an interest (11 normally-hearing students and 1 orally trained hearing impaired student).

Many projects will experience unintended side effects (either positive or negative). Such effects should be described in this section.

STATEMENT OF WORK

Program Development

During the second year the workscope will consist of eight separate steps as can be seen in the project timeline chart at the end of this section. The first task will be to revise the notetaking handbook based on the evaluative data collected during the first year. While the data showed that the program accomplished its purpose, notetakers and critical reviewers made helpful suggestions for improving the notetaking materials. The most notable of the criticisms was the lack of adequate examples to illustrate the various principles described in the handbook. More appropriate examples of the quality notes were collected during the first year pilot test and will be included in the second version of the notetaking handbook. The second task to be accomplished will be to conduct communications training for paraprofessional adults and the previously mentioned interested normally-hearing peers. This training will be conducted three weeks prior to the beginning of school and will end two weeks after the school year begins. The training will consist of sign language communications training and general techniques for communicating with hearing impaired students.

The primary development task for the second year will be to design and produce a handbook for tutors of hearing impaired students. Many of the basic principles included in the handbook will be borrowed and adapted from the structured tutoring model initially selected by the project team. It is anticipated that the handbook will consist of four primary sections: 1) a section on general techniques of tutoring, 2) tutoring techniques for specific content areas, 3) communications aides, and 4) study skills development techniques. During the design phase (task No. 3 on the project timeline), each of the major sections of the manual will be analyzed and outlined.

Once the committee has agreed on specific design specification for the tutoring handbook, sections of the manual will be assigned to various team members. During this phase, the writing and illustrations for the handbook will be produced by the team members and graphics specialists. As each section of the manual is completed, project team members will review each other's work. An English specialist, experienced in editing, will then edit the handbook for language consistency.

In the Program Development section you should explain the process you will use to create the instructional products and strategies to implement the program. Some of these tasks may involve revisions of products you began to develop last year. In this sample proposal, the notetaking handbook needed major revisions during the second year of the project.

You will also describe new development activities. In this proposal the tutoring handbook was the major focus of development efforts for the second year of the project.

After the tutoring handbook has been completed, workshops will be designed to introduce the principles to student peers and paraprofessional adults. These tutoring workshops will include role playing, the general techniques through simulation activities, general practice in communications techniques (including language modification techniques for tutoring), and study skills development. As the workshops are being designed, the project team member in charge of implementation will assign the notetaking and tutoring services to students for the following term.

At the beginning of the school year, prospective tutors will be trained using the format produced during the design phase for the workshops. It is anticipated that at least four separate workshops will be conducted for the paraprofessional adults and the student peers. Once the peers and adults have been properly trained, the tutoring services will be implemented on a pilot basis from the last week in February to the end of the school year.

During the third year, the tutoring materials will be revised, based on the data gathered during the second year field test. Minor revisions will also be made in the notetaking training materials. After the materials have been revised, the total program will be implemented and evaluated. In FY-87 the evaluation will be designed to gather primarily summative data rather than formative data as gathered in FY-86. Emphasis will be placed on determining the overall worth of the program to hearing impaired students. A comparison group will be designated who will not receive tutoring or notetaking services during the first term of school. These students' progress will be compared with students who do have access to the services.

Evaluation of Project Effectiveness

As can be seen on the project timeline chart at the end of this section, there are six primary evaluation tasks to be conducted during the second year. The first task will be to obtain competent reviewers (experts in deaf education, tutoring, and support services for deaf students) to provide critical feedback about the materials. Reviewers will critically review the materials already produced for notetakers and, more importantly, the newly produced

In all continuing developmental proposals there are some "implementation" type activities that must be included. Some of those activities fit more appropriately in the development section, and others fit more appropriately in the evaluation section. Tasks which focus on training probably belong in the development section, while tasks which focus primarily on data collection primarily belong in the evaluation section.

If you plan to continue the program a third year, briefly indicate your project plans for that year.

materials for tutors. These "face- validation" activities will provide the project team with needed information on how the materials can be improved. Reviewers' comments will be compiled by one of the project team members and used for materials revisions.

The second evaluation task will involve the videotaping of tutoring sessions conducted by both student peers and paraprofessional adults. Each of the tutors will be asked to provide the project team with a schedule of their tutoring sessions. The project team will then select tutoring sessions at random to be videotaped. These videotapes will serve two purposes: 1) as a training aide to help tutors improve their skills, and 2) as a source of specific data on the effectiveness of the training program.

There is no hard and fast rule for breaking out the activities involved in "piloting" the program. Either section might be appropriate for some tasks in your project.

After the videotapes have been gathered, they will be randomly assigned to trained raters selected from among project team members and other specialists in tutoring and deaf education. A special rating scheme will be devised to evaluate the degree to which tutors have mastered the required tutoring skills taught during the training program. Information obtained from rating the tapes will also be used as formative evaluation data in revising the workshops and the tutoring handbook materials.

The easiest way to write the evaluation (and development) sections is to plot out the various tasks on a timeline and then briefly explain each task in the text of the proposal.

The fourth task in the evaluation process will be to gather formative data from teachers, students, notetakers, and tutors. Each of the teachers, students, notetakers, and tutors involved in the project will receive a questionnaire regarding the quality of the notetaking and, more importantly, the tutoring services. One of the critical questions on the survey will ask each of the groups to determine whether or not the program should be continued in the district. For respondents who believe that the program should be continued, a further question will require them to justify their answer. In other words, respondents will be asked to explain as completely as possible the reasons they think the tutoring and notetaking program should be continued in the district. Other questions on the form will focus specifically on the quality of the tutoring and the notetaking services that have been provided during the pilot test. These data will be used to determine whether the district should continue the development of the project.

*The timeline chart at the end of this section was written first as a guide for the text. As you write your own proposal, you should think of the **major** tasks that should be included on such a chart as you plan your project. If you need assistance in writing the development or evaluation sections, assistance can be obtained from the State Office.*

The final task in the evaluation phase of the project will be to complete the final report. Each of the team members will be asked to complete a section of the final report. The team members responsible for the notetaking part of the project will focus on the data gathered on notetaking, and the team members responsible for tutoring will complete the section on tutoring.

PROJECT DELIVERABLES

During the second year, the project anticipates the production of four separate deliverables.

1. **The Revised Notetakers Handbook**. It is anticipated that this handbook will be approximately 75 pages long and will include additional examples and illustrations of quality notes for hearing-impaired students. Each of the revisions will be based on the data gathered during the first year pilot test of notetaking services.

2. **Tutoring handbook**. The Tutoring Handbook will be the first edition of training materials for paraprofessional adult and student peer tutors. While critical reviews will be obtained on the tutoring materials, it is anticipated that the guide will require substantial revisions during the third year of the project.

3. **Manager's Guidebook**. The manager's guidebook will consist of training techniques to be used during the workshops conducted for tutors and notetakers. The guidebook will be used by teachers and trainers who introduce student peers and paraprofessional adults to the tutoring and notetaking techniques in the program. This manual will allow other districts to implement the project with less assistance from the original program developers. It will make the project more exportable and more valuable to the state and schools in other states. During the second year it is anticipated that the managers guide will consist of a brief outline of objectives and training techniques. It is proposed that during the project's third year, the manager's

Your project may involve very different kinds of instructional products. You may describe a filmstrip, a videotape, a collection of posters, a set of role-playing scripts or a computer-assisted instructional package. In each case the products should fit the purposes of your program and be as "exportable" as possible. In other words, each product should be designed so that some other district could use it effectively with a minimum of training.

guide should be professionally developed and evaluated. It would be unwise to expend significant time or money on the manager's guide in the second year before the tutoring handbook has been revised and completed.

4. **Reports**. An interim report will be submitted in January. The report will briefly describe the progress in the project, emphasizing the development milestones of the project. The final report will consist of all of the evaluation data collected during the second year. Special emphasis will be placed on recommendations for improving the program and for revising the materials. The report will thus focus on formative data rather than summative data. It is proposed that a summative study of the program be conducted during the project's third year.

*Your interim report should be a **brief** summary of the progress you have made on the project by mid year.*

Your final report will be part of your proposal for the following year, if you plan to continue the project.

QUALIFICATIONS OF PROPOSED STAFF

LEA Staff

Project Director: Mark Howard.
Dr. Howard obtained an Ed.D. in special education from Utah State University in 1976. He is presently employed as the Director of Special Education in the district. In the notetaking and tutoring project, Dr. Howard will be responsible for the overall coordination of the development and evaluation of the program. Dr. Howard will assist in the actual production of instructional materials. He will summarize recommendations and make materials revisions. He will assist in the training of tutors and notetakers and will act as a quality control person for the entire project. Some of Dr. Howard's past accomplishments include:

Descriptions of qualifications of your staff need not be lengthy. Give highlights of their professional accomplishments that pertain directly to the program you are proposing.

- Primary developer for the statewide program to assist homebound retarded adults.
- Director of Project Mainstream (a program to assist parents of retarded children being educated in public schools).
- Committee chairperson for the statewide assessment

Content Specialist: Leona Mortensen

Ms. Mortensen holds a Master's degree in deaf education from the University of Oklahoma. Ms. Mortensen's prime responsibility in the project will be to provide developers and the project director with needed expertise in the field of deaf education. Ms. Mortensen will review all written materials to ensure that they are appropriate for a deaf population. She will also act as a formative screener by attempting to use all newly developed techniques herself (with her own deaf students) before the techniques are used by paraprofessionals. She will also assist heavily with the training components. Her qualifications include:

The job responsibilities for the proposed project, as well as the qualifications, should be described for each of the key staff members.

- R.I.D. certification as a trained interpreter for hearing impaired people.
- Six years experience as a teacher of hearing impaired students at the Utah School for Deaf in Ogden.
- Co-author of a syllabus for training teachers in regular classrooms to accept newly transferred hearing impaired students into the classroom.
- Intern at the National Technical Institute for the Deaf in Rochester, New York, during the 1977-78 school year.

Implementation Coordinator: Sally Feld

Ms. Feld obtained a Master's degree in Special Education from the University of California at Los Angeles in 1971. She is presently employed as a resource teacher in the district. Her specialties include learning disabilities and remedial reading instruction. In 1976 she was given the exemplary teaching award for the outstanding special educator in the state. Ms. Feld's prime responsibilities in the notetaking and tutoring project will be to coordinate the details in implementing the tutoring program and coordinating activities for the program's evaluation.

- Invited participant at the National Conference on Learning Disabilities held in Washington, D.C., in 1978.

- Invited committee member for the State Assessment project on mainstreaming and Public Law 94-142.

Projected Technical Assistance

Program Developer: Dr. John Wood

Dr. John Wood holds a Ph.D. in Instructional Science from Brigham Young University. He has authored numerous instructional programs including programs for retarded and hearing impaired students. He is presently employed as an instructional scientist at the National Institute for Instructional Development in Denver, Colorado. In the notetaking and tutoring project, Dr. Wood would be responsible for the design and development of instructional materials used in the project. He will consult with the Project Director and the other team members on each of the handbooks to be developed and will also assist in the pilot testing of materials.

If you feel the specific skills you need cannot be found in the district, it may be advantageous to obtain technical expertise from outside of the district. The State Office has a list of evaluation and development specialists that you might consider as you select your technical assistants.

Evaluation Specialist: Dr. Steven Scriven

Dr. Scriven holds a Ph.D. in Research Methodology from the University of Colorado at Boulder. He is presently employed as an Associate Professor and Research Associate in the Bureau of Educational Research at the University of Utah.

Dr. Scriven's responsibility in the notetaking and tutoring project will be to assist the project director with the design and execution of the evaluation of the program. He will assist the project team in designing instruments, sampling techniques, and data analysis. Dr. Scriven will also assist with the completion of the final report which will focus on project accomplishments and the effectiveness of the program.

Proposed Budget

1. Personnel
Mark Howard	.25 FTE for 3 months	$ 5,000.00
Leona Mortensen	.17 FTE for 4 months	3,570.00
Sally Feld	.08 FTE for 1 month	1,360.00
John Wood	25 days @ $150/day	3,750.00
Steve Scriven	15 days @ $125/day	2,250.00

2. Fringe Benefits (20% of salaries) 1,986.00

3. Travel: Mileage @ 18 cents/mile 180.00
               Per Diem @ $37.50/day 525.00
               Air Fare @ $50.00 round trip Denver to SLC 350.00

4. Consumable Supplies 500.00

5. Communications: Postage 108.47
                        Telephone 335.26

6. Capital Expenditures   0

7. Total   . . . .   <u>$19,914.73</u>

Explanation of Budget Line Items

Line Item Number One: Personnel

Current annual base salaries for personnel who will be working on this project are as follows:

Project Director, Mark Howard	$20,000
Content Specialist, Leona Mortensen	$21,000
Implementation Coordinator,	
Sally Feld	$17,000

The purpose of this section is to explain the previous line items by showing how you arrived at each of the figures.

Funds budgeted for these people during the project were computed using an appropriate percentage of these current salaries. The consultant fees for Dr. John Wood and Dr. Steven Scriven were computed at $150.00 per day.

Line Item Number Two: Fringe Benefits

Fringe benefits were computed using the current school district rate of 20 percent of salaries. This figure was applied to all School District employees' salaries. Consultant fees were fixed at $150.00 per day with no allowance for fringe benefits included.

Line Item Number Three: Travel

The cost of travel was computed at the current Utah State Office of Education rate of 18 cents per mile. It is anticipated that 20 round trips of 50 miles each will be required in order to complete the project, equalling $180. It is further anticipated that Dr. Wood will be required to make seven trips from Denver, Colorado, at $50 per round trip air fare and $37.50 per day for 14 days of per diem. Thus, the per diem will total $525 and the air fare will total $350.

Where line items are not clear, you should explain the rationale behind the amount requested.

Line Item Number Four: Consumable Supplies

In order to implement the notetaking and tutoring program, instructional manuals will be required for each notetaker and tutor participating in the study. It will also be necessary to provide each of the notetakers with an ample supply of notetaking paper (pressure sensitive) so that they can provide the students with one copy of the notes, keep a copy themselves, and give a copy of the notes to the project director. The notetaking paper cost $5 per pad and the manuals will cost about $10 each. It is anticipated that we will need 40 manuals and 20 packets of notetaking paper.

Line Item Number Five: Communications

Based on historical records of similar grants, we have budgeted 0.55 percent of the total grant for postage cost and 1.7 percent of the total grant for telephone cost.

You do not need to use these specific figures when calculating your communications costs. Simply provide a reasonable estimate based on project needs and your past experience.

Line Item Number Six: Capital Expenditures

It is not anticipated that this project will require a purchase of any new capital equipment.

Line Item Number Seven: Project Total Cost

Total project cost is a simple sum of line items 1-6.

Certain line items, such as #6 and #7 are self- explanatory and need no further documentation.

PROJECT TIMELINE

July   Aug.   Sept.   Oct.   Nov.   Dec.   Jan.   Feb.   March   April   May   June

Program Development

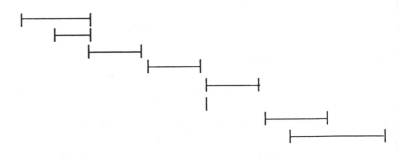

1. Revise Notetaking Handbook
2. Communications Training
3. Design tutoring handbook
4. Develop handbook
5. Design training workshops
6. Assign services to students
7. Conduct training
8. Implement services

Evaluation of Project Effectiveness

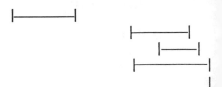

1. Critical review of materials
2. Videotape tutoring sessions
3. Rate videotapes
4. Survey teachers, students,
   notetakers and tutors
5. Submit final report

CHAPTER 3: PREPARING FOR THE PROPOSAL REVIEW

The purpose of reviewing proposal applications is to obtain the best available professional judgments regarding each application submitted for funding. The individual and panel recommendations regarding the quality of each proposal and the statements of strengths and weaknesses are a critical base upon which final funding recommendations should rest. To assure an objective, unbiased review process in which proposals will be judged strictly on their merits, each of the activities described in the following sections should be planned and conducted in preparation for the actual proposal review.

SELECTION OF REVIEWERS

Potential reviewers should be carefully selected, using nominations from funding agency staff and from known experts in the field(s) relevant to the substance and methodology with which the proposals will be concerned. For example, in the Utah Title IV proposal review, individuals nominated to serve as reviewers were required to qualify in one or more of the following areas: (1) experience in the successful conduct of Title IV projects; (2) expertise in technical areas and operations required in all proposals; or (3) membership on the Utah Title IV State Advisory Council.

It is generally wise to select additional individuals to serve as alternates in the event that last minute problems may prevent selected reviewers from meeting their commitments to participate in the proposal review. It is also wise to make certain that all selected reviewers are contacted sufficiently far in advance to schedule adequate time for the review, as well as for prior training sessions.

STRUCTURING REVIEW PANELS

Review panels are generally no better than the individual reviewers who serve on them. Yet, the selection of highly-qualified individuals to serve does not assure that their opinions can be meaningfully aggregated into sensible and equitable judgments about the quality of specific proposals. As with any team effort, the independent contributions of each team member must be merged effectively if success is to be achieved.

Where the number of proposals is relatively few and sufficient time can be allowed for each reviewer to read each proposal, there is no need to sub-divide the overall review panel into sub-panels or teams. Each individual can rate each proposal and those ratings can be aggregated to achieve consensus in a variety of ways, ranging from mathematical averaging to group discussions. In the more typical situation, larger numbers of proposals and shortage of resources and time require that the review panel be sub-divided into teams, with each team assigned responsibility for reading only a sub-set of the total proposals submitted.

In forming such teams, it is important to ensure that the total breadth of expertise and experience possessed by any given team is appropriate for the proposals assigned to it. For example, many universities have programs for funding faculty research proposals. Review teams are typically formed so that proposals from the arts and humanities can be read by persons who possess expertise in those areas, proposals dealing with chemistry are assigned to review teams where at least some of the team members possess expertise in that field, and so forth. As another example, in the Utah Title IV proposal review process, sixteen reviewers were formed into four teams. Those four-person teams were balanced insofar as possible to assure that each team included: (a) persons with experience in conducting Title IV projects, relevant technical experts, and members of the State Title IV Advisory Council, and (b) an appropriate mixture of university and public school personnel. It is also important to assign each team a leader who has experience in the content of the proposal, as well as relevant technical expertise.

There are also important considerations to assure equity and credibility in the review process by avoiding such things as selecting all team members from any one geographic area, or forming all-male or all-female review panels (unless the content of the proposals requires such team composition).

ASSIGNING PROPOSALS TO REVIEW TEAMS

Because of the varying nature of proposals in different funding competitions, there are no general guidelines for how to assign proposals to review teams. It is imperative, however, that careful thought be given to make certain that the assignment is conducted in such a way as to maximize the fairness of the review process. For example, if a particular competition is intended to result in the selection of one art project, one science project, and one physical education project, then it may be most equitable to have all the art proposals reviewed by one team, all the science proposals reviewed by a second team, and all physical education proposals reviewed by a third team.

Similarly, if funded competitions allow proposals to be submitted dealing with different functions (e.g., research vs. dissemination), it would seem that all proposals in any one category should be rated by the same team. In some proposal submissions, it is appropriate to sort proposals along some salient dimensions of the application agency (public vs. private schools, or large urban school districts vs. small rural school districts). To illustrate the above, in the Utah Title IV proposal review, all proposals in any one category (e.g., proposals for developmental projects in small rural districts) were rated by the same team so that districts would only have to compete against other districts of approximately the same size.

One potential problem which should be recognized in assigning proposals to different teams is the tendency of some teams to be more critical than other teams. This issue will be dealt with later in terms of helping teams apply listed criteria similarly to reach judgments that are fair and comparable across teams. Care must be taken to avoid a situation where proposals assigned to more rigorous teams are not placed at a disadvantage in relation to those proposals assigned to more lenient teams.

PROFESSIONAL STANDARDS FOR REVIEWERS

Proposal reviewers are privy to a great deal of information about individuals and agencies which is of a confidential nature. All reviewers should be extremely careful to never discuss -- beyond the doors of the review meeting room -- any proposals, comments, recommendations, or evaluations discussed therein. Each proposal belongs to those who develop it, and all reviewers must safeguard the rights of each applicant.

It is also important that conflicts of interest be avoided in all proposal review processes. A conflict of interest exists when the approval or non-approval of any proposal could have any financial or other advantage to any reviewer beyond that which would obtain to other persons within the same field or discipline. For example, a conflict of interest would exist in any situation where a proposal was submitted by an agency with whom the reviewer had a continuing consultant relationship. Similarly, it would be a conflict of interest if a reviewer were asked to judge a proposal submitted by the reviewer's spouse or other family member, a profit or non-profit organization with which the reviewer is associated, or any person or organization with whom the panelist has a present or anticipated relationship involving employment or financial interest.

Ideally, reviewers should be selected so that there is no possible question of conflict of interest. In some instances, however, it is not possible to identify enough qualified reviewers where some conflict of interest could not be construed. For example, there might be relatively few individuals possessing requisite expertise in some technical areas, and those individuals may have some relationship to every activity being conducted in the field. In such cases, it may be permissible to use reviewers who have known relationships with applicant agencies, but special care must be taken to avoid conflict of interest from biasing the judgments.

For example, if any reviewer or team leader feels uncomfortable about a potential conflict of interest when a proposal from an institution with which a reviewer has been associated in the past is discussed, that reviewer should be absent from the discussion (and most likely from the review room) during deliberations concerning that proposal. Professional sensitivity and good judgment will usually serve to eliminate or reduce conflict of interest situations so that they do not play a role in decisions concerning competing proposals. For example, in the Utah Title IV proposal review, it was impossible to select reviewers with prior successful Title IV experience who did not also have some affiliation with districts submitting proposals. To deal with this problem, all proposals were assigned to review teams so that no LEA staff member was asked to judge a proposal from his or her own district or a district which was competing directly with his or her district for funds.

CONTROLLING BIAS

Every effort should be made in the selection of reviewers to identify those individuals who are capable of making fair, impartial judgments -- judgments which are free of the taint of personal bias. Yet, such paragons of virtue are difficult to find. Indeed, the reviewer who is unaffected by either conscious or sub-conscious biases ranks in mythology alongside of Pegasus' winged horse. Although it may be naive to speak of eliminating bias from the proposal review process, it is paramount that bias be controlled so that it does not enter to any significant degree into the decisions rendered.

Not all individuals who are biased are malicious; most often the intrusion of biases into judgments is unintentional. It is, therefore, useful to remind all reviewers of the importance of setting their personal biases aside during the proposal review process. Reviewers should be reminded that they must be scrupulously aware of their own inevitable philosophical and methodological biases if they are to ensure each application a fair and impartial review. They should be reminded that, if they do not attend to these biases, there is a risk that applications will be judged not on their objective merits but on their degree of conformity to the reviewer's own subjective positions. All reviewers should be urged to consider all proposals in an atmosphere free of preconception, one in which reviewers remain receptive to perspectives which differ from those which they themselves espouse.

One potential source of bias is prior knowledge about individuals and agencies submitting proposals. In some cases, it is possible to conduct "blind reviews" in which the identity of the individual and/or agency submitting the proposal is kept from the reviewers, at least until after their ratings and recommendations are completed. This can be done by assigning identification numbers to each proposal and removing references to the submitting agency so as to mask identity insofar as possible and thus avoid possible bias in the review process. In other cases, the capability and track record of the submitting agency is so much a part of the decision criteria that such a "blind review" would be unwise.

PREPARATION OF PROPOSALS FOR REVIEW

A frequently overlooked but important detail in the proposal review process is the preparation of proposals for actual review. For example, adequate numbers of copies of each proposal should be provided so that reviewers are not impeded in their work by having to wait to read proposals being shared with other reviewers. Ideally, each reviewer should be provided an individual copy of each proposal which he or she is asked to review. Since resource constraints and size of proposals may occasionally make this approach impossible, care should be taken to make sufficient copies of each proposal so that the review can be conducted without undue delays. Such pedestrian planning is often viewed by funding agencies as being trivial, with the result that differential reading speeds of reviewers cause unnecessary delays, and incomplete processing of information by all reviewers -- which may have a negative effect on the final outcome of the review. Careful planning at this stage is very important if the review is to go smoothly.

DEVELOPMENT OF REVIEW INSTRUMENTS AND MATERIALS

In addition to preparing multiple copies of the proposal itself, the actual review instruments, including review forms, rating scales, and criteria must be developed. This is undoubtedly the most critical and difficult task in preparing for a proposal review. Several considerations in developing review instruments and materials are discussed briefly in the following sections.

Developing Criteria

It is important that the review and evaluation of each proposal in any funding competition be conducted in strict accordance with evaluation criteria which have been developed and publicized to potential applicants. Often legal and regulatory requirements mandate that evaluations be strictly based on published selection criteria only. Even in the absence of such legal requirements, however, fair and equitable reviews require that: (1) applicants are informed in advance of criteria that will be used to judge their proposals; and (2) that the proposal review be conducted in accordance with those established standards. Allowing additional considerations to intrude at the point of review and evaluation would be grossly unfair.

The actual criteria to be employed will vary with the nature of the activities called for in the solicitation. Therefore, it would be pointless to try to prescribe specific criteria or even categories of criteria in this book. The following are offered merely as examples of categories of criteria that might be included:

- IMPORTANCE (the potential importance of the project to particular target groups)

- IMPACT (the probable effects of proposed activities)

- SOUNDNESS (technical soundness of the proposal and adequacy of procedures)

- QUALIFICATIONS OF KEY PERSONNEL (the extent to which proposed key personnel are qualified for the task proposed)

- COST BENEFIT (the extent to which costs are consistent with the activities proposed and the potential value of outcomes).

Samples of criteria used in the Title IV project review are included in the RFP in Exhibit 2.1 in Chapter 2 and are discussed further in subsequent sections of this chapter.

Developing the Review Form

It is necessary to develop a review form to assist each reviewer in providing a detailed review of each proposal and to serve as a device by which the reviewer's judgment can be best communicated. Review forms should include the following:

1. a cover page which contains: (a) identifying information (e.g., applicant institution, proposal number; (b) a listing of the criteria and possible points; (c) a space for final ratings of each criterion to be recorded; (d) designated space for the overall recommendation and the rationale for that recommendation; and (e) a place for the signature of the reviewer and others as appropriate;

2. worksheets which contain: (a) specific criteria, along with an explanation of the range of possible points to be assigned on each criterion; (b) an explication of how each criterion is to be interpreted; (c) space to list strengths and weaknesses of the proposal in relation to each criterion; and (d) a space for a final point rating on each criterion; and,

3. instructions for use in filling out the review form.

A sample of the proposal review form used for the DD Council project is included at the end of this chapter as Exhibit 3.1. The review forms used to evaluate two different types of proposals in the Title IV program are shown in Exhibit 3.2. Finally, an example of a useful form published in the U.S. Department of Education's Special Education Program's 1983 Grant Announcements for Research in Education of the Handicapped is shown in Exhibit 3.3. Although all of the forms have some similarities and other differences, it is clear that each provides a way for transforming subjective judgments into quantitative ratings and summarizing that information for final decisions. More about how that process occurs is discussed below.

Dealing With Scaling Problems

Reviewers have expressed more concern about the assignment of numerical ratings than any other aspect of the review process. In one sense, this is the most critical determination in the evaluation. There is some evidence to suggest that the overall recommendation (e.g., approved, conditionally approved, disapproved) is the most reliable judgment, and that the narrative documentation is the most generally useful information provided by reviewers. Nevertheless, at the critical decision point where funding agencies are forced to distinguish between the last application to be funded versus the first one placed in the unfunded category, the decision is likely to hinge on the numerical rating. Thus, it is vital to give careful consideration to these numerical ratings.

The major problem with ratings is that of determining appropriate anchor points. One reviewer may assume that all applications are basically good and thus start by positioning each proposal initially at the most positive extreme of the scale, and then subtract points for specific weaknesses. Another reviewer may assume that the applicant must prove everything, thus starting each proposal at the negative end of the scale and awarding points for demonstrated strengths in the proposal. While either system will array proposals in essentially the same order, the absolute numerical values obtained may be quite different. Such differences may present difficulties when ratings must be aggregated across many panels and reviewers, any one of which judges only a small portion of the total pool of applications.

Establishing clear anchor points for the rating scales is sometimes complicated by the fact that some federal regulations prohibit setting arbitrary cut-off scores for acceptability. One acceptable procedure for dealing with this problem is to assume that a proposal that is "just adequate" on a given criterion should fall at the mid-point of the rating scale for that criterion. From this anchor point, ratings can be increased or decreased on the basis of strengths and weaknesses of the proposal. Adherence to this general approach to ratings will help to assure that numerical scores are consistent with recommendations and narrative and are relatively reliable across reviewers.

One difficulty with the above approach is that it does seem to produce scores which are "bunched together" around the midpoint. The problem is compounded by an apparent reluctance of many reviewers to assign extreme scores. The ideal reviewer does not hesitate to assign a maximum score or a zero if such score can be reasonably justified.

It is also important to be certain that readers are provided not only the overall range of points, but also a conversion scale to assist them in translating judgments into the number of points to be assigned. For example, the conversion tables used in the DD Council and Title IV projects (shown on the first page of each rating form in Exhibits 3.1 and 3.2) helped reviewers increase their consistency to the point that inter-rater and inter-team reliabilities were extremely high in applying this particular instrument. A sample of another excellent method for dealing with conversion of judgments to points appears in Exhibit 3.4.

Developing Instructions to Reviewers

In addition to providing reviewers with specific instructions for how to use the rating form, it is important to provide them with step-by-step instructions for carrying out the entire review process. In addition, it is also helpful to provide them with reminders about things that they should keep in mind as they approach their review task. Examples of such step-by-step instructions and general reminders, drawn from the Title IV proposal review process, appear in Exhibit 3.5.

Training Reviewers

Once qualified reviewers have been selected and good rating scales and instructions have been developed, the final step prior to conducting the review is to train the reviewers to use the review forms and supporting materials. If there were one cardinal principle to be followed in training reviewers, it is that **the review form does not speak for itself!** Far too frequently, proposal review chairpersons or coordinators select competent reviewers, develop excellent review forms and materials, and then hand them to reviewers who apply them so differently as to defy combining their ratings into any meaningful decision. It should not be insulting to any competent reviewer to receive specific training in the use of a particular review form.

It is generally wise to send advance information to reviewers to enable them to thoroughly read documents which describe the basic purpose of the funding authorization, as well as copies of the RFP and any model proposals which may have been sent to potential applicants. Sending such advance information to reviewers can also serve as a reminder of the upcoming event for those few persons who may otherwise forget or "double schedule" their time. Samples of materials that might be sent to reviewers in advance are suggested by materials shown in Exhibit 3.6.

To assist reviewers in attaining maximum consistency in rating proposals, it is often wise to have all reviewers rate one or more sample proposals during the training session, applying all criteria as would be the case in a real review. Any differences in application of criteria, scoring, or recommendations concerning the proposal should be discussed until those differences can be resolved.

It is also often wise to withhold from reviewers information about the total dollar amounts available to be awarded, at least until after they have conducted an initial review of each proposal and reached a summary rating. Otherwise, their judgments may be unduly influenced by the fiscal issue. Admittedly, there are some cases, for other reasons, where it is important for reviewers to be informed of the total amount of available resources; however, whether or not information about the overall dollars available is shared in advance with the reviewers is a decision that should be carefully considered.

An Example of Reviewer Training

To provide a brief example of how the above considerations can be integrated in an effort to provide good training to reviewers, the following example is drawn from one annual Title IV proposal review process.

The following list of materials provided the core materials for training of proposal reviewers:

- a detailed step-by-step summary of the review and rating process to be followed by each team member

- a summary sheet of important things to keep in mind when reviewing Title IV proposals

- general instructions to help standardize reviewers' ratings

- a rating sheet for adoptable projects for use by individual team members

- a rating sheet for continuing developmental projects for use by individual team members

- a summary sheet for composite team ratings and recommendations for each adoptable project

- a summary sheet for composite team ratings and recommendations for each continuing developmental project.

All reviewers received and read, prior to the review, copies of the RFP and model proposal sent to all districts. In addition, they received explicit and intensive training on the purpose of Title IV, the criteria and procedures to be used in judging the proposals, and the rating sheets and instructions designed to standardize the ratings and eliminate scaling problems. Federal regulations and state compliance requirements were also reviewed by all team members. Lists and descriptions of Federal and State validated projects were provided to teams scheduled to review adoptable projects. Finally, examples of ratings from the previous Title IV review were used to identify effective and ineffective techniques for using and summarizing the rating sheets. Training was conducted in three phases: (a) reading RFP materials and model proposals by all team members prior to the proposal review; (b) training of team leaders in the rating and summarizing procedures on the evening before the proposal review; and (c) training of all team members during the first morning of the two-day proposal review.

This training, in conjunction with the review forms and other instructions provided reviewers, resulted in an extremely high degree of consistency in team ratings, as will be described in the next chapter.

EXHIBITS FOR CHAPTER 3

EXHIBIT 3.1: DD COUNCIL PROPOSAL REVIEW FORM

GENERAL INSTRUCTIONS

Each application should be independently rated by each panel member using the appropriate rating forms. Brief justification for each rating should be provided. The explanation accompanying each rating category on the forms as well as the contents of the memorandum "Project Funds Available Under DD Act" should provide sufficient information about what should be contained in each proposal. Each proposal should be given a total number of points by summarizing the points given in each of the following categories.

I	STATEMENT OF NEED	(0 - 20)	_____
II	QUALITY OF OBJECTIVES	(0 - 5)	_____
III	WORK PLAN	(0 - 20)	_____
IV	EVALUATION PLAN	(0 - 20)	_____
V	CAPABILITY OF APPLICANT	(0 - 15)	_____
VI	PROSPECTS FOR FUTURE FUNDING	(0 - 10)	_____
VII	APPROPRIATENESS OF BUDGET	(0 - 10)	_____
	TOTAL RATING	(0 - 100)	_____

A general strategy to use in assigning points to each of the categories follows:

IF, WITH REGARD TO THIS CATEGORY, THE PROPOSAL EXHIBITS:

a. No or almost no problems or weakness → assign approximately 90% to 100% of possible points

b. Minor problems or weaknesses which could likely be corrected as a condition of funding → assign approximately 75% to 89% of possible points

c. Moderate problems which could jeopardize the success of the project in meeting the objectives of DD Council funding → assign approximately 50% to 74% of possible points

d. Major problems which definitely will jeopardize the success of the project in meeting the objectives of DD Council funding → assign approximately 25% to 49% of possible points

e. Little of no compliance with what the proposal should have contained for this category → assign approximately 0% to 24% of possible points

RATING OF APPLICATION
FOR DD COUNCIL FUNDS FOR FY87

Title of Proposal	Application #

RATINGS				RECOMMENDED ACTION (check one)
	I STATEMENT OF NEED	(0 - 20)	_____	
	II QUALITY OF OBJECTIVES	(0 - 5)	_____	_____ APPROVAL
	III WORK PLAN	(0 - 20)	_____	_____ DISAPPROVAL
	IV EVALUATION PLAN	(0 - 20)	_____	_____ CONDITIONAL APPROVAL (conditions must be explained below)
	V CAPABILITY OF APPLICANT	(0 - 15)	_____	
	VI PROSPECTS FOR FUTURE FUNDING	(0 - 10)	_____	
	VII APPROPRIATENESS OF BUDGET	(0 - 10)	_____	DO YOU CONSIDER THIS PROJECT AS: (check one)
	TOTAL RATING	(0 - 100)	_____	Direct Service? _____ or Indirect Service? _____

RATIONALE FOR RECOMMENDED ACTION

(continue on next page)

RATIONALE FOR RECOMMENDED ACTION (continued):

RECOMMENDATIONS FOR TECHNICAL ASSISTANCE:

_____

Signature of Reviewer

I. STATEMENT OF NEED (20 points)

YES	SOMEWHAT	NO	
‾‾‾	‾‾‾	‾‾‾	Is the need for such a project clearly established?
‾‾‾	‾‾‾	‾‾‾	Does the project fall within one of the Council's service priorities.
‾‾‾	‾‾‾	‾‾‾	Is there a high probability that the results of the project will be valuable for other service providers?
‾‾‾	‾‾‾	‾‾‾	Is this a need that no one else is mandated to meet?

RATING

STRENGTHS		WEAKNESSES

II. QUALITY OF OBJECTIVES (5 points)

YES	SOMEWHAT	NO	
‾‾‾	‾‾‾	‾‾‾	Are objectives clearly stated in measurable terms?
‾‾‾	‾‾‾	‾‾‾	Are objectives related directly to the identified need?
‾‾‾	‾‾‾	‾‾‾	Are objectives focused on outcomes rather than processes?

RATING

STRENGTHS		WEAKNESSES

III. WORK PLAN (20 points)

YES	SOMEWHAT	NO	
____	____	____	Are procedures for <u>development</u> and <u>implementation</u> appropriate, technically adequate, and sufficient for the scope of the project?
____	____	____	Will the project result in outcomes or deliverables which are programmatically important, adequately meet the identified need(s), and can be effectively disseminated?
____	____	____	Is a reasonable time line included?
____	____	____	Is cooperation from necessary agencies or persons assured?
____	____	____	If direct service is proposed, is the estimated number of DD people to receive service stated?
____	____	____	Are deliverables which would be useful for other agencies/persons described?

RATING

STRENGTHS		WEAKNESSES

IV. EVALUATION PLAN (20 points)

YES	SOMEWHAT	NO	
____	____	____	Is the evaluation plan technically adequate and appropriately conceptualized to provide valid information about the effectiveness of the project?
____	____	____	If this is a direct service project, will objective measures of development progress (appropriately coordinated with the client's IHPs) be utilized?
____	____	____	Does the evaluation plan provide information about each project?

RATING

STRENGTHS		WEAKNESSES

V. CAPABILITY OF APPLICANT (15 points)

YES	SOMEWHAT	NO	
_____	_____	_____	Are there personnel proposed for the project (either those on the agency staff or others proposed via consultancies or technical assistance) who possess the necessary expertise and experience?
_____	_____	_____	Is there evidence that the efforts of various staff members will be effectively coordinated and managed?
_____	_____	_____	Are responsibilities of each staff member specified?
_____	_____	_____	If this is a continuation proposal, does past performance justify continued funding?

RATING

STRENGTHS		WEAKNESSES

VI. PROSPECTS FOR FUTURE FUNDING (10 points)

YES	SOMEWHAT	NO	
_____	_____	_____	If the project is successful, is there a strong potential that alternative funding will be available to support the project after DD Council funding is completed?
_____	_____	_____	If this is a second or third year project, has the offeror made concrete progress in securing funds from other sources?

RATING

STRENGTHS		WEAKNESSES

EXHIBIT 3.1: DD COUNCIL REVIEW FORM (continued)

VII. APPROPRIATENESS OF BUDGET (10 points)

YES	SOMEWHAT	NO	
———	———	———	Is the overall budget reasonable and appropriate to adequately implement and test the effectiveness of the program?
———	———	———	Are individual budget line items appropriate and supported by sufficient justifications?
———	———	———	Is the proposed approach at least as cost effective as the alternative?

RATING

STRENGTHS		WEAKNESSES

EXHIBIT 3.2: TITLE IV PROPOSAL REVIEW FORM

GENERAL INSTRUCTIONS

Each application should be independently rated by each panel member using the appropriate rating forms. Brief justification for each rating should be provided. The explanation accompanying each rating category on the forms as well as the contents of the memorandum "Request for Title IV - Part C Proposals for FY81" should provide sufficient information about what should be contained in each proposal. Each proposal should be given a total number of points by summarizing the points given in each of the following categories.

CONTINUING DEVELOPMENTAL PROPOSALS

	Category	Range of Points
I	Past Performance	0 - 30
II	Statement of Need	0 - 10
III	Quality of Objectives	0 - 10
IV	Statement of Work	0 - 20
V	Qualification of Personnel	0 - 20
VI	Cost Effectiveness	0 - 10
	TOTAL	0 - 100

ADOPTABLE PROPOSALS

	Category	Range of Points
I	Statement of Need	0 - 35
II	Quality of Objectives	0 - 10
III	Statement of Work	0 - 25
IV	Qualification of Personnel	0 - 20
V	Cost Effectiveness	0 - 10
	TOTAL	0 - 100

IF, WITH REGARD TO THIS CATEGORY, THE PROPOSAL EXHIBITS:

ASSIGN POINTS WITHIN THE FOLLOWING RANGES:

Points Possible:

	10	20	25	30	35
a. No or almost no problems or weakness	9 - 10	18 - 20	23 - 25	27 - 30	32 - 35
b. Minor problems or weaknesses which could likely be corrected as a condition of funding	7 - 8	15 - 17	19 - 22	23 - 26	27 - 31
c. Moderate problems which could jeopardize the success of the project in meeting the objectives of Title IV - Part C	5 - 6	10 - 14	13 - 18	15 - 22	18 - 26
d. Major problems which definitely will jeopardize the success of the project in meeting the objectives of Title IV - Part C	3 - 4	6 - 9	7 - 12	8 - 14	9 - 17
e. Little of no compliance with what the proposal should have contained for this category	0 - 2	0 - 5	0 - 6	0 - 7	0 - 8

Application for Funds under Title IV - Part C

ADOPTABLE PROJECTS

District Title			Application #	
RATINGS	I STATEMENT OF NEED	(0 - 35)	_____	RECOMMENDED ACTION (place an "X" in appropriate space)
	II QUALITY OF OBJECTIVES	(0 - 10)	_____	
	III STATEMENT OF WORK	(0 - 25)	_____	_____ APPROVAL
	IV QUALIFICATION OF PERSONNEL	(0 - 20)	_____	_____ DISAPPROVAL
	V COST EFFECTIVENESS	(0 - 10)	_____	_____ CONDITIONAL APPROVAL (conditions must
	TOTAL RATING	(0 - 100)	_____	be explained below)

RATIONALE FOR RECOMMENDED ACTION (recommendations must relate specifically to above ratings. Consideration should not be given to any other factors)

_____   _____
Signature of Chairperson   Date

I. STATEMENT OF NEED (0 - 35) Is the project responding to a priority area of need within the LEA? Is there evidence that some type of systematic process was used to establish this area of need and that the project has the support of LEA administration and other key personnel?

RATING

STRENGTHS		WEAKNESSES

II. QUALITY OF OBJECTIVES (0 - 10) Are objectives clearly stated in measurable terms, obviously related directly to the need identified by the LEA, and focused on outcomes rather than processes?

RATING

STRENGTHS		WEAKNESSES

III. STATEMENT OF WORK (0 - 25) Was the process used to select this particular adoptable adequate to ensure that the selected project will meet the identified need? Are adequate provisions built into the adoption process to ensure that key elements of the validated project are maintained and appropriate contact is had with the original developer or certified trainer? Are procedures for implementation and evaluation appropriate, technically adequate, and sufficient for the scope of the project? Will the project result in outcomes or deliverables which are educationally important and which adequately meet the identified need(s)?

RATING

STRENGTHS		WEAKNESSES

IV. QUALIFICATION OF PERSONNEL (0 - 20)   Do the personnel currently proposed for the project (either those on the LEA staff, or others proposed via consultancies or technical assistance) possess the necessary expertise and experience to carry out the proposed project? Is there evidence that the efforts of various staff members will be effectively coordinated and managed?

RATING

STRENGTHS		WEAKNESSES

<u>V. COST EFFECTIVENESS (0 - 10)</u>   Is the overall budget reasonable and appropriate to adequately implement and test the effectiveness of the program within the adopting LEA? Do any individual budget line items seem inappropriate or lack sufficient justification?

RATING

STRENGTHS		WEAKNESSES

Application for Funds under Title IV - Part C

CONTINUING DEVELOPMENTAL PROJECTS

District Title			Application #
RATINGS	I PAST PERFORMANCE	(0 - 30) _____	RECOMMENDED ACTION (place an "X" in appropriate space)
	II STATEMENT OF NEED	(0 - 10) _____	
	III QUALITY OF OBJECTIVES	(0 - 10) _____	_____ APPROVAL
	IV STATEMENT OF WORK	(0 - 20) _____	_____ DISAPPROVAL
	V QUALIFICATIONS OF PERSONNEL	(0 - 20) _____	_____ CONDITIONAL APPROVAL (conditions must be explained below)
	VI COST EFFECTIVENESS	(0 - 10) _____	
	TOTAL RATING	(0 - 100) _____	

RATIONALE FOR RECOMMENDED ACTION (recommendations must relate specifically to above ratings. Consideration should not be given to any other factors)

_____   _____
Signature of Reviewer   Date

I. PAST PERFORMANCE (0 - 30) Does the project's past performance provide convincing evidence that there is a high probability that the project will be successful in accomplishing the purpose of Title IV - Part C? Have previous activities conformed with original projections and have timelines been met? Does previous work provide an adequate foundation for what is being proposed?

RATING

STRENGTHS		WEAKNESSES

II. STATEMENT OF NEED (0 - 10) Although it is central to the success of Title IV - Part C that projects respond to priority LEA needs, it can usually be assumed that continuing developmentals have already demonstrated such a need -- hence the relatively low weighting. However, the needs statement is so critical that some consideration is still important. Has this area been identified as a priority LEA need through some type of systematic and comprehensive process? Is there evidence that the project has prior support of LEA administration and other key LEA personnel?

RATING

STRENGTHS		WEAKNESSES

III. QUALITY OF OBJECTIVES (0 - 10) Are objectives clearly stated in measurable terms, obviously related directly to the need identified by the LEA, and focused on outcomes rather than process?

RATING

STRENGTHS		WEAKNESSES

IV. STATEMENT OF WORK (0 - 20)   Are program development and evaluation procedures clearly described, adequate to respond to the previously identified need(s), and sufficiently conceptualized? Will the proposed activities and deliverables build appropriately on what has been accomplished and learned previously?

RATING

STRENGTHS		WEAKNESSES

<u>V. QUALIFICATIONS OF PERSONNEL (0 - 20)</u> Do the personnel currently proposed for the project (either those on the LEA staff, or others proposed via consultancies or technical assistance) possess the necessary expertise and experience to carry out the proposed project? Is there evidence that the efforts of various staff members will be effectively coordinated and managed?

RATING

STRENGTHS		WEAKNESSES

<u>VI. COST EFFECTIVENESS (0 - 10)</u>   Is the overall budget reasonable and appropriate for the work which is proposed? If this is the 2nd or 3rd year of the project, is LEA financial support increasing and Title IV - Part C support decreasing; or if not, is there appropriate justification? Do any individual line items seem inappropriate (too high or too low)?

RATING

STRENGTHS		WEAKNESSES

EXHIBIT 3.3: U.S. DEPARTMENT OF EDUCATION PROPOSAL REVIEW FORM

APPLICATION TECHNICAL REVIEW

HANDICAPPED RESEARCH AND DEMONSTRATION, CFDA 84.023

AUTHORITY: Chapter III-2. Grants Administration Manual, Sections 641 and 642 of Part E Of the Education of the Handicapped Act (20 U.S.C. 1441, 1442)

INSTRUCTIONS: See the "Application/Proposal Review" brochure.

PRINT OR TYPE	APPLICANT INSTITUTION	APPLICATION NUMBER 023 _ _ _ _ _ _ _

Each criterion score may range from the minimum to the maximum indicated. Score a criterion that is "barely adequate" at the midpoint.

Criteria		Independent Rating	Final Rating
1. IMPORTANCE	(0-15)	_____	(1) _____
2. IMPACT	(0-15)	_____	(2) _____
3. SOUNDNESS	(0-30)	_____	(3) _____
4. PLAN OF OPERATION	(0-10)	_____	(4) _____
5. EVALUATION PLAN	(0- 5)	_____	(5) _____
6. QUALITY OF KEY PERSONNEL	(0-10)	_____	(6) _____
7. ADEQUACY OF RESOURCES	(0- 5)	_____	(7) _____
8. BUDGET AND COST EFFECTIVENESS	(0-10)	_____	(8) _____
TOTAL RATING	(0-100)	_____	(T) _____

OVERALL RECOMMENDATION

(Enter an "X" in the appropriate space provided below)

___ APPROVAL   ___ DISAPPROVAL   ___ CONDITIONAL APPROVAL
(Conditions must be included with *required* JUSTIFICATION on the next page.)

REVIEWER (print name below)	PROJECT OFFICER (print name below)
SIGNATURE OF REVIEWER	DATE	

OE FORM 9020 REVISED 10/80   PREVIOUS EDITIONS ARE OBSOLETE

JUSTIFICATION. (Justification for OVER-ALL RECOMMENDATION must relate specifically to the RATINGS on the preceding page. Consideration should *not* be given to any other factors.)

1. IMPORTANCE (0 to 15 points)

Potential importance of the project to the education of the handicapped. Look for information that shows that:

(i) The area of research is important to the particular target group(s) addressed, *and* that

(ii) This particular project will make an important contribution in that area.

STRENGTHS	WEAKNESSES

COMMENTS

L. IMPORTANCE   (0-15) _____

2. IMPACT (0 to 15 points)

The probable impact of proposed research and development products and the extent to which products can be expected to have a direct influence on the handicapped or personnel responsible for the education of the handicapped.

Look for information that shows that:

(i) The products are usable by schools, teachers and others responsible for educating the handicapped.

(ii) The results of the project will be widely disseminated to those interested in making use of them.

STRENGTHS	WEAKNESSES

COMMENTS

2. IMPACT   (0-15) _____

3. SOUNDNESS (0 to 30 points)

Technical soundness of the research and development plan and adequacy of specification of procedures.

Look for information that shows that:

(i) The research design will yield answers to the research questions the project addresses.
(ii) The sample is selected to represent the target group(s) that the project's product will be used for.
(iii) The data are analyzed sufficiently to provide answers to the research questions.

STRENGTHS	WEAKNESSES

COMMENTS

3.   SOUNDNESS   (0-30) ____

4. PLAN OF OPERATION (0 to 10 points)

Look for information that shows:
(i) High quality in the design of the project;
(ii) An effective plan of management that insures proper and efficient administration of the project;
(iii) A clear description of how the objectives of the project relate to the purpose of the program;
(iv) The way the applicant plans to use its resources and personnel to achieve each objective; and

(v) A clear description of how the applicant will provide equal access and treatment for eligible project participants who are members of groups that have been traditionally underrepresented such as —

(A) Members of racial or ethnic minority groups;

(B) Women;

(C) Handicapped persons; and

(D) The elderly.

STRENGTHS	WEAKNESSES

COMMENTS

4. PLAN OF OPERATION (0-10) ____

5. EVALUATION PLAN (0 to 5 points)

Look for information that shows methods of evaluation that are appropriate for the project and, to the extent possible, are objective and produce data that are quantifiable.

STRENGTHS	WEAKNESSES

COMMENTS

5. EVALUATION PLAN (0-5) ____

6. QUALITY OF KEY PERSONNEL (0 to 10 points)

Look for information that shows:
(i) The qualifications of the project director (if one is to be used);
(ii) The qualifications of each of the other key personnel to be used in the project;
(iii) The time that each person referred to in paragraphs (i) and (ii) plans to commit to the project; and
(iv) The extent to which the applicant, as part of its nondiscriminatory employment practices, encourages applications for employment from persons who are members of groups that have been traditionally underrepresented such as —

(A) Members of racial or ethnic minority groups;

(B) Women;

(C) Handicapped persons; and

(D) The elderly.

To determine the qualifications of a person, consider evidence of past experience and training in fields related to the objectives of the project as well as other information that the applicant provides.

STRENGTHS	WEAKNESSES

COMMENTS

6. QUALITY OF KEY PERSONNEL (0-10)___

7. ADEQUACY OF RESOURCES (0 to 5 points)

Look for information that shows that:
(i) The facilities that the applicant plans to use are adequate;
(ii) The equipment and supplies that the applicant plans to use are adequate;

(iii) Access is available to subject samples; and
(iv) There is a commitment of cooperating schools or agencies to the project.

STRENGTHS	WEAKNESSES

COMMENTS

7. ADEQUACY OF RESOURCES (0-5) ____

8. BUDGET AND COST EFFECTIVENESS (0 to 10 points)

Look for information that shows that:
(i) The budget for the project is adequate to support the project activities; and

(ii) Costs are reasonable in relation to the objectives of the project.

STRENGTHS	WEAKNESSES

COMMENTS

8. BUDGET AND COST EFFECTIVENESS (0-10)

EXHIBIT 3.4 : INSTRUCTIONS FOR CONVERTING JUDGMENTS TO NUMERICAL RATINGS (EXCERPT)

3. SOUNDNESS   **MAXIMUM 30 POINTS**

Technical soundness of the research and development plan and adequacy of specification of procedures.

The important point here is to consider both the appropriateness of procedures and the extent to which they are specified. Are the problems, objectives, procedures, and expected products, and the relationships among these all clearly and logically stated? Does the statement of the procedures to be followed include all applicable design components? Are the criterion measures appropriate for the questions asked and analyses used? Are the proposed timelines realistic? Factors generally meriting consideration include:

(1) Population description

(2) Sampling procedures

(3) Specification of variables

(4) Instrumentation

(5) Data collection, procedures, and related training

(6) Experimental treatments

(7) Data analysis

(8) Timelines

SOUNDNESS

0   Proposed procedures are not appropriate to the questions posed.

0   **What** is to be done is well specified but the document provides virtually no information on **how** the project will be carried out.

5-10   Procedures are generally sound, but sampling procedures and data reduction procedures are not appropriate.

5-10   The general procedural plan seems appropriate but specific details are lacking.

15   Technical aspects are generally appropriate and well specified, but better techniques are available for training of data collectors and for statistical analysis.

20-25   Procedures are appropriate and adequately specified for the most part, but more detailed timelines would have clarified the design.

20-25   All procedural elements are appropriate and adequately specified but it is unclear why these particular techniques were selected.

30   Every procedural element is appropriate to the question, completely detailed, and carefully considered. Possible alternative approaches have been considered but the selected procedural plan has been documented as the most appropriate.

30   The design is so well specified that a stranger should be able to complete the project to the satisfaction of the investigator.

EXHIBIT 3.5:   GENERAL INSTRUCTIONS FOR TITLE IV PROPOSAL REVIEW

 WASATCH INSTITUTE
FOR RESEARCH AND EVALUATION

TO: John Bennion

FROM: Blaine Worthen

RE: Proposal Review

I am enclosing two items for your perusal before our proposed review meeting next week.

The first is a brief list of reminders the State Title IV Program Officer wants you and your team members to keep in mind in reviewing the Title IV proposals. I know all of us are probably aware of most of these things, but it would be easy to forget them when we start dealing with the piles of proposals next week.

The second item is a summary of the proposal review process which I prepared as an information item for the State Office of Education administrators. It occurred to me that it might also serve as a useful summary for our use during our pre-review training of the proposal reviewers.

I'll bring copies of both to our training session, but I thought you might like to see them in advance.

THINGS TO KEEP IN MIND IN REVIEWING TITLE IV - C PROPOSALS

1. All proposals should meet minimum criteria for a Title IV - C adoptable or continuing developmental proposal (e.g., for adoptables, there should be an identifiable validated project which is being adopted).

2. Title IV - C projects should supplement, not **supplant**, local district expenditures for personnel, etc.

3. Proposals should contain all the important elements outlined in the RFP. If any are missing, final funding authorization should not be given until and unless the district satisfactorily addresses the missing elements in a proposal addendum.

4. Where proposals are inadequate in technical areas (e.g., evaluation design, statement of objectives, timelines, statement of work) but the proposed project is judged as worthy of funding, the reviewer should stipulate that districts must obtain technical assistance. This might relate to the categories of "Approve" or "Conditionally Approve" as follows:

> APPROVE: (A) - need no technical assistance
>   (B) - **suggest** specific technical assistance to district, let district decide whether to request funds.
>
> CONDITIONALLY
> APPROVE: **require** specific technical assistance; and build budget for TA into approved proposal budget.

TITLE IV - C PROPOSAL REVIEW PROCESS SUMMARY

1. All proposals submitted to USOE will be given identification numbers and references to specific LEAs will be removed to avoid possible bias in the review process. In preparation for the review, proposals will be duplicated in four copies and bound for use by reviewers (USOE).

2. All reviewers will be given explicit training on (a) the purpose of Title IV, (b) criteria to be used in judging the proposals, and (c) the review rating sheets and procedures. General instructions for using the rating sheets will be used to help standardize ratings of reviewers and eliminate scaling problems (USOE/WIRE[*]).

3. Proposals will be assigned to review teams so that no LEA staff member will be asked to judge a submission from his/her own district (WIRE).

---

[*]"WIRE" represents the Wasatch Institute for Research and Evaluation, the agency which coordinated this particular proposed review process.

4. All proposals in any one category (e.g., adoptables in districts in Category C) will be assigned so as to be rated by the same team; thus, districts will only have to compete against other districts of approximately the same size (WIRE).

5. Each proposal will be read and rated independently by each member of the four-person team rating proposals in that category. Each reviewer will fill out the rating sheet (shown hereafter) with both numerical rating and written comments about the proposal's strengths and weaknesses on each criterion. The written comments **must** be interpretable and readable, since they will be provided to the USOE staff (Reviewers).

6. After all proposals have been read by a team, the team members will discuss each proposal at length, comparing their ratings and individual lists of strengths and weaknesses. An attempt will be made to reach a consensus on ratings for each category. In a few instances when team members cannot reach complete agreement on a rating, the individual reviewer ratings will be averaged to produce the team's rating on that criterion (Teams).

7. After team ratings of each proposal are completed, the team chairperson will assign for each proposal a team member to summarize the team members' comments and ratings on one rating form (same color as individual rating forms). These should be shared with other team members to assure that it accurately reflects all team members' sentiments. It is particularly important that team suggestions concerning required technical assistance or proposal modifications be clearly spelled out in this document (Team Chairperson).

8. Team chairpersons will fill out a summary rating form (blue or green) which contains: (a) the team's rating on each criterion and for the project as a whole; (b) the team's recommendation concerning whether to approve, conditionally approve, or disapprove the proposed project; and (c) comments which summarize the team's rationale for their ratings and recommendations. This summary will depend heavily on the multi-page summary described in #7 above. (Team Chairperson)

9. When each team has completed their ratings, all summary rating forms and individual reviewer ratings and more detailed lists of strengths and weaknesses will be given to USOE officials to aid in their deliberations. The four team chairmen will debrief with USOE officials to (a) respond to any questions about any of the ratings or recommendations, and (b) check and standardize scaling across teams so that ratings from all teams will be on a comparable scale for comparative purposes. (WIRE)

Reviewers of proposals for Title IV - C funding

USOE - April 10, 8:00 - 5:00; April 11, until completed

Rooms: East and West Board - B and C Conference Rooms

Teams -

#1	Glenn Latham Lynn Haslam Jerry Peterson Bruce Owens	Category W Proposals
#2	Russell Osguthorpe Maria Detrio Sharon Beck JoAnn Seghini	Category X Proposals
#3	Adrian VanMondfrans Marian Karpis Morgan Hawks Colleen Colton	Category Y Proposals
#4	Blaine Worthen Betty Cowley Gary Carlston John Bennion	Category Z Proposals

Dinner Meeting - Team Chairpersons, Bill Cowan

At: Hilton Hotel
Towne Hall Restaurant
6:00 p.m.

Meet Bill Cowan at USOE at 5:30 to review materials to see if all is in order.

Per diem - $37.50
Per mile - $ .23

Honorarium - $135.00
41 proposals reviewed

EXHIBIT 3.6: ADVANCE TRAINING MATERIALS FOR REVIEWERS

 WASATCH INSTITUTE FOR RESEARCH AND EVALUATION

TO: TITLE IV PROPOSAL REVIEW PANEL MEMBERS

FROM: Blaine R. Worthen

RE: Materials to Review Prior to our Meeting in Salt Lake

By now each of you should have received a call from Barbara, our project coordinator, to confirm arrangements for our upcoming review of Utah's Title IV - C proposals for 1981-82. I trust she was able to answer any questions you may have had concerning details of scheduling, reimbursements, and the like.

I am enclosing a copy of the Request for Proposals (RFP) which was sent to each district in early February. Since this RFP outlines precisely what should be in every Title IV - C proposal submitted to the State, I think it is important that you familiarize yourself with the guidelines and criteria contained in this document. Please read it **before** you arrive at our first team meeting on April 10. The short training session we will have at 8:00 a.m. that morning will assume you have already read the RFP, and the training will focus on more detail concerning criteria and ratings which will not be very meaningful unless you have already read the RFP.

We will start our training session **promptly** at 8:00 a.m. on Friday morning in Room 201 of the Utah State Office of Education at 250 East 5th South in Salt Lake City. For those of you who live in outlying areas, it would seem wise to travel to Salt Lake on Thursday evening so as to be "bright-eyed" for Friday's session.

For those of you who participated in last year's review, there have been some alterations in the RFP and in the rating scales and procedures, so please plan to be in attendance for the entire training session.

I look forward to seeing you there!

P.S.   Regarding Room # above, the proposal review will use several rooms, consequently the best procedure would be to go to Bill Cowan's office and his secretary will direct you from there.

CHAPTER 4: CONDUCTING THE PROPOSAL REVIEW PROCESS AND PRESENTING THE RESULTS

The importance of all prior preparation notwithstanding, no amount of careful groundwork will be profitable if the actual review process is conducted in a haphazard fashion. Procedures and considerations important to assure a smooth, effective, and objective review process are discussed briefly in this chapter.

COORDINATION AND SUPPORT

The proposal review process should be directed and coordinated by someone who possesses the following characteristics:

- substantive and/or methodological knowledge relevant to the work called for in the proposals

- experience in writing and evaluating proposals

- experience in managing prior review panels or similar efforts

- credibility and respect of other professionals who will serve as reviewers.

The review coordinator may be either an officer or staff member from the funding agency (referred to hereafter as the program officer) or a consultant hired by the funding agency to direct this particular review. In many instances, it is wise to have both persons present, the consultant to coordinate the review effort and the program officer to answer questions that may arise about the funding authorization and to oversee the process to assure the funding agency that the review was conducted appropriately.

In cases where the program officer coordinates the proposal review, s/he normally should not sit as a reviewer, share the results of his/her analysis of the proposal, vote on scoring or rating the proposal, or make statements that the reviewers could construe as a preference for either approval or disapproval. The program officer should answer requests for information about program regulations and assure that only the published criteria are used in individual and panel reviews.

In cases where a consultant serves as coordinator of the review process, s/he can also serve as a reviewer. If multiple panels are being used however, there may be some merit in having the coordinator free to roam from panel to panel during the review process to watch for difficulties that might arise and can be rectified by early intervention and, if necessary, on-the-spot retraining.

It is also often important to have clerical support available during proposal reviews. This is obviously necessary if there is an expectation that the review process will end with finished products in the hands of the program officer. Even if that is not the case, it is often helpful for reviewers to have photocopies of one another's hand-written summaries and rating sheets as they discuss particular proposals and attempt to reach consensus on their ratings and recommendations.

INDIVIDUAL RATING OF PROPOSALS

External reviews of proposals are typically composed of two parts: individual reviews and panel or team summaries. All individual reviews should be completed prior to aggregating into total panel reviews. Each individual review should result in the following:

- a specific recommendation as to whether a project merits support or not (approval, conditional approval, or disapproval)

- ratings of each proposal which accurately reflect the reviewer's judgment regarding the merits of each proposal reviewed

- detailed documentation of specific strengths and weaknesses of each application which substantiates the rating.

In completing the review process, the individual reviewer should complete a cover page for each proposal in which the overall recommendation and overall rating on each major criterion are given. In support of this summary information, the reviewer should provide his/her answer to each review question or criterion by entering an appropriate numerical score within the range given and providing narrative comments regarding the strengths and weaknesses of each criterion in support of the rating. These responses are important in providing feedback to applicants as well as to funding agency personnel. Whenever possible, comments should be supported with specific examples from the proposal, including page numbers, if appropriate.

Ratings should be consistent with written comments; e.g., disapproval and approval recommendations should be consistent with the ratings and written narrative. If there is a discrepancy between the reviewer's rating/comments and the recommendation, an explanation for that discrepancy should be provided. For example, few things are more difficult to defend than a proposal which has **not** been approved for funding, even though all of the comments and numerical ratings by the individual reviewers are quite positive.

Evaluation comments are important components in the review process. Such comments provide valuable input into the decision making process, and also provide helpful feedback to the applicants, both those who are funded and those who are unsuccessful. Whether or not it is required by law for a particular funding program, it is a good idea to make available to applicants the reviewers' evaluation of their proposals. The easiest way to do this is to conduct the review in such a way that the same material submitted to the funding agency can also be given to requesting applicants after reviewers' names have been deleted to preserve anonymity. Consequently, full and fair justification of reviewers' judgments is of utmost importance.

High-quality reviews and summary statements typically possess the following characteristics:

- justification in complete sentences

- objectivity of judgment

- specific reconciliation when an overall judgment is based on a mixture of strengths and weaknesses

- specification of exactly what elements of a given criterion were considered

- differentiation of comments based on fact from those based on professional judgment

- consideration of all criteria.

Low-quality reviews and summaries are characterized by the following:

- too little documentation (i.e., "yes", and "no", or "good")

- comments which cannot be clearly related to the criteria

- comments which are inconsistent with the ratings or recommendations

- comments which are inaccurate

- comments which are facetious or derogatory, biased, or otherwise inappropriate or unprofessional

- judgments which are outside the scope or responsibility of the review (for example, "the indirect cost rate is too high").

As an example, in the Utah Title IV proposal review process, each proposal was read and rated independently by each member of a four-person team assigned to rate proposals within that particular category. Each reviewer filled out each review form with both a numerical rating and written comments about the proposal's strengths and weaknesses on each criterion. Proposals that clearly failed to meet minimal federal guidelines for a Title IV proposal were identified by individual reviewers and did not receive completed ratings. These individual ratings of proposals served as a basis for the subsequent panel ratings.

TEAM RATINGS OF PROPOSALS

After all proposals have been read and judged by individual reviewers, the next step is to bring the individual reviewers together as teams or as a total panel to discuss their individual perceptions. The decision of whether to convene teams or the total panel depends upon how proposals were distributed to readers. If all members of the panel read the same proposals, then the entire panel would convene to discuss those proposals. If, however, members of a sub-panel team were the only ones to read specific proposals, then only those team members would meet to discuss those specific proposals. In the remainder of this section, the process will be described as it would occur within proposal review teams. The same principles would, however, apply if total panel discussions were under consideration.

The purpose of the team discussions is to provide for consideration of each proposal by the individual reviewers, each of whom has appropriate experience but who may bring a different perspective to bear on the discussion. Team members should discuss each proposal in turn at whatever length is necessary. The team leader should give a brief summary of the objectives of the proposal and all of the reviewers should have an opportunity to share their evaluations of that proposal, comparing their ratings and individual listings of strengths and weaknesses. If serious disagreements exist, an attempt should normally be made to reach a consensus on ratings for each category. In those cases, it is not necessary for team members to change their written individual ratings or comments during or as a result of the group discussion, unless those individual comments are to be submitted separately to the funding agency. In those cases, if a reviewer does change his or her view of a proposal as a result of the discussion, it would be appropriate to add the changed ratings and list the major reason(s), then date and sign the amendment to the original rating as well. In any instance where team members cannot reach complete agreement on a rating, the individual reviewer ratings might be averaged to produce a team rating on that criterion.

After team ratings of each proposal are completed, it is generally desirable for the team chairperson to assign a team member to each proposal to summarize the team's comments and ratings on **one** rating form. These summaries should be shared with other team members to assure that they accurately reflect all team members' sentiments. Team suggestions concerning required technical assistance or proposed modification should be clearly spelled out in this document.

Team chairpersons should fill out a summary rating for each proposal which contains: (a) the team's rating on each criterion and for the proposal as a whole; (b) the team's recommendation concerning whether to approve, conditionally approve, or disapprove the proposal; and (c) comments which summarize the team's rationale for its rating and recommendations. This summary will depend heavily on the summary described in the preceding paragraph.

Team Recommendations

The overall team recommendation concerning the final disposition of the proposal is of such importance as to deserve some additional comment. Over the years, reviewers have offered recommendations ranging from "This proposal should be enshrined" to "This proposal should be entombed." In most cases, however, it is best to limit the team to three choices: approval, conditional approval, or disapproval. Distinctions among these three categories can generally be made very reliably if the review has been appropriately conducted. One way of defining these categories which seems to have worked quite well is reproduced below from the U.S. Department of Education's Special Education Program's 1983 Grant Announcement.

a) **Approval** - The application is worthy of support essentially as submitted. Minor modifications may still be suggested in your narrative justification, but this recommendation (approval) assumes that the project merits support even if such suggestions are rejected by the applicant.

b) **Conditional Approval** - This recommendation is not necessarily inferior to a recommendation of "Approval." Conditions (required modifications) must be very precisely noted, and it should be assumed that the application will have equal promise as a straight "Approval" if the conditions are accepted by the applicant even though the original application requires modification.

c) **Disapproval** - This recommendation should be used when the application is not viewed as acceptable as submitted, nor is it susceptible to a judgment of approval except with substantial modifications.

When the team has completed its ratings, all summary rating forms and, where appropriate, individual reviewer ratings and more detailed listings of strengths and weaknesses should be given to funding agency officials to aid in their deliberations. Samples of completed summary rating forms from the Utah Title IV Proposal Review for an approved, conditionally approved, and disapproved project are shown in Exhibit 4.1 at the end of this chapter. These samples show the general level at which team leaders summarized and reported team ratings and recommendations. District and project names and other identifying information (including the name of the chairperson) have been deleted from these samples to preserve anonymity. Exhibit 4.2 shows a model for an individual reviewer's rating sheet from the DD Council project, also changed where necessary to preserve anonymity.

It is also helpful to funding agency officials to have some estimate of how consistently the individual reviewers and team apply the criteria in rating and making recommendations about the proposals. For example, efforts were made in the Utah Title IV Proposal Review to assess the extent to which all teams were applying the criteria and awarding points in a comparable manner. Each of three proposals were read and rated independently by the different teams and the summary ratings compared. In no instance did the results vary by more than four points (on a scale of 100 possible), demonstrating that a high degree of consistency in teams' ratings can be achieved by using the procedures outlined in this chapter.

PRESENTATION OF PROPOSAL REVIEW RESULTS

It is generally useful to provide funding agency officers with more than the individual proposal summary rating sheets described in the previous section. It is generally also helpful to provide a summary of ratings and recommendations across all proposals such as the example shown in Table 1 on the next page.

In some funding agencies, political considerations exert an undue influence, often resulting in final decisions about proposal approval being made more on the basis of politics than review panel ratings. If the funding agency is aware of this problem and wishes to correct it, it can be largely handled by using a "double blind" review process in which the decision makers and the funding agency are left unaware of the identity of the proposing agency or individual until after decisions and funding recommendations have been made. For example, proposal numbers such as those shown in Table 1 could be assigned by a trusted staff member who keeps proposal identity confidential until such time as final decisions are made. In this case, funding agency officers would receive only information comparable to that shown in Table 1 and in Exhibit 4.1 in which the identity of the proposer is omitted. However, in such cases, it is almost impossible to consider the applicant's history of success with similar projects as a part of the approval criteria because doing so would almost always reveal the applicant's identity.

Table 1

1981 Title IV Ratings/Ranking

Proposal Number	Team Rating	*Recommended Action	Proposal Number	Team Rating	*Recommended Action
125-2	94	C	204-2	70	C
101-2	93	A	200-2	70	C
102-2	89	A	201-2	69	D
302-2	87	A	107-2	60	C
208-2	87	A	126-2	60	C
108-2	86	A	111-2	59	C
105-2	85	A	116-2	59	C
206-2	85	A	121-2	58	D
207-2	85	A	109-2	56	D
203-2	85	A	122-2	46	D
128-2	83	A	115-2	46	D
209-2	81	C	100-2	43	D
129-2	81	C	112-2	32	D
117-2	79	C	124-2	20	D
104-2	79	C	303-2	19	D
110-2	78	C	103-2	19	D
127-2	78	C	301-2	18	D
111-2	76	C	120-2	12	D
300-2	76	C	123-2	NR	D
113-2	73	C	119-2	NR	D
205-2	73	C	106-2	NR	D
202-2	71	C			

*Key to Recommended Action: A = Approve
C = Conditional Approval
D = Disapprove
NR = Not Rated (Failed to Qualify as Title IV Proposal)

Subsequent to the completion of the panel review, funding agency officers will typically prepare a technical summary for each of the applications recommended for funding, including a pre-funding cover memorandum to present to the official responsible for approval. Such a pre-funding cover memorandum will generally include a description of the review process, the ranking, the summary review form with written justification for ratings, a discussion of the issues regarding the review and the funding competition, and a final recommendation, including the dollar amount of the award. This document will generally serve as the final document for approval of each grant or contract.

It is also appropriate, following each proposal review, to communicate appreciation to reviewers who are often interested in the outcomes of the review. Samples of such letters to reviewers and team leaders are contained in Exhibit 4.3.

EXHIBITS FOR CHAPTER 4

EXHIBIT 4.1: COMPLETED PROPOSAL REVIEW TEAM SUMMARIES

Application for Funds under Title IV - Part C

ADOPTABLE PROJECTS

District Title				Application #	
RATINGS	I STATEMENT OF NEED	(0 - 35)	28	RECOMMENDED ACTION (place an "X" in appropriate space)	
	II QUALITY OF OBJECTIVES	(0 - 10)	8		
	III STATEMENT OF WORK	(0 - 25)	22	X APPROVAL	
	IV QUALIFICATION OF PERSONNEL	(0 - 20)	17	____ DISAPPROVAL	
	V COST EFFECTIVENESS	(0 - 10)	8	____ CONDITIONAL APPROVAL (conditions must	
	TOTAL RATING	(0 - 100)	83	be explained below)	

RATIONALE FOR RECOMMENDED ACTION (recommendations must relate specifically to above ratings. Consideration should not be given to any other factors)

This is a good project and well worthy of approval. The need, objectives, work statement, personnel qualifications and budget are all high quality.

There are, however, several suggestions which the team would strongly urge the district to consider and, hopefully, accept. They include:

1. Increase the criterion level for objective 2 to a minimum of 10%, and possibly higher, depending on the items below;

2. Have criterion levels on objectives reviewed and approved by district administrators to make certain that they agree that they are appropriate cut-off points to demonstrate success and failure, and that the rationale for setting these levels is acceptable;

3. Strengthen the evaluation design in specific areas noted in section III of the team's critique "synthesis";

4. Remove "books" from the "capital expenditures" category and transfer it to an appropriate budget category. (i.e. - O.k. to buy books, but not O.K. to label them as capital expenditures).

Philip Brown   April 3, 1986
Signature of Chairperson   Date

Application for Funds under Title IV - Part C

ADOPTABLE PROJECTS

District Title				Application #
RATINGS	I STATEMENT OF NEED	(0 - 35)	5	RECOMMENDED ACTION (place an "X" in appropriate space)
	II QUALITY OF OBJECTIVES	(0 - 10)	2	
	III STATEMENT OF WORK	(0 - 25)	3	_____ APPROVAL
	IV QUALIFICATION OF PERSONNEL	(0 - 20)	0	X DISAPPROVAL
	V COST EFFECTIVENESS	(0 - 10)	2	_____ CONDITIONAL APPROVAL (conditions must
	TOTAL RATING	(0 - 100)	12	be explained below)

RATIONALE FOR RECOMMENDED ACTION (recommendations must relate specifically to above ratings. Consideration should not be given to any other factors)

This proposal suffers from the following serious weaknesses

1) There is no evidence that the project meets a priority need within the district, that the proposed adoptable project meets the alledged need, that key district personnel are committed to the project, or that the project would or could be continued with district funds once Title IV funds are expended.

2) The concept of "seed money" and increasing financial particip by the district (across years of the project) does not appear to be understood by the offeror. Nor do they appear to be aware that adoptable projects are slated for only one year of funding, except in extreme circumstances. Thei

(over)

Jack Keevel   4-3-86

Signature of Chairperson   Date

request for a three year project, without a <u>compelling</u> justification, is inappropriate.

3) There is little if any impact on students proposed or measured The objectives are vague, replete with jargon, and pre-occupied with processes.

4) The statement of work says little and promises nearly nothing

5) Budget information is incomplete and the required narrative is missing

6) Timelines are missing

7) The proposal ignores the "guidelines for proposals" sent out by the state office of Education -- deviating in almost all particulars from that model

Application for Funds under Title IV - Part C

ADOPTABLE PROJECTS

District Title				Application #	
RATINGS	I STATEMENT OF NEED	(0 - 35)	27	RECOMMENDED ACTION (place an "X" in appropriate space)	
	II QUALITY OF OBJECTIVES	(0 - 10)	8		
	III STATEMENT OF WORK	(0 - 25)	20	_____ APPROVAL	
	IV QUALIFICATION OF PERSONNEL	(0 - 20)	15	_____ DISAPPROVAL	
	V COST EFFECTIVENESS	(0 - 10)	9	X CONDITIONAL APPROVAL (conditions must	
	TOTAL RATING	(0 - 100)	79	be explained below)	

RATIONALE FOR RECOMMENDED ACTION (recommendations must relate specifically to above ratings. Consideration should not be given to any other factors)

THIS PROJECT IS RECOMMENDED FOR APPROVAL IF THE FOLLOWING CONDITIONS ARE MET:

1. CERTIFICATION THAT THE DISTRICT WILL CONTINUE THE PROJECT IF IT IS SUCCESSFUL SHOULD BE OBTAINED FROM THE SUPERINTENDENT;

2. OBJECTIVES SHOULD BE REVIEWED, REFINED TO FOCUS MORE SPECIFICALLY ON OUTCOMES, AND PERHAPS SCALED DOW IN SCOPE TO THE POINT WHERE THEY AR CLEARLY FEASIBLE WITHIN THE AVAILABLE RESOURCES; AND

3. THE EVALUATION PLAN (AND MEASUR NEED TO BE EXTENDED TO COLLECT DATA THAT BEAR DIRECTLY ON THE PROJECT OBJECTIVES. QUALIFI - CATIONS OF THE PROPOSED EVALUATOR

_____Mary Evans_____ _April 3, 1_
Signature of Chairperson   Date

MUST BE ESTABLISHED AND/OR OUTSIDE
TECHNICAL ASSISTANCE FROM WELL-
QUALIFIED EVALUATION PERSONNEL SHOULD
BE OBTAINED TO PERFORM THIS TASK. THE
MEASUREMENT ISSUES ARE DIFFICULT
AND SEASONED EVALUATORS/PSYCHO-
METRICIANS WOULD BE OF HELP. IT IS
SUGGESTED THAT $500 BE ADDED TO THE
BUDGET TO OBTAIN SUCH ASSISTANCE.

OTHERWISE, THE PROJECT PLAN IS
VERY GOOD. NEEDS APPEAR TO BE SUF-
FICIENTLY ESTABLISHED; INDEED, THE
PROPOSAL APPEARS TO GROW OUT OF A
BROADLY BASED EXPRESSION OF A STRONG
DISTRICT NEED. THE OBJECTIVES ARE
CLEAR. CONTACT WITH THE PARENT
(DAVIS) PROJECT IS VERY ADEQUATE. IMPLE-
MENTATION PLANS AND TIME LINES ARE
GOOD. THE BUDGET REQUEST IS REASONABLE
AND THE JUSTIFICATION APPEARS SOUND.
THE PROJECT IS, ON BALANCE, QUITE
WELL-CONCEIVED.

EXHIBIT 4.2: COMPLETED INDIVIDUAL REVIEWER'S RATING OF PROPOSAL

RATING OF APPLICATION
FOR DD COUNCIL FUNDS FOR FY87

Title of Proposal Hillsdale Case Management	Application # 87-12

RATINGS				
	I STATEMENT OF NEED	(0 - 20)	18	RECOMMENDED ACTION (check one)
	II QUALITY OF OBJECTIVES	(0 - 5)	3	
	III WORK PLAN	(0 - 20)	8	_____ APPROVAL
	IV EVALUATION PLAN	(0 - 20)	16	_____ DISAPPROVAL
	V CAPABILITY OF APPLICANT	(0 - 15)	5	X CONDITIONAL APPROVAL (conditions must be explained below)
	VI PROSPECTS FOR FUTURE FUNDING	(0 - 10)	7	
	VII APPROPRIATENESS OF BUDGET	(0 - 10)	7	DO YOU CONSIDER THIS PROJECT AS: (check one)
	TOTAL RATING	(0 - 100)	64	Direct Service? X or Indirect Service? _____

RATIONALE FOR RECOMMENDED ACTION

Evidence for need is well presented, and everything except for "fringe benefit" costs seem reasonable. The evaluation plan, though brief, is quite good (particularly for objective #1). The most serious weaknes[s] are the lack of detail in the work plan (e.g. how will materials for training be developed, what procedures will be used for soliciting work opportunities, how will outreach and dissemination be done?); the absence of a time line and budget narrative, and the uncertain nature of applicant capability because of the lack of a project director and the absence of a management plan for quality control.

(continue on next page)

RATIONALE FOR RECOMMENDED ACTION (continued):

Although not a high priority for funding, the need to which the project would be responding makes it worth further consideration if the following issues can be resolved:

1) workplan needs to be specified in greater detail

2) Objectives (especially #2) need to be worded more clearly

3) An acceptable timeline must be submitted

4) Budget items (especially fringe benefits) need further justification

5) An acceptable project director must be hired (they might consider .25 FTE from someone currently on staff for the first year)

RECOMMENDATIONS FOR TECHNICAL ASSISTANCE:

Until project staff are hired its virtually impossible knowing whether the project will require technical assistance from the DD Council. Because the agency has not previously conducted a DD Council project, they probably will need assistance with the evaluation and monitoring procedures.

Karl R. White
_____
Signature of Reviewer

I. STATEMENT OF NEED (20 points)

YES	SOMEWHAT	NO	
✓	—	—	Is the need for such a project clearly established?
✓	—	—	Does the project fall within one of the Council's service priorities.
—	—	✓	Is there a high probability that the results of the project will be valuable for other service providers?
✓	—	—	Is this a need that no one else is mandated to meet?

RATING

STRENGTHS	18	WEAKNESSES
• Cites White House conference report -- convincing data • Hillsdale's survey suggests a pool of 55 adults in need of service (see chart A) • Conclusions from Task Force on Institutional Options is very supportive		No discussion of how others could use the materials or "model" developed by this project -- hence its unclear whether this would assist others. If the project is successful, this could be remedied however

II. QUALITY OF OBJECTIVES (5 points)

YES	SOMEWHAT	NO	
✓	—	—	Are objectives clearly stated in measurable terms?
—	✓	—	Are objectives related directly to the identified need?
—	—	✓	Are objectives focused on outcomes rather than processes?

RATING

STRENGTHS	3	WEAKNESSES
objectives are specifically stated and are related to the needs Outcomes can be inferred from most objectives, but are now states as processes or activities		objectives are not linked to individual developmental progress made by clients objective #2 about developing staff capability is overly vague -- whose staff, in what areas, how measured?

III. WORK PLAN (20 points)

YES	SOMEWHAT	NO	
___	✓	___	Are procedures for <u>development</u> and <u>implementation</u> appropriate, technically adequate, and sufficient for the scope of the project?
___	✓	___	Will the project result in outcomes or deliverables which are programmatically important, adequately meet the identified need(s), and can be effectively disseminated?
___	___	✓	Is a reasonable time line included?
___	___	✓	Is cooperation from necessary agencies or persons assured?
✓	___	___	If direct service is proposed, is the estimated number of DD people to receive service stated?
___	✓	___	Are deliverables which would be useful for other agencies/persons described?

RATING

STRENGTHS	8	WEAKNESSES
# of DD people to be served was specified Each objective was discussed in the workplan -- it all sounds logical, but was not supported by enough detail Project deliverables were specified		• Advisory council plans too vague • No indication of how 2nd & 3rd years will build on 1st • No timeline, or letters of support • obj. #2 -- procedures to support & provide administrative assistance are unclear • obj. #3 -- needs more detail on content of training manual, & field testing

IV. EVALUATION PLAN (20 points)

YES	SOMEWHAT	NO	
___	✓	___	Is the evaluation plan technically adequate and appropriately conceptualized to provide valid information about the effectiveness of the project?
___	✓	___	If this is a direct service project, will objective measures of development progress (appropriately coordinated with the client's IHPs) be utilized?
✓	___	___	Does the evaluation plan provide information about each project?

RATING

STRENGTHS	16	WEAKNESSES
Basic ideas for evaluation of objective #1 are quite good. It's somewhat sketchy about how data will be collected, but not bad Measures are individually referenced		Evaluation for objectives #'s 2 & 3 are much weaker -- this may be because both are really more important in later years Procedures for measuring counselor and trainee satisfaction are overly vague

V. CAPABILITY OF APPLICANT (15 points)

YES	SOMEWHAT	NO	
____	____	✓	Are there personnel proposed for the project (either those on the agency staff or others proposed via consultancies or technical assistance) who possess the necessary expertise and experience?
____	✓	____	Is there evidence that the efforts of various staff members will be effectively coordinated and managed?
____	✓	____	Are responsibilities of each staff member specified?
____	____ N/A ____		If this is a continuation proposal, does past performance justify continued funding?

RATING

STRENGTHS	5	WEAKNESSES
Plans for training new staff sound good Job descriptions have been developed		Project Director unspecified – given importance of this position, this is a critical weakness No description of organizational capability or track record; or how quality control will be assured

VI. PROSPECTS FOR FUTURE FUNDING (10 points)

YES	SOMEWHAT	NO	
____	✓	____	If the project is successful, is there a strong potential that alternative funding will be available to support the project after DD Council funding is completed?
____	____ N/A ____		If this is a second or third year project, has the offeror made concrete progress in securing funds from other sources?

RATING

STRENGTHS	7	WEAKNESSES
Agency has some ideas for obtaining continuation funds, but they lack specificity. Since this is a first year project, that's not too serious. The idea is one that should be fundable through a state agency if it is successful		

VII. APPROPRIATENESS OF BUDGET (10 points)

YES	SOMEWHAT	NO	
✓	___	___	Is the overall budget reasonable and appropriate to adequately implement and test the effectiveness of the program?
___	✓	___	Are individual budget line items appropriate and supported by sufficient justifications?
✓	___	___	Is the proposed approach at least as cost effective as the alternative?

RATING

STRENGTHS	7	WEAKNESSES
Required match -- most of it in hard money, is already available Most line items seem reasonable		Individual categories included in fringe benefits account for 42% of salaries -- this seems excessive No budget narrative to justify line items Projected salaries may be too low to attract qualified people

EXHIBIT 4.3: SAMPLE LETTERS OF APPRECIATION TO REVIEWERS

**WASATCH INSTITUTE
FOR RESEARCH AND EVALUATION**

Dr. Glenn Latham
UMC 68
Utah State University
Logan, Utah 84322

Dear Glenn:

This is an overdue note of appreciation to you for your participation as a chairman in the review of Title IV-C proposals on April 10 and 11. Although I know those were two grueling work days, it seems the results were worth the effort. Bill Cowan and other State Office of Education officials have indicated several times that this is the best review of Title IV proposals they have had. I attribute the success of the review primarily to the contribution made by you and your colleagues.

Perhaps you will be interested in the enclosed list, which summarizes the points and recommendations for the proposals we evaluated. I think it is impressive that the merged point distribution and recommendations of the four teams flowed together so smoothly. With two minor exceptions (e.g., the highest rated program was recommended for **conditional** approval only because of one inappropriate budget item that has to be changed), the ratings and recommendations of the teams fit together beautifully, as you can see. These results, and the excellent syntheses your team prepared will be extremely useful to the U.S.O.E. as they make their final decisions about which Title IV-C proposals to fund.

Again, many thanks for your excellent help. You and your colleagues were a tremendous group of reviewers and a real joy to work with.

Sincerely,

Blaine R. Worthen
Director

BRW:baw

Enclosure

TITLE IV RATINGS/RANKING

Number	District	Project	Rating	**Recommended Action
125-2			94	C
101-2			93	A
102-2			89	A
*D-302-2			87	A
*D-208-2			87	A
108-2			86	A
105-2			85	A
*D-206-2			85	A
*D-207-2			85	A
*D-203-2			85	A
128-2			83	A
*D-209-2			81	C
129-2			81	C
117-2			79	C
104-2			79	C
110-2			78	C
127-2			78	C
111-2			76	C
300-2			76	C
113-2			73	C
*D 205-2			73	C
*D-202-2			71	C
*D-204-2			70	C
*D-200-2			70	C
*D-201-2			69	D
107-2			60	C
126-2			60	C
111-2			59	C
116-2			59	C
121-2			58	D
109-2			56	D
122-2			46	D
115-2			46	D
100-2			43	D
112-2			32	D
124-2			20	D
303-2			19	D
103-2			19	D
301-2			18	D
120-2			12	D
123-2			NR	D
119-2			NR	D
106-2			NR	D

*D = Development Grant

**Key to Recommended Action:
A = Approve
C = Conditional approval
D = Disapprove

WASATCH INSTITUTE FOR RESEARCH AND EVALUATION

Albert Augustus, Principal
Westside Elementary School
150 South 14th Street
Tooele, Utah 84074

Dear Al:

This letter is to formally express our appreciation for the superb job of Title IV - Part C proposal reviewing to which you contributed on April 18th and 19th. From all the feedback we have received, the Utah State Office of Education staff were very pleased with the results - in large part because of the conscientiousness with which you and your colleagues worked.

As you may be aware, there is a possibility that the Title IV program will sustain significant budget cuts next year. If such budget cuts do occur, the detailed and objective way in which the proposals were reviewed and the resulting judgments documented will make the difficult task of deciding which projects to fund as fair, equitable, and defensible as possible. We believe that the value of your contribution to this year's proposal review process will be even more apparent as the negotiations and funding process proceeds.

As a final note, we are very interested in obtaining your feedback about how the proposal review process could be improved in the future. Your perception as to the strengths and weaknesses of this year's process as well as suggestions for improvement would be most welcome.

Thanks again for all of your help.

Sincerely,

Karl R. White
Project Director

Blaine R. Worthen
Associate Project Director

SECTION II: ONSITE EVALUTION GUIDELINES AND PROCEDURES

Bob Stake observed over fifteen years ago:

> The shortage of procedures for making systematic observations of educational activities is particularly dismaying because the **site visit** is a widely used evaluation method. When a large-scale program is under way at some distant place, the most common way to evaluate it is to appoint a small number of respected persons to go there and inspect it. This method receives a proper share of criticism. It is evident that the program staff works hard to make the operation atypically handsome during the visit and the visitors grasp at the slimmest shred of evidence for something to report. Despite these defects, the method of site visits deserves its eminence because it is designed for the most sensitive instruments available: experienced and insightful men. Furthermore, it is capable of quick adaptation to local circumstances [13, pp. 192-193].

What was true then is still true today, on two counts. First, site visits remain one of the most useful evaluation techniques available for judging the worth of programs, projects, and processes, as well as providing input to project managers that can be used to improve the quality of the program. Secondly, there remains a shortage of available procedural guidelines for use by those responsible for planning and implementing such a program of site visits. Although there is a fair amount of literature dealing with the conduct or philosophy of accreditation site visits and their use in evaluation [14-16], this literature focuses primarily on particular accreditation agency requirements and procedures tailored to meet these requirements. Consequently, these writings are not particularly relevant to designing and conducting onsite evaluations of projects of the nature described in this book.

Based on experience with designing, implementing, and monitoring programs of site visits to various funding programs in multiple states, this section provides a description of procedures and processes necessary to operate a high-quality system of onsite evaluations and gives examples of many of the materials that can serve as a foundation for creating a similar system for any specific program. The value of the procedural guidelines in this section is attested to by their impact on the programs for which they were designed and to which they were applied. For example, the Utah Title IV program (where many of these materials were first used) showed steady progress in terms of accomplishing the goals of the funding agency during the three-year period in which the onsite evaluations were conducted. In fact, the resultant evaluation system was selected by federal officials as one of two exemplary statewide Title IV evaluation systems. Furthermore, the threat and aversiveness that staff of individual projects so frequently associate with onsite evaluations was reduced dramatically by the particular procedures used in this system. As a result, project directors expressed increasingly positive attitudes towards evaluation in general and suggested that the particular onsite evaluation procedures tend to play an important instructional function in addition to the more typical accountability function associated with such evaluation activities.

What was true in these projects is probably also true for onsite evaluations of many other educational and social services programs and projects operated under guidelines which are rigorous and/or technical in nature. In short, the better the onsite evaluation, the more likely it is that projects will succeed in meeting the objectives for which they were funded.

It does not necessarily follow, however, that merely conducting onsite evaluations automatically results in improved programs. If one major purpose of onsite evaluation visits (indeed, all evaluation) is to determine worth in order to differentiate among effective and ineffective programs and procedures, then it seems that the processes and methodologies used in the conduct of many onsite evaluations are failing. For example, in an evaluation study of the Colorado state administration of ESEA Title III, it was noted that no Title III project in Colorado had ever been terminated as a result of an onsite visit [17]. Two alternative hypotheses obviously emerge. Either all projects were above average and worthy of continuation, or the Title III onsite evaluation procedures being used failed to differentiate good projects from the bad projects that should have been terminated. Somehow, the latter conclusion seems more plausible.

Similar patterns of non-functional, non-discriminating onsite evaluations have occurred and continue to be prevalent in many onsite evaluation systems. Closer analysis reveals that such failures frequently stem from poor onsite procedures that produce unreliable and invalid information. Perhaps the greatest single factor that contributes to the abundance of abysmal evaluations is the widely shared misconception that any educated person can do an onsite evaluation, since it requires only that a competent professional spend time onsite, examining the program of interest, and thereafter report on the program's quality and effectiveness. This innocence is nearly as rampant as the naivete' that leads many to believe they are experts on educational matters simply because they survived twelve years of schooling in the elementary and secondary schools.

This problem is further exacerbated by the commonly held (and erroneous) notion that the person familiar with the content or substance of the program need know little or nothing of evaluation techniques, per se, to be an effective onsite evaluator. Such notions have been debunked elsewhere [18] and will not be repeated here. Suffice it to say that "onsite strolls" of content specialists have resulted in such broadspread misapplication of the professional judgment approach to evaluation as to render such an approach suspect, on its face, to many professional evaluators.

In this context, the importance of guidelines that will help improve and standardize onsite evaluation procedures should be obvious. They will also go far toward streamlining onsite visits and making them as non-disruptive as possible, thus helping to reduce the resentment which so often accompanies clumsily handled and intrusive onsite visits.

PURPOSE AND ORGANIZATION OF THIS SECTION

This section includes a variety of procedures that can be used by individual onsite evaluators or by funding agencies charged with the responsibility for arranging or conducting onsite evaluation. The section is subdivided into three chapters, which deal with the following general topics:

- Chapter 5: Various uses and functions of onsite evaluations

- Chapter 6: Considerations and activities preceding the onsite visit

- Chapter 7: Conducting, reporting, and evaluating onsite evaluations

CHAPTER 5: USES AND FUNCTIONS OF ONSITE EVALUATIONS

Onsite evaluation is one of the most frequently employed strategies to evaluate programs in education, social services, and related areas. Its popularity is doubtlessly due, at least in part, to the fact that it can be a simple and straightforward approach that is not dependent on extensive technical expertise in psychometrics, statistics, or data manipulation. For those who view professional judgment as constituting the core of evaluation, onsite evaluation is often the preferred approach. Further, onsite evaluation is a flexible method that can be used as a part of a wide variety of evaluation methods.

There are two related reasons why onsite evaluation visits are made: (1) because they are often required by legislation or by some funding or regulatory agency; and (2) because onsite evaluation is viewed as a valuable technique in assisting programs and projects to reach their full potential.

USING ONSITE EVALUATION TO IMPROVE EDUCATIONAL PROGRAMS

Evaluations of an educational/social service program or project are conducted to determine the worth or value of that program or project in attaining a particular goal. Such evaluation requires that information be collected in relation to specified criteria, leading to determination of the value of the program or project and, therefore, leading to informed decisions about those enterprises. In other words, evaluation should provide relevant evidence beyond the usual rhetoric or unsupported opinions typically offered as the basis for judgments about the worth of educational and social service programs or processes.

Evaluation should discriminate among successful and unsuccessful programs or projects. This discriminative function of evaluation should assist national, state, and local agencies in making various decisions concerning the programs and projects they operate -- decisions about which programs are sufficiently exemplary to warrant dissemination, which areas need improvement, and whether to continue or terminate a project.

The Utah Title IV evaluation provides a good example of how onsite evaluation visits can contribute to the success of educational activities. As illustrated in Table 2, once the onsite evaluation system described in this chapter was implemented, the quality of funded projects steadily improved, according to the ratings made by independent external evaluators, as a function of the accountability and feedback that represented the central thrusts of the onsite visits over this particular three-year period.

Table 2

Comparison of Overall Ratings for Utah Title IV Projects
Over a Three-Year Time Period

Type of Project	Year #1	Year #2	Year #3
Developmental Projects	77.8	87.4	90.2
Adoptable Projects	70.6	75.3	85.0

NOTE: The scale permitted ratings from 0 to 100, with 100 being high.

Project directors, state officials, and onsite chairpersons agreed that the improvement noted was due primarily to the onsite evaluation visits. These beneficial effects of the onsite visits were evident in both developmental and adoptable projects. If the assumption holds that better project ratings are a reflection of better projects, and if better educational projects yield higher benefits to children, then the benefits of high quality onsite evaluations are evident.

The value of such onsite evaluations was emphasized by the state officials in their report to the federal government at the conclusion of that three-year period, as indicated by the following excerpt from that report.

Conducting external onsite evaluations to a sample of all funded projects does represent a significant investment of resources by the State Office of Education. However, these evaluations, when conducted in a systematic and consistent manner, appear to have substantial impact on the quality of projects which are operated. The prespecified criteria and written reports produced by the external onsite evaluation teams have provided important guidance for project directors and appear to have assisted them substantially in understanding the purposes and requirements of Title IV - C funding. In addition, information from the external onsite evaluations have provided project directors with information which appears to have been beneficial in helping them to improve their project in subsequent years. Finally, information from these evaluation visits has provided a wealth of information which can be used by the State Office of Education in improving and monitoring and management of Title IV - C type funding. Therefore, it is recommended that the state continue some form of external onsite evaluation visits as they look for ways to continue to provide support for innovative and exemplary program development and implementation [19, pp. 49].

MANDATED ONSITE EVALUATIONS

The apparent utility of onsite evaluations in improving educational programs and projects has led to onsite visits frequently being required by congressional or regulatory agencies or by the federal and local agencies who implement their mandates. For example, in Title III of the Elementary and Secondary Education Act, later modified to become Title IV, it was required that "the State Educational Agency shall develop procedures and criteria for the on-site evaluation, at least annually, of all Title III projects in the State . . . . Such procedures shall also provide affected projects with recommendations made as a result of on-site evaluations and follow-up methods to ensure proper implementation" [20, pp. 30-31].

Each state, therefore, developed a plan to conduct onsite evaluations as part of its overall evaluation of Title III. For example, the Colorado State Plan differentiated two types of evaluation for fulfilling the requirements specified by the Federal mandate: internal evaluation (usually done by project personnel), and external evaluation (generally conducted through onsite visits). The following guidelines for external onsite evaluations were outlined in the Colorado Plan:

> The State Title III Director and his staff in consultation with the State Advisory Council will administer a program of annual on-site evaluations of Title III projects.
>
> On-site evaluations provide not only valuable information related to the operation of the project but also an opportunity for two-way communication between project personnel and persons of other communities. The specific objectives of on-site evaluations in Colorado are as follows:
>
> • Local school personnel will have increased knowledge of their Title III project through discussions with members of the visitation team and analysis of the written evaluation report.
>
> • Project personnel will be able to plan project activities more effectively utilizing evaluation reports of observed strengths, areas of needed improvements, and recommended changes.
>
> • Project personnel will be able to prepare continuation proposals and year-end reports.

- The evaluation of projects will provide reliable information which will be utilized in the dissemination program.

- Members of the evaluation team will gain first-hand information on the State Title III program and individual projects and will thus be able to assist in dissemination of information.

- By analyzing results of project evaluations, the State Title III Advisory Council and the professional staff will have increased information on needed educational innovations.

- The State Title III Advisory Council and Title III staff will be able to make informed decisions regarding continuation of project activities and budget requirements [21, p. 3].

Requirements for onsite evaluations have continued and spread to other educational and social service programs; today, many state and federal funding authorizations carry with them legal expectations of external evaluation, through onsite visits, of each funded project.

FORMATIVE VERSUS SUMMATIVE ONSITE EVALUATIONS

Conceivably, onsite evaluation visits might serve two functions: formative evaluation (providing information to help a project during its operation) and summative evaluation (gathering information at the end of a project to determine its final worth and impact). An additional function which might be served by an outside team is formative **help** (not evaluation). In this instance, one or more persons with expertise directly relevant to the content or the processes in the project might be called in to provide consultative help to the project director between the time the proposal is funded and the time the project begins. This activity, while highly recommended, is not an evaluation function and is not discussed further in this chapter, but is considered in a later chapter dealing with technical assistance.

Formative Functions of Onsite Evaluations

If used formatively, onsite evaluation visits can improve and strengthen a project. It is imperative that an objective, "cold, hard look" be taken by external evaluators during the course of the project. It need not be an unfriendly look, but it should introduce outside reality into a project before time, money, and all types of human and material resources have been expended in vain. It is little help to introduce such evaluations when the project has reached or nearly reached completion. It may simply be too late to save it. Of course, formative onsite evaluation visits may uncover many positive aspects of a project, in which case information concerning such strengths can be appropriately disseminated to assist other projects or agencies working on similar programs.

In one of the earlier evaluations of the administration of an onsite evaluation system, Goodwin emphasized the value of using the evaluation for formative purposes.

> Facilitation of project activities can be enhanced by providing annually an on-si.. team to evaluate **formatively** each Title III project. The team will be tailored to fit the project and will include a director from some other Title III project in the state. The on-site team will file a written report of its recommendations, a report that will be responded to in writing by project personnel within two months (indicating the project's response to each recommendation). If an on-site team determines that unsatisfactory progress is being made toward achievement of objectives, it can recommend that the Title III Office commission a further evaluation, of a summative nature, for the project. Failure to so recommend will indicate to the State Advisory Council that the on-site team deems the project worthy of continuation funding [17, p. 63].

Summative Functions of Onsite Evaluations

If used summatively, onsite evaluation visits can assist in determining which program, project, or process should be discontinued or continued and disseminated to other similar agencies and groups. It is essential that a funding agency determine the ultimate operational effectiveness of programs and projects supported through resources for which it is responsible. This is best done by external evaluation, which may take the form of a summative onsite evaluation visit conducted after the program or project is fully operational and has had the benefit of earlier formative evaluations and subsequent revision. Such summative onsite evaluations may certify the effectiveness of a project, thus helping to ensure its continuation and possible expansion, or it may show the project to be ineffectual, thus leading to its termination.

Formative and Summative Evaluation in Tandem

In practice, one often need not choose between formative and summative onsite evaluations. If resources permit simultaneous "cake-having" and "cake-eating," a particular educational project might receive both a formative onsite evaluation and a subsequent summative onsite evaluation. Further, the distinction between formative and summative evaluation is not always as clear in practice as it is in theory. A summative evaluation of a program that is continued will likely yield results that can be used formatively to improve the program's future operation.

If resources permit only a single onsite visit to a particular project, the choice of whether to use it for formative or summative purposes will depend on the alternative methods available to assure that both evaluation purposes will be addressed in some fashion during the life of the project. For example, if a member of the project staff is competent to conduct an internal, formative evaluation, but no mechanism for summative evaluation exists, it would seem wise to plan a summative, external onsite evaluation to be conducted at the end of the program. Conversely, if there is an external accrediting body that will conduct an annual onsite accreditation visit, but no good system of internal evaluation exists, it would be better to conduct an earlier, formative onsite evaluation visit.

Although the evaluation questions and criteria would be different in formative and summative onsite evaluations, the procedures and other considerations in conducting the visits would be similar. Therefore, no further distinction is made in the remainder of this book between formative and summative onsite evaluations.

PROGRAM AND FINANCIAL ONSITE AUDITS

Onsite visits have also been used to conduct evaluation-related activities such as program and financial audits. Program audits (of the type relevant here) focus on the extent to which a program or project is in compliance with specific guidelines or regulations. Financial audits focus on the extent to which project expenditures are in accordance with the amounts approved for specific budget categories. Either type of audit can be conducted as part of an onsite evaluation, and examples of onsite evaluation systems with embedded program and financial audits are given later in this chapter. With the exception of the specific questions and instruments, the procedures used in such audits are sufficiently similar that no separate onsite guidelines or procedures are offered herein.

CONSIDERATIONS IN USING ONSITE EVALUATIONS

Several issues need to be considered as one determines how to make the best use of onsite evaluations. The way in which each of the following issues is resolved will impact on the specific way in which the onsite evaluation is designed. However, the procedures and materials presented in this chapter establish a foundation from which such modifications can be readily made.

Nature of the Project(s) to be Visited

If a project to be evaluated is "one of a kind," and no similar projects are to be assessed, the onsite evaluation approach will be tailored to fit that project and the purposes to be served by its evaluation. If, however, the project is one of a class of projects which share a common funding source and similar expectations, general onsite evaluation procedures and instruments might be designed for use in each of the separate onsite evaluations of those projects. The main difference in these two situations lies in the fact that the questions, criteria and instruments in the first instance will be created **de novo** for each evaluation, while in the second, a general set of questions, criteria and instruments can be developed at the outset and evaluators can be trained to use them thereafter with multiple projects.

In the remainder of this chapter, it is assumed that the onsite evaluations under consideration are part of an overall evaluation system, such as the Title IV or DD Council evaluation systems. In most instances, the more generalizable guidelines and procedures proposed here can be readily adapted for use in the one-shot site visit.

Visiting a Sample of All Projects

If resources are limited, it might be necessary to conduct onsite evaluations of only a sample of the total population of projects or programs of interest. In such instances, the projects to be visited should be selected from among the operational projects to provide as much variability as possible along dimensions such as: (a) funding level; (b) geographical location of project; and (c) type of project. Whether the selection of projects is systematic or random, it is important that it be conducted in such a fashion that all projects have an opportunity of being included so that the need for accountability is felt by all projects.

Combining Onsite Evaluations With Other Data Collection

An onsite evaluation is often only one facet of an overall evaluation design; site visits can be used very effectively in conjunction with mailed questionnaire surveys, administration of cognitive and affective measures, and the like. In such cases, the guidelines and procedures presented in this book are still relevant. One of the primary advantages of using onsite evaluations in conjunction with other data collection activities is that the results of questionnaires, surveys, or other data collection might provide clues of possible problems or issues that should be probed in greater depth during onsite visits.

Duration of Site Visit

Onsite evaluation visits can vary in duration and intensity from a brief, informal stroll through a project, to an intensive and extensive week-long observation and examination of virtually every facet of the project's operation and activities. Although the guidelines and procedures presented hereafter in chapters 6 and 7 would have some relevance for an onsite visit of almost any duration or intensity, they are proposed primarily for use in comprehensive, thorough onsite evaluations of one to three days in duration.

Number of Evaluation Team Members

Onsite teams can obviously vary in size from a single evaluator to a large team presided over by a team leader or coordinator. It seems obvious that, all things being equal, larger, more complex programs or projects require larger numbers of team members to provide adequate coverage. It is also apparent that greater diversity of expertise can be represented in onsite teams with more team members. Although most of the guidelines and procedures presented in chapters 6 and 7 could be used by a lone onsite evaluator, with only minor adaptations, they are designed for use by onsite evaluation teams. Many of the procedures assume a two or three person team and some minor adjustments would be necessary with larger onsite teams.

Responsibility for Managing a System of Onsite Evaluations

Onsite evaluation systems can be managed directly by the funding agency or they can be managed by an agency contracted to coordinate the overall onsite evaluation system.

Management of onsite evaluations by either the funding agency or a contracted agency is infinitely preferable to having the programs or projects being evaluated arrange for their own external evaluations. This latter arrangement has little more to recommend it than does the dubious practice of allowing a bank to audit its own books.

CHAPTER 6: CONSIDERATIONS AND ACTIVITIES PRECEDING THE ONSITE VISIT

The utility of onsite evaluation visits will typically vary in direct proportion to the thoroughness and care that went into the evaluators' preparations for those visits. The several issues and activities that should be considered in preparing for onsite evaluations are discussed in the following sections.

FOCUSING THE ONSITE EVALUATION

A poorly focused onsite evaluation visit will produce no better result than will a poorly focused camera lens. "Focusing," as used here, refers to efforts to attain clarity at the outset as to the purposes to be served by the onsite visit, the general procedures to be used, and the evaluative questions to be answered.

To focus the onsite evaluation, it is necessary to answer, as a minimum, the following questions:

- Is the onsite evaluation to serve primarily a formative or a summative purpose?

- Is a financial audit or program compliance audit to be included as part of the onsite visit?

- Is the onsite visit part of an onsite evaluation system which contains extant guidelines and instruments, or must evaluative questions, criteria and instruments be developed specifically for this one onsite visit?

- Is the onsite visit a part of a broader evaluation of the program or project and, if so, how do the several pieces of the evaluation fit together to enhance the study and avoid duplication of effort?

- What is the duration of the onsite visit? What activities will occur?

- How many persons will be on the onsite team, what expertise need they possess, and how will they be prepared?

- Who is responsible for actually directing the onsite evaluation activities? To whom is that person ultimately responsible -- i.e., who is sponsoring the onsite evaluation?

Answers to these questions constitute the basic message in the remainder of this chapter.

DEVELOPING EVALUATION QUESTIONS

It is possible to use a variety of approaches to decide what questions should be answered during an onsite evaluation. For example, one might aim data collection techniques at determining the extent to which specific program or project objectives have been met. This is a perfectly respectable and useful way to approach an evaluation. However, it may miss some of the most important issues.

One very useful approach is to use those people affected by the program to identify the major evaluative questions which, if answered, will tell whether or not the program or project is working. Program sponsors, administrators and staff, and participants will each have specific questions they would like to see answered by the onsite evaluation. An easy first step is to ask everyone directly or indirectly involved in the program what they would like to learn from the onsite visit. Evaluators should feel free to inject their questions (and may need them for "pump-priming" so others get a feel of what is meant by "evaluative questions"), but a major portion of these questions should be drawn from those with a stake in the outcome of the study.

To illustrate this point, the following fictional diary entry of an evaluator planning the evaluation of a humanities program is offered, along with excerpts from a resulting draft of an evaluation plan as shown in Figure 1.

November 16. I spent part of today working with the evaluation steering committee, laying out the skeleton of an evaluation plan, which I suggested we do together. Some of the committee wanted the evaluation to focus on the curriculum goals and objectives, using those as organizers for collecting and reporting the data. But the board president noted that the objectives were really only part of the program, and she listed several important questions she felt would be overlooked if we were bound by the objectives. That was tremendous! It usually takes a fair bit of Rogerian counseling to get people to look beyond their written objectives, so I was quick to take the opportunity to tout the advantages of using evaluative questions as key organizers in an evaluation study. To illustrate, I put on the blackboard the questions I had gleaned over the past two days that they and others had said they would like the evaluation to answer. They got involved, started categorizing and collapsing questions, added others, and before we knew it, we had 17 evaluative questions that they all agreed should be dealt with in the study, plus a handful that were left in but viewed as lower in priority.

With time running out, we took a few of the questions and, using a matrix I offered, went through the exercise of identifying information we would need to answer them, listing where and how we would obtain the information, and so on. It was great to see the enthusiasm of several of the group when they began to realize how simple and straightforward it was. Once they had the hang of it, I suggested they fill out as much of the matrix as they could for the remaining questions and then send it to me. I would try to refine it, flesh out the evaluation plan, and send it back to them for their final approval.

Didn't get the plan finished, but I feel good about what we were able to accomplish. More important, this isn't going to be my evaluation plan, it is at least ours, if not theirs, built on questions they posed, and answered by information from sources they specified [22, p. 74].

Evaluative Questions	Information Required	Source of Information	Strategy/Method of Collecting Information
1. To what extent are the program objectives shared by important groups?	Ratings of importance of objectives.	a. Board of education b. Hum. Curr. Review Comm. c. Teachers d. Parents e. Other community members	a-b. Individual interviews c-e. Mailed questionnaire survey to all teachers, samples of others, using Phi Delta Kappa Goal Ranking Procedure
2. To what degree does the curriculum address all the stated objectives?	Coverage of stated objectives in lesson plans and other materials.	a. Humanities faculty b. External humanities experts	a. Faculty analysis of curriculum, match to objectives b. Review/critique of faculty analysis above
4. Is the content of the lesson plans faithful to the humanities?	Substantive adequacy of lessons and other materials.	External humanities experts	Expert review of lesson plans and materials
5. Are social attitudes in the community such that the curriculum can be successfully implemented here at this time?	Attitudes of Community members and influence groups toward humanities.	a. Community members b. Community influence groups (for example, PTA and service club officers)	Mailed questionnaire survey to sample of community's citizens plus all identified "influence leaders"
9. Do the lesson plans and other curriculum materials use sound instructional theory?	Knowledge of instructional theory and methods.	Expert in instructional theory	Expert review of lesson plans and materials
13. Do student attitudes demonstrate that the curriculum is producing the desired results?	Attitudes of students toward the values and concepts taught in the curriculum.	Students	a. Comparative design, using attitude scales, observation, and unobstrusive measures; and? b. Simulated situations, role-playing to get at real student attitudes (for example, attitudes toward elderly, stereotyping of elderly)

Figure 1: Excerpts From a Draft Evaluation Plan

Project sponsors and staff ostensibly will know what important questions about project activities and effects should be posed. Not so the onsite evaluator(s), at least not at the outset. This requires that onsite evaluators absorb in advance all the information they can about the project and its various facets. This will generally require that evaluation team members read all available project descriptions and other materials. This advance preparation is discussed in greater detail later; it is mentioned here because it serves as a basis for each team member generating tailored questions for use in obtaining particular information about the project during the course of the onsite visit. These questions should be sent to the onsite team leader so that they can be integrated with other questions during the development of onsite evaluation instruments. This activity is especially important in "one-shot" onsite visits where general evaluation guidelines and instruments do not exist **a priori.**

An additional example of onsite evaluation questions may help to illustrate the point. During the Utah Title IV onsite evaluation visits, data and information were collected relative to several evaluative questions. The specific questions about which information was collected are summerized below for both developmental and adoptable projects. For developmental projects the following questions were addressed.

1. Do project activities conform with approved plan or approved modifications?

2. Is the project responding to a priority area of significant need or weakness within the LEA?

3. Has an evaluation plan been implemented which will provide valid information about project effectiveness or impact?

4. If the project is effective, is there evidence that the LEA plans to continue the project after Title IV - Part C funding is completed?

5. Are appropriate and sufficient efforts being made to include private schools?

6. Do relevant LEA personnel sufficiently understand the purpose of Title IV and are they sufficiently aware of the expectations and requirements associated with accepting a Title IV - Part C grant?

7. Did the LEA make sufficient efforts to identify existing projects which may have met their needs?

8. Do project expenditures and financial accounting procedures conform with state and federal requirements?

For adoptable projects, the following questions were addressed.

1. Did project activities conform with approved plan or approved modifications? Were activities implemented in a quality-like manner that should lead to improved educational practice? If an adoptable project, were the key components of the original validated project implemented?

2. Was the project responding to a priority area of need or weakness within the LEA?

3. Did the project evaluation provide valid information about project effectiveness or impact? Did evaluation yield information which can assist the district in making decisions about project continuation?

4. If the project was effective, is there evidence that the LEA plans to continue the project after Title IV - C funding is completed?

5. Were appropriate and sufficient efforts made to include private schools?

6. Are relevant LEA personnel sufficiently aware of and do they understand the purpose of Title IV - C; and are they aware of the expectations and requirements associated with accepting a Title IV - C grant?

7. In selecting an adoptable program to meet their identified need, did the LEA sufficiently consider other options besides the one ultimately selected?

8. Did the project have sufficient contact with the original developer or with certified second generation trainers?

9. Do project expenditures and financial accounting procedures conform with state and federal requirements?

As can be seen from the preceding example, questions asked during onsite visits to developmental and adoptable projects differed somewhat because of different expectations for the two types of projects. These questions served as the driving force behind the evaluation instruments that were used during the onsite data collection activities.

DEVELOPMENT OF ONSITE EVALUATION INSTRUMENTS

One problem with many onsite evaluations is that judgments resulting from them are indefensibly subjective. If left unguided, it is easy for each member of an evaluation team to approach the onsite visit with inherently different values, priorities, and preferences, with the result that the "blind men" will report the elephant rather differently. This same problem extends to situations where different teams are assigned to conduct onsite visits of similar projects. If left to develop their own procedures and instruments, one team, guided by feelings of mercy, may end up rating a poor project more generously than the rating received by an excellent project which is evaluated by another team prone to identify and focus on project weaknesses.

In both of the above examples, lack of standardization of data collection procedures and instruments effectively prevents any sensible summarization across judgments of onsite team members or teams. To prevent such divergent perspectives of onsite teams or individual team members from reducing the utility of onsite evaluations, the way in which evaluation information is collected by each external onsite evaluation team should be standardized to allow for better summarization across projects or across individual team member's ratings where only one project is involved.

To achieve such standardization, it is necessary to develop instruments that incorporate the previously agreed-upon evaluative questions, to standardize criteria and data collection techniques insofar as possible, and to help onsite evaluators understand the type of information needed for the final onsite evaluation reports. By providing more structured training and instrumentation, the equity and uniformity of evaluative judgments can be enhanced and statements about the quality and impact of projects evaluated will be much more systematic and comprehensive.

A complete discussion of the principles of instrument development is far beyond the scope of this chapter. However, a few comments about matters of particular concern in constructing instruments for use in onsite evaluations will be offered in conjunction with several examples of instruments used in previous onsite evaluations. First, onsite data collection efforts will generally use a variety of data-collection methods in answering the evaluative questions posed. Onsite evaluators frequently interview members of the project and supervisory agencies, examine project records and materials, examine test scores or questionnaire data, observe the project in operation, and interview recipients of the service. Consequently, interview schedules, content analysis guides, and observation rating scales may all be a part of the instrumentation used during an onsite visit to collect the information which is summarized on the onsite evaluation instrument.

Secondly, in developing onsite rating scales, it is imperative that typical scaling problems (where different interpretations by different raters result in their assigning different weights and points on the same criterion) be eliminated or reduced to a minimum. This can be done by careful use of anchor points and careful standardization of what is meant by assignment of a particular score value or evaluative label. For example, if one were developing a rating scale item to be used by onsite evaluators to judge the **importance** of a particular research project in the area of special education, the use of anchor points outlined in Table 3 on the following page could be used to help standardize ratings of different evaluators.

Copies of one set of onsite evaluation instruments used with the Title IV project appear as Exhibit 6.1. Another set of materials, used with the DD Council project, which took a

Table 3

An Example of the Use of Anchor Points

Assign the points below IF:	This description reflects your conclusions about the **importance** of this project
0	The project has little or nothing to do with education of the handicapped.
0	The general area of investigation is undoubtedly important but the project fails to specify any particular research problem in Special Education to be addressed.
5	On face value the project is important, but there is no documentation, on the basis of either research or theory, that investigation in this area would prove fruitful.
5	This project would provide information of some interest, but the issue addressed is of relatively little consequence to the field of Special Education.
8	The project is justified in terms of the current state of the art. The issue is of interest and results should be of some value, but this is not a pressing problem in Special Education.
10	The research problem is clearly stated, well-justified on the basis of previous research, and of significance in a narrow area of Special Education.
10	While not one of the most critical problems in the field of Special Education, this is an area where additional data would be of definite value to the field.
15	This project has built an extremely strong case for the importance of the research being conducted, based on theory, previous research and current practice.
15	The results of the research activities conducted on this project to date demonstrate that it is clearly one of the most critical projects in Special Education to date.

somewhat different approach appears as Exhibit 6.2 at the end of this chapter. A sample of a more typical onsite evaluation instrument which is useful, but is more susceptible to scaling problems, appears as Exhibit 6.3.

Several points are important to note about the two onsite evaluation instruments included as Exhibits 6.1 and 6.2. First, although there are similarities between the two instruments, it is obvious that they were developed for different projects in which different evaluative questions were important. Thus, it becomes clear how important it is to specify the correct evaluative questions, as pointed out above.

Secondly, both instruments include forms used in collecting budgetary information necessary to answer one of the broader evaluative questions posed during the onsite visit. This is a good example of how the onsite instrument can be used to collect, synthesize and summarize complex information into a single rating of merit. In both cases the budget data collection form was designed not only to standardize the collection of budget information, but also to document that onsite evaluators had actually examined the records (previous experience had suggested that this was one part of the evaluation that was often left to the last minute and thus skipped altogether, trusting in the project director's assurances that everything was in order). In addition, both forms also served to establish a documentable "audit trail" which could be used in case federal officials raised questions about the adequacy of the procedures.

It is also interesting to note that the DD project evaluation form contained a section to collect information related to the adequacy of client's individualized habilitation plans. Because it would not have been possible for the evaluators to examine each client's individualized habilitation plan, a format was included in the evaluation instrument to do a sampling of those plans. Because of the technical nature of those plans, it was decided that it was best to provide a standard format that could be used by all onsite evaluators in examining those records.

Finally, the Title IV evaluation form contains a rating scale designed to solicit information from the onsite evaluation team about those factors that may have contributed to the successes or problems encountered by the project. This is a good example of tailoring the onsite evaluation form to the particular issues that different audiences find most valuable. That page was added to the onsite evaluation form in the third year of the project because the onsite evaluation system reported some projects to be more successful than others. The funding agency officials were particularly interested in finding out what factors contributed to the success or problems that a project experienced, and it was decided that this information could be efficiently collected during the onsite evaluation.

There are obviously also a great many similarities between the two forms shown in Exhibits 6.1 and 6.2. Based on the experience of these two projects, this particular approach appears to be a very usable approach that can be modified to meet the individual needs of a given funding program or project. In doing onsite evaluations of other types of programs, modifications obviously would need to be made, but this particular format provides a foundation upon which others can build.

Finally, a great deal of time and energy can be saved during the onsite evaluation if the sponsoring agency or the team leader will take time to prepare sufficient numbers of tailored data-collection forms for use by each evaluator. This is vastly preferable to the more typical situation where each team member receives an omnibus list of questions, only some of which are appropriate to any one interviewee. A large packet of questions requires the evaluator to flip through the data-collection forms during the interview to locate the questions that should be addressed, for example, to the school principal as opposed to the parents of participants. It is far better if the team leader assembles in advance the questions for particular categories or classes of interviewees and duplicates copies of separate, tailored interview schedules for team members to use with different types of individuals with whom they talk.

Similar thought and foresight in preparing for other aspects of data collection can go far toward making better use of time spent during onsite evaluations.

SELECTION OF THE ONSITE TEAM LEADER

The selection of the team leader will influence the outcome of an onsite evaluation more than almost any other factor. Even the best evaluation procedures and instruments can become useless tools in an ineffectual hand. It is important that the onsite team leader be someone who is not only credible but also someone with experience and demonstrated competence in onsite evaluation. There is no place for "cronyism" or political appointments in selecting onsite team leaders. Individuals and agencies who make such choices reveal clearly that their intent is either patronage or whitewashing, not honest evaluation.

Team leader selection for **formative** onsite evaluations could be a function of either the sponsoring agency or of the program or project staff. For **summative** onsite evaluations, team leader selection should be a function of the sponsoring or regulatory agency faced with making the final decision about the project or program.

Recommended criteria for the selection of team leaders include the following, in descending order of importance.

1. Team leaders should have no known close personal or professional relationship with the project director or staff.

2. Team leaders should have a general understanding of evaluation procedures, specifically with regard to onsite procedures. Ideally, team leaders will be able to point to previous successful experience and demonstrated competence in directing onsite evaluations. As a minimum, team leaders should be able to point to previous successful experience as a member of an onsite evaluation team.

3. Under certain circumstances, it may be appropriate to select team leaders with academic background and expertise in the major content or activities of the project.

SELECTION OF ONSITE TEAM MEMBERS

As is true of teams in other areas of human endeavor, evaluation teams can ill afford to carry a "weak player." Evaluation resources are generally so limited that it is already difficult to finance as many team members as necessary to do a thorough evaluation. In such a context, it is wasteful, in terms of real cost, to allow an unproductive or inexpert person to fill one of the team positions. In terms of **opportunity** cost, this is an even more serious mistake, for it not only wastes resources but also prevents that team slot from being filled by a competent individual who may make the difference between a successful or unsuccessful evaluation.

Recommended criteria for selecting team members include the following:

1. Team members should have no prior association with the project in a consultant, project participation, or advisory capacity.

2. Team members should be **known** to be professionally competent persons with expertise either as evaluators or in areas directly related to the substance of the project.

3. Team members should have no known biases concerning the project.

4. Team members must be willing to spend adequate time for advance preparation as well as for the onsite visit and subsequent debriefings and report writing, as required.

Team members should be selected by mutual consent of the team leader and the sponsoring agency. Where either party is unfamiliar with the person, letters of inquiry and recommendations would be in order.

COMPOSITION AND BALANCE OF THE ONSITE TEAM

As was noted earlier, an onsite evaluation team can range in size from two members upward. For larger projects, at least four to six persons (according to the nature and complexity of the entity being evaluated) should ideally be included on the team. Resource constraints often dictate, however, that team size be limited to two or three persons. Team size should be negotiated between the team leader and the sponsoring agency. In fact, all details connected with team members' selection should ideally be decided cooperatively between the team leader and the funding agency sponsoring the evaluation. Some general suggestions concerning selection of team members follow.

1. The team may include members of the appropriate advisory bodies (e.g., in the Title IV evaluation, all members of the Title IV State Advisory Council were invited to accompany one of the external onsite evaluation teams, and in the DD Council project at least one member of the team was required to be a council member).

2. Content and/or process specialists should be included on teams, as appropriate.

3. Team members should understand and be able to use sound evaluation processes.

4. There should be institutional balance by providing team member representation from institutions such as the sponsoring agency, advisory councils, local and state agencies and groups, and universities and colleges, where such balance seems advantageous.

5. The possibility exists of using one or two team members from a prior onsite team which has visited the same project (if this is a second or third onsite visit to a project) for purposes of continuity. This, however, should be negotiable between the team leader and the sponsoring agency.

6. Lay persons and directors of similar projects or programs may be included on the team as the team leader and the sponsoring agency deem appropriate.

RECRUITING PERSONS TO SERVE ON ONSITE TEAMS

As noted earlier, the selection of the team leader is usually the province of the sponsoring agency. Ideally, such selection would involve personal or telephone contact with each individual sought as a team leader. Given practical constraints, however, it may be necessary to recruit team leaders by mail. A sample of one letter previously used for that purpose appears in Exhibit 6.4.

After team members have been selected cooperatively by the team leader and sponsoring agency, they should be invited to serve on the team. Which party issues that invitation is another matter for negotiation, since each form of recruitment has its advantages. Again, personal or telephone contacts would be preferable, but letters similar to that referenced above, modified as necessary in details, could be used if necessary.

PRE-VISIT ARRANGEMENTS

Suggestions concerning some of the most important preparations for onsite evaluation visits are provided in this section dealing with advance notification and other communications, materials preparation, team training, and the like. Many of the suggestions are supported by examples which appear in the exhibits at the end of the chapter.

Prior to discussing specific communications and arrangements that are important in preparing for an onsite visit, it may be helpful to portray a general conception of how the various "actors in the drama" relate to one another. Figure 2 provides such a conception, which underlies some of the suggestions that follow.

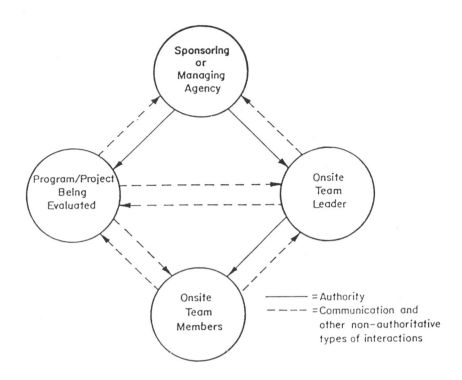

Figure 2
Relationships Among Groups and Individuals Involved in An Onsite Evaluation

Funding Agency Notification of Sites About the Upcoming Onsite Evaluation

Nothing undermines an onsite evaluation visit's ultimate success more than to have it burst onto a program or project unannounced. Indeed, project and program administrators and staff members should be informed well in advance of the fact that an onsite evaluation is planned, the purpose of that visit, when (generally) the visit will take place, and the general focus, evaluative questions, and activities which will take place during the onsite. A good example of how this might be accomplished comes from the Title IV project evaluation. At the time of funding, each project director was invited to a half-day seminar at which the various evaluation and reporting activities associated with Title IV projects were discussed. Five months later, a follow-up memorandum was sent to each project director reminding them of much of this same information (see Exhibit 6.5). Then, shortly before the scheduled evaluation visit, another memorandum was sent to remind them specifically about the evaluation visit (see Exhibit 6.6). In this way, project directors were fully aware from the beginning what was to happen, and periodic reminders helped to ensure that they would be adequately prepared.

Once program or project administrators have been advised of the general purposes and parameters of the onsite evaluations, it is appropriate for the funding agency (or team leader, as discussed in the next section) to notify the site administrator(s) of the specifics necessary to prepare for the onsite visit. This communication should include the following:

1. The date(s) of the onsite evaluation team visit.

2. The name of the team leader (including background).

3. The composition of the team (including addresses and background information).

4. A request to supply the team leader with materials available (or an annotated list of materials) which might provide background on the project and its achievements.

5. A request that the project director and staff complete and return a "Pre-visitation Information" form (described hereafter) at least two weeks prior to the onsite visit so that each onsite team member can receive a copy prior to the actual visit.

6. A request that the project director send the team leader a list of the following:

   • names of project staff

   • membership of advisory boards

   • lists of staff members, administrators, and consultants working with the project (where feasible).

7. A request that the project director and staff cooperate fully with the team leader in setting an agenda and facilitating the team visit.

Two sample letters which can be used when protocol or policy requires that official notification be made by the sponsoring agency appear at the end of this chapter in Exhibit 6.7. The first letter is designed to be followed by the second. In cases where the funding agency has contracted with another agency to manage its onsite evaluation system, the contact about specifics of the onsite may come from an individual within that agency, as shown in the third example in Exhibit 6.7.

Initial Team Leader Contact With Site Administrator(s)

Once the project administrator is aware of a pending site visit and the identity of the team leader, it is often best to leave it to the team leader to initiate contact to explain the specifics of the onsite preparation and activities. Depending on geography and resources available, this may be a personal or telephone contact or it may be a written communication. Whatever the format, the initial team leader contact with the project director should accomplish the following purposes:

- To introduce the team leader to the project director.

- To request that the project director send the desired materials to other team members.

- To discuss a tentative agenda, including: (1) kinds of persons the team should interview; (2) sampling of interviewees within each category; and (3) arrangements and sites for interviewing people (interview rooms).

- To set the tone for evaluation by indicating the desire and responsibility for collecting as much information as possible in the time allotted in order to be constructive and helpful to the project and the sponsoring agency.

- To indicate a desire to avoid sophisticated and lengthy "dog and pony show" types of briefings. Because the materials have been sent to and read by all team members in advance, the time for project briefing of the onsite team should typically be held to a minimum (briefing no longer than one hour, including time for discussion).

- If necessary, to discuss lodging accommodations, which should be convenient to project site(s).

- To confirm the onsite visit agenda with the project director.

In some instances, unusual problems or circumstances will require significant acceleration or delay of the onsite visit. Such rescheduling should be approved by the sponsoring agency, since there is often a specific and important rationale for the time period originally slated for the onsite evaluation. For example, in the Utah Title IV onsite evaluation system, onsite visits were conducted in March for developmental projects and October for adoptable projects. The March timing for visits to developmental projects was because all of these projects were eligible for continuation funding during the following school year and continuation proposals were due on April 1. By conducting the onsite evaluations in March, it was hoped that the results of the external onsite evaluations would be helpful to projects in writing their continuation proposals and to the proposal review teams in deliberating about continued funding. Visits to adoptable projects were scheduled in October so that projects (which were funded from July through June of the prior year) would be completely finished and would have had time to close out their financial records and complete any internal evaluation reporting prior to the onsite evaluation visits. In addition, by scheduling the visit in October, external onsite evaluation teams were able to more accurately determine the degree to which districts were actually continuing the project beyond the period supported by Title IV funds.

Similar rationales would often make extensive shifts in the schedules for onsite visitation dysfunctional.

Advance Preparation by Site Personnel

As was implied in previous comments and noted in the sample letters in Exhibit 6.7, project or program administrators and staff can reasonably be expected to engage in some advance preparation to make the evaluation team's time on site as productive and efficient as possible.

First, project staff should be reminded to assemble and mail in advance, as requested, all descriptive project materials, any prior evaluation reports, or any other documents they or the team leader may view as useful to the team members. Second, it is often useful to ask program or project administrators to complete and return a "Pre-visitation Information Form," such as that shown in Exhibit 6.8.

Finally, it is probably inevitable (and to only some degree inappropriate) that site personnel will feel compelled to make advance preparations intended to present their project in the "best possible light." To some extent, this can be useful, such as time spent posting all current expenditures in preparation for a financial audit. Over-anxiety about upcoming onsite visits can also lead to unfortunate, sometimes pitiful, efforts to prepare an artificial "show and blow" presentation, complete with rehearsals, advance censoring designed to prevent interviewees from speaking freely on certain topics or issues, and the like. Fortunately, such travesties are usually as transparent to any qualified evaluation team as they are rare.

Team Leader Communication With Team Members
Prior to the Onsite Visit

It is not the purpose of this discussion to prescribe how a team leader should orchestrate the preparation of his or her team, for every qualified team leader will have preferred methods for contacting and preparing their team colleagues. It does seem, however, that some minimal guidelines might be suggested. For example, the team leader will doubtlessly wish to communicate to other team members, in some fashion, information on the following points:

- Necessary introduction of team members.

- Confirmation of the dates, places, and expected hours of the onsite visit.

- A caution that team members cannot anticipate being present for only a portion of the onsite visit (and a suggestion that, if a team member cannot meet for the entire time, the team leader must be informed immediately so that a replacement can be obtained).

- Notification of what materials to expect from the project director or the team leader. It is also wise to urge that the team leader or project director be notified immediately if the materials are not received by a specified date.

- The requirement that, because of the limited time on site, all materials should be read completely in advance.

- A request that the team member jot down (as project materials are read) any general or specific questions which should be posed to interviewees and send those questions to the team leader as soon as possible so that they might be incorporated in onsite instruments.

- Details about financial arrangements, expense forms, and the like, including specification of honoraria and travel reimbursements.

It is often useful to communicate as much of this information as possible in writing so that team members will have it available for later reference. For example, in the DD Council project, each evaluator was provided with a packet of written materials outlining the purpose, procedures, and intended data to be collected during the visits. An example of these materials is shown in Exhibit 6.9. Staff from the coordinating contractor held a meeting with each of the team leaders to discuss these materials to be certain each onsite team was well prepared to implement the outlined procedures.

Advance Preparation and Training of Team Members

Adequate preparation of the onsite team will typically depend on three interrelated but separate activities, as described below.

1. First, the team leader should review all available project or program materials (e.g., the original proposal and any subsequent revisions, written descriptions of project activities or products, or prior evaluation reports). The purpose of this review is twofold: (a) to familiarize the team leader thoroughly with the project; and (b) to enable the team leader to select the materials that should be sent to all team members before the onsite visit. There need be no apology for asking team members to read a substantial quantity of materials in preparation for a site visit if all of those materials are relevant and helpful. It is inexcusable, however, to burden busy professionals with the task of wading through reams of superfluous printed materials to find the one, succinct twelve-page document that summarizes all important information about the project.

2. Second, the team leader should send to team members all advance preparation materials (under cover of a memorandum explaining what they are and what each team member should do with them, as in Exhibit 6.10) including as a minimum the following:

- a brief description of the purposes of the funding and of the onsite review

- all project or program materials (as described in the previous section)

- copies, as appropriate, of correspondence among project director, funding agency, and team leader concerning the onsite evaluation (see Exhibits 6.4 - 6.8)

- a step-by-step list of procedures for conducting the onsite visit (see example included in Exhibit 6.10)

- forms which will be used in constructing a summary rating of the project on each criterion (see Exhibits 6.1 and 6.2), along with instructions for how to rate on each criterion (see Exhibit 6.9)

- any guidelines for allowable expenditures within the funding authorization and, if appropriate, financial audit forms and instructions as described earlier and shown in Exhibit 6.1 and 6.2

- a format for the final report along with a description of the contents to be included in each section of the report (see Exhibits 6.9 & 6.10)

- other materials uniquely relevant to the particular onsite visit (for example, the **Standards for the Ethical Conduct of Psychologists and Psychiatrists** may be relevant preparation for evaluation of a community mental health clinic).

3. Third, a training session should be scheduled to make certain that all team members understand and are prepared to use the onsite procedures and instruments. For one-shot onsite evaluations, this initial session may also include the task of reaching agreement on evaluative questions and instruments to be used during the onsite visit. Depending on proximity and resources, this training may occur on a date prior to the onsite or in a conference telephone call. In some cases, however, such training will occur as the first activity once the team is assembled at the site, often on the morning of the first day (or on the preceding evening).

The time at which training is scheduled is less important than the need for such training to receive adequate time and attention. Strangely, many team leaders seem reluctant to spend much time making certain all team members are in agreement about how to apply the various criteria and carry out the onsite procedures. This reluctance is occasionally reinforced by a prima donna team member who exhibits impatience at being told how to do what s/he obviously feels very well prepared to do. Fortunately, such behavior is rare among experienced and knowledgeable evaluators. The most expert (and often the best reputed) onsite evaluators are not only tolerant of time spent on training but are often insistent on it, for they understand full well the subjectivity and unreliability that creep into onsite evaluative judgments when scaling and similar difficulties are not controlled.

Model Onsite Evaluation Reports

"A picture is worth a thousand words" is as applicable in evaluation as elsewhere. The use of a model report is among the best ways to communicate expectations to those who will write up an onsite evaluation report and to achieve desirable consistency among the reports. Although it may be possible to use an actual evaluation report, selected for its quality, it is often difficult to disguise the program or project well enough to avoid breaches of confidentiality. Another strategy is to construct a hypothetical model report which displays the format, level of detail, and style of exposition desired. This model report may be annotated to describe the rationale for the various report sections (an example of such annotation for a different purpose is shown in Exhibit 2.4). It can also be helpful to include examples of both good and unacceptable ways of reporting, so readers can also be forewarned of what not to do. Exhibit 6.11 contains an example of a model report used in conjunction with the Title IV project. In some cases, particularly where it is not possible to prepare a model report, it is worthwhile to provide a fairly detailed outline of the format and information which should be included in the final report. An example of such an outline taken from the DD council project is shown in Exhibit 6.9.

An Onsite "Pre-visit"

Some funding agencies urge each team leader to make a pre-evaluation visit to the site in advance of the full team visit. This has been suggested in order to facilitate communication, set the schedule for the onsite team visit, clarify points connected with the visit, and so on. Although these activities are doubtlessly useful, they may not always be sufficiently compelling to outweigh the possible disadvantages of such a visit that might result if the team leader develops extensive camaraderie with project director and staff. The difficulty of maintaining objectivity under such conditions should not be minimized. Also, these same outcomes might be attained in many cases through more efficient, less expensive, non- biasing techniques outlined earlier in this chapter. Given those concerns, a pre-visit to the site by the team leader is not recommended as a part of all site visits, although it is left optional to the team leader who has a particular rationale for pre-visitation and has that rationale approved by the funding agency.

Where there is no reason to believe a pre-visit would have the deleterious biasing effects described above (and where proximity and resources make it feasible), an advance onsite visit by the team leader can be useful. The purpose of this visit is not to evaluate, but rather to establish a climate and take care of details that, collectively, will enhance the actual onsite evaluation. Used properly, a pre-visit should allow the team leader to accomplish the following:

- Establish rapport with the project/program director to attain necessary cooperation.

- Convince the project/program director that the onsite evaluation will be fair and professional in all particulars.

- Reach agreement with the project/program director about advance preparations for the site visit and details relating to the onsite activities.

- Obtain available project/program materials.

- Inform the project/program director of how results of the onsite evaluation will be reported.

A sample agenda used in one pre-visit in the Title IV onsite evaluations is shown in Figure 3 to illustrate the items that can be accomplished during such an interview.

PRE-VISIT INTERVIEW AGENDA

Agenda Item	Material To Give Project Director
1. Introduction; provide for future contact	Business card
2. Inform project director of team composition and rationale for selection.	NA
3. List of team members and institutional affiliation.	List of team members
4. Review purposes of onsite visit	Feb. 14 memo to project director
a. federal requirement - summary evaluation of Utah Title IV.	
b. Utah's focus on onsite evaluation as primary mode.	
c. twenty-five percent of adoptables selected for onsite on the basis of a stratified random sample.	
d. onsite visits of one-day duration to collect data and review records with exit interview.	
e. this pre-visit intended to make onsite evaluation more productive.	
f. a written report sent to USOE, after review by project director.	
5. Review evaluation questions to be addressed during the onsite.	Summary Rating Sheet
6. Review preparations for fiscal audit.	Allowable Expenditures Summary and Financial Audit Sheet
7. Review schedule for onsite visit.	Draft of onsite schedule
8. Agree on sampling procedures (if any) to to used to select interviewees.	NA
9. Obtain (or have project director send):	NA
a. project proposal	
b. any prior reports	
c. budget information	
d. descriptions/project materials	
e. any funding agency approval for deviations from original proposal	
f. any evaluation plans or instruments currently in use	
10. Confirm arrival time and logistic arrangements as necessary	NA

Figure 3
Sample Pre-visit Agenda

EXHIBITS FOR CHAPTER 6

EXHIBIT 6.1: TITLE IV - PART C ADOPTABLE PROJECTS EXTERNAL ONSITE EVALUATION SUMMARY RATING SHEET

Project Name:_____

District: _____ Project Director:_____

Answers to each of the questions listed below will provide information about how successful a project has been in accomplishing the purpose of Title IV - C funding. A project which is completely successful would receive the maximum number of points associated with each question. Note that many questions have both <u>quantitative</u> and <u>qualitative</u> dimensions which should be reflected in the rating. For example, a project which implements each of the projected activities, but does so in a slipshod manner which will not likely lead to improved educational practice, should not be rated highly on question #1. For each question, assign the appropriate number of points and summarize briefly on this form your rationale. The table below provides approximate guidelines for assigning points associated with various levels of performance.

Range of points associated with each level of compliance	QUESTIONS WORTH 60 POINTS	Range of points associated with each level of compliance	QUESTIONS WORTH 30 POINTS	Range of points associated with each level of compliance	QUESTIONS WORTH 10 POINTS	
	54 - 60		27 - 30		9 - 10	Complete or near complete compliance in meeting the purposes of Title IV - Part C suggested by this question
	45 - 53		23 - 26		8	Minor problems in this area, but not serious enough to jeopardize the success of the project in accomplishing the purposes of Title IV - Part C suggested by this question.
	30 - 44		15 - 22		5 - 7	Moderate problems in this area which may be serious enough to jeopardize the success of the project in accomplishing the purpose of Title IV - Part C suggested by this question.
	15 - 29		8 - 14		3 - 4	Major problems in this area which are definitely serious enough to jeopardize the success of the project in accomplishing the purposes of Title IV - Part C suggested by this question.
	0 - 14		0 - 7		0 - 2	Little or no compliance in this area. Project is not accomplishing the purposes of Title IV - Part C suggested by this question.

_____
Date of Visit

Possible Points	Rating	
60		1. Did project activities conform with approved plan or approved modifications? Were activities implemented in a quality-like manner that should lead to improved educational practice? If an adoptable project, were the key components of the original validated project implemented?
10		2. Was the project responding to a priority area of need or weakness within the LEA?
30		3. Did the project evaluation provide valid information about project effectiveness or impact? Did evaluation yield information which can assist district in making decisions about project continuation?
30		4. If the project was effective, is there evidence that the LEA plans to continue the project after Title IV - C funding is completed?
10		5. Were appropriate and sufficient efforts made to include private schools?

Possible Points	Rating	
10		6. Are relevant LEA personnel sufficiently aware of and do they understand the purpose of Title IV - C; and are they aware of the expectations and requirements associated with accepting a Title IV - C grant?
10		7. In selecting an adoptable program to meet their identified need, did the LEA sufficiently consider other options besides the one ultimately selected?
10		8. Did the project have sufficient contact with the original developer or with certified second generation trainers?
30		9. Do project expenditures and financial accounting procedures conform with state and federal requirements? (see attached worksheet and instructions)

TOTAL POINTS POSSIBLE   TOTAL RATING   %

200   ____   ____

Signatures: Project Director _____

Chairperson of
Onsite Team _____

Team Member _____

Team Member _____

TITLE IV-C PROJECT BUDGET WORKSHEET

| Budget Category (a) | Information from Ledger | | | Back-up Documentation | | | | | Was expenditure consistent w/approved budget (j) | Comments (k) |
| | Date (b) | Payee (c) | Description of Expenditure (d) | Amount (e) | P.O. or Requisition | | Invoice or Warrant | | | |
					Amount (f)	Approval (g)	Actual Cost (h)	Goods Received (i)		
1.										
2.										
3.										
4.										
5.										
6.										
7.										
8.										
9.										
10.										
11.										
12.										
13.										
14.										
15.										

INSTRUCTIONS:

This worksheet is to be used in gathering information regarding question #9 on the Summary Rating Sheet . . . "Do project expenditures and financial accounting procedures conform with state and federal requirements?" This worksheet should be completed for a random sample of at least 8 entries from the project ledger plus any entries which seem questionable or unusually large. Additional information about how to complete the worksheet for each selected entry is given below.

(a) List the main budget categories in which the selected expenditure falls (e.g., travel, supplies, consulting, etc.). The "random" selection should include an entry from as many of the main budget categories as possible except for "personnel", "fringe benefits", and "indirect costs."

(b) (c) (d), & (e) This information is to be taken from the project ledger (i.e., official listing of expenditures for that project, which may be handwritten, computerized, or typed as long as it is an official listing of a part of the official accounting records). Enter the date of the expenditure (b), the payee ("c" -- the person or vendor to whom project funds were transmitted), what the money was spent for ("d" -- e.g., typewriter ribbons, travel to project meetings, etc.) and the amount of the expenditure listed in the ledger (e).

(f) & (g) For each expenditure, the project should have a Purchase Order (P.O.) or Requisition. List the amount for which the P.O. or Requisition was written (f) and whether the P.O. or Requisition was approved by and appropriate person ("g" -- e.g., Project Director, Business Adminstrator, etc.).

(h) & (i) For each expenditure in the sample, indicate the actual cost of the goods/services ("h" -- it is not unusual for the actual cost to vary slightly from the cost noted on the P.O.) and whether the goods/services were actually received ("i" -- e.g., in some instances you may want to see the item, in others a signed invoice ackowledging receipt).

(j) Make a judgment as to whether the expenditure was consistent with the orginally proposed or modified budget.

(k) In this section note any comments you have about the degree to which the project expenditures conform with state and federal requirements as indicated by the information about that particular item. For example, any "no" answers in (g) or (j); discrepancies between (e) and (f) or (e) and (h); items which do not have appropriate back-up documentation; or any other irregularities or exceptions with federal and/or state guidelines should be explained. Use the back of the page if necessary.

COMPARISON OF BUDGET WITH

FINANCIAL RECORD*

a Category Title	b Budgeted For Line Items	c Actual Expenditure For Line Items	d Percent Discrepancy	e Written Approval (if discrepancy is 10% or more)

*Ensure that the record is part of the official accounting records.

NOTE: This is not to be shared with project personnel

Listed below are a number of factors that may have contributed to the successes or problems encountered by the project. In addition to the factors listed, you have probably identified other factors during your visit. First, list any additional factor you have identified in the blanks listed "other". Then go through and rate each item as to whether and to what degree it contributed to the project's successes, strengths, weaknesses, or problems.

	A Major Contributor to Problems	Not a Factor	A Major Contributor to Success	Don't Know
1. Technical expertise/qualifications of LEA staff	1 2 3 4 5 6 7 8 9 10			_____
2. Expertise of outside consultants or technical assistants	1 2 3 4 5 6 7 8 9 10			_____
3. Enthusiasm and commitment of project staff	1 2 3 4 5 6 7 8 9 10			_____
4. Contact with and support from USOE	1 2 3 4 5 6 7 8 9 10			_____
5. Human and financial resources	1 2 3 4 5 6 7 8 9 10			_____
6. Commitment and support of LEA administration	1 2 3 4 5 6 7 8 9 10			_____
7. Appropriate conceptualization	1 2 3 4 5 6 7 8 9 10			_____
8. Political pressure/involvement	1 2 3 4 5 6 7 8 9 10			_____
9. Relevance to district needs	1 2 3 4 5 6 7 8 9 10			_____

Other (specify)

_____   1 2 3 4 5 6 7 8 9 10 ___

Other (specify)

_____   1 2 3 4 5 6 7 8 9 10 ___

Other (specify)

_____   1 2 3 4 5 6 7 8 9 10 ___

EXHIBIT 6.2: DD COUNCIL EXTERNAL ONSITE EVALUATION SUMMARY RATING SHEET FOR DIRECT SERVICE PROJECTS

Project Name:_____

Agency: _____ Project Director:_____

Evaluation Team Members: _____

Date of Onsite Visit:_____

    On the following pages are a series of questions designed to provide information about how successful a project has been in accomplishing the purposes of funding from the DD Council Formula Grant Program. A project which is completely successful would receive the maximum number of points associated with each question. Note that many questions have both quantitative and qualitative dimensions which should be reflected in the rating. The table below provides approximate guidelines for assigning points associated with various levels of performance. Also, attached to this document is a set of more detailed guidelines onsite evaluation teams may wish to follow in determining the number of points to be assigned to each question. For each question the onsite team should assign the appropriate number of points and provide a brief rationale explaining its rating. The rating given each question should then be summarized on the chart at the bottom of this sheet.

Range of points associated with each level of compliance	QUESTIONS WORTH 50 POINTS	Range of points associated with each level of compliance	QUESTIONS WORTH 35 POINTS	Range of points associated with each level of compliance	QUESTIONS WORTH 15 POINTS	
	45 - 50		32 - 35		14 - 15	Complete or near complete compliance in meeting the purposes of DD Council funding suggested by this question
	38 - 44		26 - 31		11 - 13	Minor problems in this area, but not serious enough to jeopardize the success of the project in accomplishing the purposes of DD Council funding suggested by this question.
	25 - 37		18 - 25		8 - 10	Moderate problems in this area which may be serious enough to jeopardize the success of the project in accomplishing the purpose of DD Council funding suggested by this question.
	13 - 24		9 - 17		4 - 7	Major problems in this area which are definitely serious enough to jeopardize the success of the project in accomplishing the purposes of DD Council funding suggested by this question.
	0 - 12		0 - 8		0 - 3	Little or no compliance in this area. Project is not accomplishing the purposes of DD Council funding suggested by this question.

EVALUATION SUMMARY

Question	Rating	Percent
1. Conformity of Activities to Approved Plan	———	/50 = ———
2. Evidence of Response to Priority Need	———	/15 = ———
3. Appropriate Evaluation Including Documentation of Developmental Progress	———	/35 = ———
4. Efforts Toward Continuation Funding	———	/35 = ———
5. Completion of IHPs	———	/15 = ———
6. Procedures for Assuring Confidentiality	———	/15 = ———
7. Fiscal Accountability	———	/35 = ———
Total	———	/200 = ———

Possible Points	Rating	
50		1. Do project activities conform with approved plan or approved modifications? Are activities being implemented in a quality-like manner that should lead to high-quality service for the developmentally disabled?
15		2. Does evidence exist that the project was responding to a priority area of need or weakness within the DD service system which meets one of the Council priorities for this funding year?
35		3. Are evaluation activities being properly implemented which will provide valid information about project effectiveness or impact? Does the evaluation design document individual developmental progress that is tied directly to IHP's?

Possible Points	Rating	
35		4. If the project is effective, is there evidence that the contractor plans to continue the project after DD Council funding is completed? Are appropriate plans currently being made to identify and secure continuation funding?
15		5. Are appropriate Individual Habilitation Plans properly maintained for each client being served?
15		6. Is an effective system being used to protect the confidentiality of records and information describing DD persons served by the project?
35		7. Do project expenditures and financial accounting procedures conform with state and federal requirements?

TOTAL POINTS   TOTAL
POSSIBLE   RATING   %

_200_   ____   ____

Signatures: Project Director _____

Chairperson of
Onsite Team _____

Team Member _____

DD COUNCIL FORMULA GRANT PROGRAM
BUDGET WORKSHEET

Budget Category (a)	Information from Ledger			Back-up Documentation				Was expenditure consistent w/approved budget (j)	Comments (k)
	Date (b)	Payee (c)	Description of Expenditure (d)	Amount (e)	P.O. or Requisition		Invoice or Warrant		
					Amount (f)	Approval (g)	Actual Cost (h)	Goods Received (i)	
1.										
2.										
3.										
4.										
5.										
6.										
7.										
8.										
9.										
10.										
11.										
12.										
13.										
14.										
15.										

INSTRUCTIONS:

This worksheet is to be used in gathering information regarding question #7 on the Summary Rating Sheet . . . "Do project expenditures and financial accounting procedures conform with state and federal requirements?" This worksheet should be completed for a random sample of at least 8 entries from the project ledger plus any entries which seem questionable or unusually large. Additional information about how to complete the worksheet for each selected entry is given below.

(a) List the main budget categories in which the selected expenditure falls (e.g., travel, supplies, consulting, etc.). The "random" selection should include an entry from as many of the main budget categories as possible except for "personnel", "fringe benefits", and "indirect costs."

(b) (c) (d), & (e) This information is to be taken from the project ledger (i.e., official listing of expenditures for that project, which may be handwritten, computerized, or typed as long as it is an official listing of a part of the official accounting records). Enter the date of the expenditure (b), the payee ("c" -- the person or vendor to whom project funds were transmitted), what the money was spent for ("d" -- e.g., typewriter ribbons, travel to project meetings, etc.) and the amount of the expenditure listed in the ledger (e).

(f) & (g) For each expenditure, the project should have a Purchase Order (P.O.) or Requisition. List the amount for which the P.O. or Requisition was written (f) and whether the P.O. or Requisition was approved by and appropriate person ("g" -- e.g., Project Director, Business Adminstrator, etc.).

(h) & (i) For each expenditure in the sample, indicate the actual cost of the goods/services ("h" -- it is not unusual for the actual cost to vary slightly from the cost noted on the P.O.) and whether the goods/services were actually received ("i" -- e.g., in some instances you may want to see the item, in others a signed invoice ackowledging receipt).

(j) Make a judgment as to whether the expenditure was consistent with the orginally proposed or modified budget.

(k) In this section note any comments you have about the degree to which the project expenditures conform with state and federal requirements as indicated by the information about that particular item. For example, any "no" answers in (g) or (j); discrepancies between (e) and (f) or (e) and (h); items which do not have appropriate back-up documentation; or any other irregularities or exceptions with federal and/or state guidelines should be explained. Use the back of the page if necessary.

**EVALUATION CHECKLIST FOR
INDIVIDUALIZED HABILITATION PLANS (IHPs)
Required of All Direct Service Projects Funded By DD Council**

<u>Instructions:</u> Obtain a list of clients being served by the project. From this list, randomly select at least 5
clients for whom you will examine the IHPs and any supporting material. For each client
selected, assign a code #. Examine the IHP for each selected client and complete the
checklist by rating each IHP on each item according to the following scale:

2 = This person's IHP is in full compliance with this item.

1 = This person's IHP is in partial compliance with this item.

0 = This person's IHP shows little or no compliance with this item.

During the rating, comments and clarifications should be made as necessary and identified
by client # in the right hand column (use the back of the sheet if necessary). When each client's
IHP has been rated, complete the following summary.

SUMMARY

Rating Item	#	#	#	#	#	#	#	#	Total	Percentage
1) IHP in writing									__ out of__	
2) Appropriate participation									__ out of__	
3) Long-term goals									__ out of__	
4) Intermediate objectives									__ out of__	
5) Habilitation services									__ out of__	
6) Evaluation procedures									__ out of__	
7) Responsible agency									__ out of__	
8) Responsible personnel									__ out of__	
9) Initiation date and duration									__ out of__	
10) Annual review									__ out of__	
Grand Total									__ out of__	

IHP EVALUATION CHECKLIST (continued)

Evaluation Question	Ratings								Comments
	#	#	#	#	#	#	#	#	
1. The IHP is in writing.									
2. Appropriate persons participated in the development of the IHP -- at least one representative from the program responsible for delivery of services to the client, and either the client (where appropriate) or the client's parent/guardian.									
3. The IHP contains long-term goals for the client.									
4. The IHP contains intermediate objectives to be met in reaching long-term goals. These objectives are sequenced and stated in measurable terms.									
5. The IHP describes the planned activities for achieving each objective and the specific habilitation services which are to be provided.									
6. The IHP contains an evaluation procedure and schedule for determining if goals and objectives are being achieved.									
7. The IHP identifies an agency responsible for the delivery of each habilitation service.									
8. The IHP identifies a coordinator with responsibility for implementing the plan and the specific personnel necessary for the delivery of each habilitation service.									
9. The IHP states the initiation date and expected duration for each habilitation service.									
10. The IHP has been reviewed at least annually by the agency primarily responsible for the client.									

EXHIBIT 6.3: COLORADO STATE DEPARTMENT OF EDUCATION ONSITE EVALUATION FORM FOR TITLE III ESEA PROJECTS

Local Education Agency: _____

PROJECT TITLE: _____

Evaluator: _____ Visitation date(s) _____

Please return completed evaluation by: _____ to _____

_____

SECTION I - Directions: Check the position best representing your judgment of how each statement describes the project. Comment freely in the space beneath the statement*, especially when clarification of check choice is needed.

	High				Low
	1	2	3	4	5
1 a. Current direction of the project is consistent with stated objectives.					
1 b. Teachers, administrators, and pupils involved with the project are aware of the project objectives.					
1 c. Existing LEA policies and practices are conductive to accomplishment of the objectives.					
2 a. Project activities are appropriate for meeting stated objectives.					
2 b. It appears, at present, that reasonable progress is being made toward meeting objectives of the project.					
2 c. Dissemination of information about the program within the project area is appropriate and adequate. (Consider central administration, Board of Education, professional staff, and lay public and pupils.)					
2 d. Adequate safeguards prevent possible negative effects of the project on children. (Consider overexposure to visitors, subjection to questionable experimental activities, disruption of other vital learning activities, ect.)					
3 a. Physical resources are appropriate and adequate for achieving project objectives.					

*This area has been deleted for this example to conserve space

EVALUATION FORM FOR TITLE III ESEA PROJECTS

	High 1	2	3	4	Low 5
3 b. Human resources are numerically adequate for the achievement of objectives. (Consider both regular staff and possible outside consultants.)					
3 c. Project personnel have qualities essential to project success. (Consider open-mindedness, creativity, specialized knowledge, administrative ability, communication skills, etc.)					
4 a. The budget is appropriate for current operation of the project.					
4 b. Good administrative practice exists in: Leadership___ Supervision___ Fiscal Management___					
5 a. Provisions exist for integrating successful project activities into the regular school programs.					
5 b. The Board of Education and administrative staff are committed to supporting successful project activities after federal funding ends.					
6 a. Current project evaluation practices and measuring instruments are appropriate for measuring the achievement of objectives.					
7 a. Provisions for follow-up study of project pupils are appropriate and adequate.					

SECTION II - Directions: Following are guidelines for the narrative portion of the evaluation report. Please respond fully to each item using additional sheets of paper as needed. Be as objective as possible and cite specific areas where good and poor practices are taking place.

1. What are the strengths of this project?
2. What are the weaknesses of this project?
3. What suggestions have you for improving the project?
Suggestions should be based on weaknesses listed on No. 2 and/or strengths, No. 1.
4. Additional comments.

EXHIBIT 6.4: EXAMPLE OF LETTER TO RECRUIT TEAM LEADERS

Dr. Adrian Van Mondfrans, Professor
College of Education
Brigham Young University
Provo, Utah 84602

IN RE: Onsite Evaluation of **Project TALENT, Franklin County Schools, October 10**

Dear Adrian:

We would appreciate your assisting with our onsite evaluation efforts this year. We would like you to lead an evaluation of the project noted above and in the attached letter copy.

Team leaders will receive a stipend of $500 plus expenses for completion of each onsite visitation and the submission of a satisfactory evaluation report.

Please return the enclosed card indicating your response. If these dates are inconvenient for you, advise us at once so that we can reschedule them. If the project directors respond similarly, we will contact you and rearrange the schedules as soon as possible.

Sincerely yours,

Ralph M. Johnson, Division Director

Enclosure - Letter to Project Director

EXHIBIT 6.5: EXAMPLE OF ONSITE EVALUATION INSTRUCTIONS FOR PROJECT DIRECTORS

250 EAST 500 SOUTH STREET · SALT LAKE CITY, UTAH 84111 · TELEPHONE (801) 533-5431

UTAH STATE OFFICE OF EDUCATION

MEMORANDUM

TO: Title IV - Part C Project Directors
FROM: Bill Cowan
DATE:
SUBJECT: Project Operation and Evaluation

The school year is approximately one-half over and those of you who are responsible for Title IV - Part C projects are hopefully well along your way to accomplishing the goals you established last Fall. As we have reviewed the past functioning of Title IV - Part C projects in Utah, there are a number of areas we want to bring to your attention. Some of you are already aware of much of this information as a result of past involvement with Title IV - Part C, or from orientation meetings held earlier in the year. We thought it worthwhile, however, to make doubly sure that all Project Directors were well informed about the topics discussed in this memo, since the information bears directly on the success of Part C projects. We encourage you to read the memo carefully and to contact the designated people should you have further questions.

Technical Assistance to Projects

As you know, a major purpose of Title IV - Part C is to provide initial funding for LEAs to develop and implement programs to meet previously identified critical needs within their system. As a part of Title IV - Part C projects, it is intended that LEAs will carefully evaluate the effectiveness of each program so that successful programs can be continued with LEA funds after Title IV funding has been completed.

During the past several years, the Title IV State Advisory Council has recognized that some LEAs, who are otherwise qualified to conduct a project meeting the purpose and priorities of Title IV - C, may not be able to readily identify people with specific technical expertise in one or two areas. Consequently, a system has been established whereby LEAs can receive additional technical assistance in areas where their own staff may lack experience and/or expertise. Additional technical assistance is usually most helpful to LEAs in assisting with the design and conduct of internal evaluations of project effectiveness or assisting in writing a project final report or continuation proposal. However, technical assistance has also proved invaluable for some projects in tasks such as developing or revising curriculum, identifying additional program resources, and monitoring project progress.

In response to input from past project directors, a system has been established whereby LEAs can obtain additional technical assistance to properly implement and/or evaluate Title IV - Part C projects (either developmental or adoptable). A pool of people has been identified from around the state (mostly university personnel) who have experience and expertise in the requisite areas. To assist LEAs in selecting a person who would be most appropriate for their project, Bill Cowan's office maintains for each person in the pool a brief resume showing previous experiences of a similar nature. If an LEA would like to obtain additional technical assistance for their project, they should contact Bill Cowan's office. After reviewing the available people and perhaps checking with LEAs for whom these people have previously worked, an application can be made by the LEA to Bill Cowan's office for project-related technical assistance services. Typically, this application would make available to the LEA an additional amount of money (usually no more than 5 - 10% of the project budget) which could be used to purchase consultant technical assistance services for the project. Any of this money not used for technical assistance would revert back to the state at the end of the project.

Evaluation of the Title IV - Part C Program

Each year the Federal Government allocates approximately $650,000 to the Utah State Office of Education to be used for Title IV - Part C projects. As some of you are already aware, the Title IV State Advisory Council is required every three years to submit to the Federal Government a summary evaluation of the operation and effects of Title IV - Part C expenditures in Utah. To assist in accomplishing this task, the State Advisory Council has approved a contract with Wasatch Institute for Research and Evaluation (a Logan-based consulting firm which specializes in educational research and evaluation, program planning, and project monitoring) to assume the primary responsibility for conducting this evaluation.

In conducting this evaluation, staff members of Wasatch Institute for Research and Evaluation (WIRE) will be contacting many of you to collect information. We think you will be pleased with the way the evaluation activities have been structured to reduce the burden on project staff members, while at the same time providing the necessary information for a comprehensive evaluation of the operation and effects of Title IV - Part C expenditures in Utah.

The remainder of this memo summarizes the major parts of the evaluation which will involve LEA participation, and summarizes again for you the various reports and records which are required of you in regard to Title IV- Part C projects.

Onsite evaluation visits. Onsite visits to Title IV - Part C projects from external evaluators will again be used as a major source of information about the operation and effects of Title IV - Part C. However, in order to reduce the amount of time required from LEA personnel, not all projects will receive an onsite evaluation visit each year. These onsite evaluation visits will occur shortly after the end of the contract completion date. Three-year developmental projects which are funded for less than $5,000/year will only be visited once, at the conclusion of the final year of the project. During the first two years, the onsite visit will occur in March so that project staff and the State Advisory Council can receive feedback in time to effect continuation proposals and decisions. The final onsite visit for these larger developmental projects will occur shortly after the end of the contract completion date for the third year.

During the external onsite evaluation visits, information will be collected regarding a number of evaluation questions. The summary rating forms which will be used by the external onsite evaluation teams as they visit projects are attached.

LEA project staff who are involved in an onsite evaluation visit should plan on having the external evaluation team onsite for one full day. During this time, external evaluator(s) will want to meet with various project staff, observe the program in operation (if possible), examine records, and collect other data relevant to the questions listed above. The specific onsite evaluation activities will vary somewhat from project to project depending on the nature of the project but each project director will be contacted well in advance so he or she will have ample time to prepare.

Financial Accountability. During the external onsite evaluation visit, the external evaluator will want to see evidence that budget expenditures conform with the requirements of the grant. In other words, the evaluator will need to examine the LEA's financial records to verify that funds granted to the LEA were spent on project-related activities in conformance with federal guidelines for expenditures. This part of the evaluation is mandated by Federal law as a condition upon which Title IV -Part C funds are given.

To facilitate the financial monitoring aspect of the onsite visit, LEAs should make sure that their accounting procedures allow for a clear "audit trail" of Title IV - Part funds. LEAs who have questions whether their current accounting system is satisfactory, should contact Bill Cowan as soon as possible to avoid any unnecessary complications during the onsite visit. The Federal guidelines which govern Title IV - Part C monies are attached to this memo. A good rule of thumb is that any contemplated expenditure which deviates significantly from the approved project plan should be cleared beforehand in writing by the Project Officer from USOE.

Annual Project Report. Each Title IV - Part C project is required to submit to the Utah State Office of Education an annual report summarizing the accomplishments of the project. This report is due within 30 days of the project completion date for that year (for most projects, the due date would be July 31st). Although the LEA may receive technical assistance in completing this report, the final responsibility for the contents and the timely delivery of the report rests squarely on the LEA as the grant recipient.

This report should contain sufficient detail to demonstrate how successfully the LEA has conducted the activities outlined in the proposal (1) for that year, (2) summarize evaluation data relevant to the effectiveness of the project, and, (3) if the report covers the final year of the project, outline briefly LEA plans for continuing the project. Although the report need not be lengthy, at least 15-20 pages will be necessary in most cases for a complete report. Examples of the type of report which is anticipated were provided to each project director at the Project Director's Meeting in Provo last September.

Additional Evaluation Activities. In addition to their role of being the "ones being evaluated", it is important that project directors and other LEA staff members have an opportunity to be the "evaluators" of Title IV - Part C. As a part of the comprehensive three-year evaluation of the operation and effects of Title IV - Part C expenditures in Utah, information will be solicited from LEA staff members concerning questions such as:

1. How meaningful and helpful is LEA contact with external evaluators, consultants for technical assistance, and State Office of Education personnel?

2. How effectively is the dissemination process for information related to adoptable programs functioning?

3. Is sufficient technical assistance, information, and opportunity provided to all LEAs in Utah for equitable participation in Title IV - Part C programs should they so choose?

4. How effectively are private schools being involved in Title IV - Part C programs?

Much of the information related to these questions will be collected during the external onsite evaluation visits referred to previously. However, some additional information will need to be collected via questionnaires, telephone and person-to-person interviews, and site visits. Most of the evaluation information described in this section is "formative" evaluation data which will feed directly back into the system to improve the functioning of Title IV - Part C programs within Utah on a year-to-year basis.

We appreciate your patience in reading such a lengthy memo. We feel that it contains important information which is essential for Title IV - Part C project directors to know if Title IV - Part C is to be effective in Utah. Should you have further questions, please do not hesitate to contact Bill Cowan or Ken Lindsay at the USOE or one of the members of the State Advisory Council.

EXHIBIT 6.6: REMINDER TO PROJECT DIRECTORS ABOUT ONSITE EVALUATIONS

250 EAST 500 SOUTH STREET · SALT LAKE CITY, UTAH 84111 · TELEPHONE (801) 533-5431

UTAH STATE OFFICE OF EDUCATION

MEMORANDUM

TO: Title IV - Part C Project Directors
FROM: Utah State Title IV Advisory Council
DATE:
SUBJECT: Upcoming Evaluation Onsite Visits

Each year the Federal Government allocates resources to the Utah State Office of Education to be used for Title IV - Part C projects. As some of you are already aware, the Title IV State Advisory Council is required every three years to submit to the Federal Government a summary evaluation of the operation and effects of Title IV - Part C expenditures in Utah. To assist in accomplishing this task, the State Advisory Council has approved a contract with the Wasatch Institute for Research and Evaluation, a Logan-based consulting firm which specializes in educational research and evaluation, program planning, and project monitoring, to assume the primary responsibility for conducting this evaluation.

In conducting this evaluation, staff members of Wasatch Institute for Research and Evaluation will be contacting many of you to collect information. We think you will be pleased with the way the evaluation activities have been structured to reduce the burden on project staff members, while at the same time providing the necessary information for a comprehensive evaluation of the operation and effects of Title IV - Part C expenditures in Utah.

The remainder of this memo summarizes the major parts of the evaluation which will involve LEA participation and summarizes again for you the various reports and records which are required of you in regard to Title IV- Part C projects.

Onsite evaluation visits. Onsite visits to Title IV-Part C projects from external evaluators will again be used as a major source of information about the operation and effects of Title IV-Part C. Not all projects will be visited during this year; those projects to receive a site visit will be contacted no later than April 15.

During the onsite evaluation visits information will be collected regarding the following evaluation questions.

1. Did budget expenditures conform to the requirements of the grant?

2. Did project activities conform to the approved plan?

3. Is there evidence of project effectiveness or impact?

4. Was the project responding to identified needs?

5. Is there evidence the LEA will continue effective projects?

6. Did the project have sufficient contact with the original developer?

7. Were key components of the original validated project implemented?

8. Were sufficient efforts made to include private schools?

9. Was the project innovative, or merely supplementary funding for existing LEA services?

10. Were LEA personnel aware of the expectations and requirements associated with grant acceptance?

11. How aware are LEA personnel of the validation/dissemination process at the beginning of the developmental process?

12. Are internal evaluation reports an accurate representation of project activities and impact?

Title IV - C projects selected to receive an onsite visit will be notified by the Wasatch Institute for Research and Evaluation. LEA project staff who are involved in these visits should plan on having the external evaluation team onsite for one full day. During this time, the external evaluator(s) will want to meet with various project staff, observe the program in operation (if possible), examine records, and collect other data relevant to the questions listed above. The specific onsite evaluation activities will vary somewhat from project to project depending on the nature of the project but each project director will be contacted well in advance so he or she will have ample time to prepare.

Financial Accountability. During the external onsite evaluation visit, the external evaluator will want to see evidence that budget expenditures conform with the requirements of the grant. In other words, the evaluator will need to examine the LEA's financial records to verify that funds granted to the LEA were spent on project related activities in conformance with federal guidelines for expenditures. This part of the evaluation is mandated by Federal law as a condition upon which Title IV - Part C funds are given.

To facilitate the financial monitoring aspect of the onsite visit, LEAs should begin now to make sure that their accounting procedures allow for a clear "audit trail" of Title IV- Part C funds. LEAs who have questions whether their current accounting system is satisfactory, should contact Bill Cowan as soon as possible to avoid any unnecessary complications during the onsite visit. The federal guidelines which govern Title IV - Part C monies are attached to this memo. A good rule of thumb is that any contemplated expenditure which deviates significantly from the approved project plan would be cleared beforehand in writing by the project officer from USOE.

We appreciate your patience in reading such a lengthy memo. We feel that it contains important information which is essential for Title IV - Part C project directors to know if Title IV - Part C is to be effective in Utah. Should you have further questions, please do not hesitate to contact Bill Cowan at the USOE or one of the members of the State Advisory Council.

EXHIBIT 6.7: LETTERS TO ESTABLISH SCHEDULE AND ARRANGMENTS FOR ONSITE EVALUATION

Colorado Department of Education
State Office Building
201 East Colfax
Denver, Colorado 80203
Telephone: (303) 892-2211

Donald D. Woodington, Commissioner

Dear Project Director:

The dates of _____ have been set for the annual onsite evaluation of your project. Activities on the first date will consist of a morning meeting with the visitation team with the balance of the day spent in data collection; second day activities will continue with project visitation and a final meeting between the team and project staff.

Procedures will include your sending project materials (current proposal, schedule of activities, dissemination materials and other pertinent data available on your project) to each team member, completion of a pre-visitation information form (a format for this will be sent to you later), and interviews of project personnel--including evaluators and school administrators--with the visitation team. We will contact you later regarding the details of the visitation, along with a list of the team members.

If you have any questions about these procedures, or if the date scheduled is not satisfactory, pleased contact our office within the week.

Sincerely yours,

State Coordinator
Development and Demonstration Services
892-2238

Colorado Department of Education
State Office Building
201 East Colfax
Denver, Colorado 80203
Telephone: (303) 892-2211

Donald D. Woodington, Commissioner

Dear Project Director:

    This letter confirms our arrangments made for the onsite evaluation of your project. The evaluation will take place on _____. The team will meet alone at your site headquarters at 8:00 a.m. for thirty minutes. At 8:30 a.m. they will wish to meet with you and the project staff for a briefing for a maximum of sixty minutes. The team will have thoroughly prepared for the onsite visit so there will be no need for a lengthly briefing or extended general comments concerning the project. Rather, the purpose is to seek clarification regarding misperceptions and learn of components which are particulary idiosyncratic to your project.

    The remainder of the day will be spent in data collection whereby the team members will interview and talk with selected people who are directly or perhaps indirectly associated with the project. Later on the second day we will share with you and your staff our team's impressions concerning your project.

    We are enclosing a copy of the Pre-visitation Information Form. Please complete and return this form to this office two prior to the visit. We will supply copies to all members of the team.

    The team is composed of: (Names: Leader, followed by members)

Sincerely yours,

State Coordinator
Special Programs Unit
(892-2223)

Enclosure - Pre-visitation Form

WASATCH INSTITUTE FOR RESEARCH AND EVALUATION

TO: Title IV - Part C Project Directors for Developmental Projects
FROM: Glenn Latham
SUBJECT: Scheduling for Onsite Evaluation Visits
DATE:

As you probably know, a sample of Title IV - Part C developmental projects are scheduled each year to receive an external onsite evaluation. Your project, _____, funded during the 1981 - 82 school year, is one of the projects which has been selected for an onsite evaluation visit this Spring. Enclosed in this mailing is a copy of the Summary Rating Sheet which will be completed by the team during the external onsite evaluation, along with a memorandum from the State Title IV Advisory Council providing additional information about Title IV evaluation activities and expectations.

As we discussed on the phone, the visit for your project is scheduled for _____. The evaluation team chairperson for your project is _____. He will be contacting you soon to schedule the date of the onsite visit. Prior to the actual visit, _____ _____ will be contacting you to answer any questions you have provided additional detail concerning the visit.

Please do not feel that you need to entertain the evaluators. It is our hope that the site visit can take place with as little inconvenience and disruption for you and your staff as possible. If you have any questions, please feel free to contact our office.

EXHIBIT 6.8: PROJECT PRE-VISITATION INFORMATION

This evaluation form should be completed by the project director in cooperation with others directly associated with the project immediately preceding the annual site visitation. A copy of this completed report should be made available to each member of the evaluation team prior to the onsite visitation.

The purposes of this report are to (a) provide a basis for systematic appraisal of the project by local school personnel; (b) to help prepare project personnel for the types of questions that might be asked by members of the visitation team; and (c) provide information to members of the visitation team.

Sponsoring School District _____

Project Title _____

Project Director _____

Please respond **briefly** and **candidly** to the following items: (use additional paper as necessary).

1. A. Which of the specific objectives for the project are being most satisfactorily attained? (Abbreviated statement of objectives).

   B. Which specific objectives are not being satisfactorily attained?

      What factors have prevented their attainment?

   C. To what extent are the following aware of the stated objectives for the project?

   1. Teachers _____   4. Project Personnel _____

   2. Administrators _____   5. Board of Education _____

   3. Pupils _____

D. What district policies and practices have been a hindrance to the project: (e.g., required district-wide grading or reporting practices which have a negative effect on attempts to individualize instruction).

2. A. List project activities which have been most satisfactorily carried out.

B. List intended project activities which have been least satisfactorily carried out.

What factors have prevented their satisfactory implementation?

C. List local dissemination techniques as they pertain to:

1. The Board of Education

2. Administrators

3. The professional staff

4. The lay public

5. Pupils

D. Has any aspect of the project had a negative effect on pupils? ___ If yes, describe the aspect and the effect.

3. A. Indicate the limitations, if any, that physical resources have placed on the project.

    B. Indicate ways available physical resources have encouraged expansion or refinement of the project.

    C. To what extent have human resources been adequate for the project?

    D. To what extent have human resources been inadequate for the project?

4. A. What budgetary limitations, if any, have you experienced which prevented implementation of project activities?

5. A. List procedures and provisions for integration of successful project activities into the regular school program.

    B. List evidence that various administrative units are committed to the support of successful project activities after federal funding discontinues.

6. A. List evaluative techniques and measuring instruments being used to measure achievement of project objectives. (Attach samples, if appropriate).

7. A. Briefly, what changes are under consideration for the continuation proposal, provided the project is not in its final year of intended operation?

Exhibit 6.9   Onsite Report Guidelines   181

EXHIBIT 6.9: GUIDELINES FOR EXTERNAL ONSITE REPORTS OF DD COUNCIL FUNDED PROJECTS

This document outlines the sections which should be included in the report of the external onsite evaluation. It is expected that the text of your report will be 15-25 pages long.

Prior to Onsite Visit

Describe in this section what activities were undertaken to prepare for the onsite evaluation visit, including what reports and documents were obtained and reviewed. Although very brief, this section provides important information to the DD Council which enables them to know that appropriate preparation and contact with project staff occurred prior to the actual visit. Be specific about dates and people where possible.

During Onsite Visit

A chronological description of the activities which occurred during the onsite visit provides information about the context in which the evaluation was conducted and the adequacy of the data upon which conclusions are based. Included in this section should be the names and titles of people who were interviewed during the visit.

PROJECT DESCRIPTION

A brief description of the project is important so that the external evaluator's report can be understood without reference to other documents which may not be readily available. Additionally, projects will occasionally change substantially from what is described in the original application, or the description in the application will be somewhat vague or incomplete. This section should be complete enough to give someone who is totally unfamiliar with the project a basic understanding of the project. As appropriate, include reference to objectives, timelines, and specific activities.

OBSERVATIONS REGARDING EVALUATIVE QUESTIONS

The focus of each onsite evaluation should be to provide as much information as possible in response to the questions discussed below. These questions will also be the focal point of the exit interview and the External Onsite Evaluation Summary Rating Sheet which is attached to this memo. The exact procedures for collecting information about each of the evaluative questions have purposely not been specified in greater detail. Because projects vary dramatically, evaluation team leaders will need to be flexible in planning and designing the exact procedures which will be necessary for a specific project.

A substantial part of the data for the evaluation will need to be gathered via interviews with various people. It may be helpful for the evaluator to consider a matrix such as the following in preparing for the onsite visit. Specific questions under each main evaluative questions and the appropriate interviewees will vary so much from project to project that the evaluation team leader will be in a better position to construct the specific questions which need to be asked after reviewing the project materials.

	Project Director	Project Staff	Clients	Parents	Other Staff	Agency Administrator	Other
1. Did Project activities conform with approved plan or approved modifications? a. b. c.							
2. Was the project responding to a priority area of need or weekness? a. b. c.							
3. Are evaluation studies being properly implemented which will provide valid information about project effectiveness or impact? a. b. c.							
4. Etc. a. b. c.							

Exhibit 6.9 Onsite Report Guidelines (continued) 183

In addition to the information gathered during the interviews, evaluation team members may need to observe the project in operation, examine materials and products developed by the project, and consider various project reports and results of internal evaluations, if the main evaluative questions are to be responded to accurately and completely.

The intent of each of the main evaluative questions is discussed briefly below.

1. **Do project activities conform with approved plan or approved modifications? Are activities being implemented in a quality-like manner that should lead to high quality services for the developmentally disabled?**

Each project, as a part of its proposal for FY86 was to develop a **Work Plan** that described and timelined the procedures and activities necessary for accomplishing its objectives. This section of the proposal and any related documents (proposal amendments, evaluation plans, etc.) can be reviewed prior to the onsite visit. During the onsite visit you should interview people, observe the program in operation if appropriate, and examine materials and records to determine if the project activities are being conducted in conformance with the original or modified plans. It is not unusual for projects to encounter some problems in accomplishing all tasks in accordance with the original timeline, but it is essential that the proposed project be completed by the end of the grant period unless an extension has been formally approved. Your rating of this question should reflect the degree to which the project is accomplishing the original activities or the approved modifications in the project plan.

This question, as many of the following ones, has both a **quantitative** and **qualitative** dimension. Projects should not be rated high if they merely stumble through all of the activities which were promised. High ratings should be reserved for those projects which not only do the promised activities, but do them in a high quality manner which is likely to lead to improvement in the quality of programs funded by the DD Council. To be rated in the top category (i.e., complete or near complete compliance) any modifications to the original activities should have been approved in writing by the DD Council, the project should be on schedule in implementing the originally proposed (or approved modified) activities, and you should be convinced that the activities are being implemented in a high quality, state of the art, professional manner. For example, suppose a project was to have developed a handbook to be used by case managers in helping DD clients by March 1, 1986. Even though the original timeline and list of activities may not have detailed all of the steps that should go into the development of such a handbook (e.g., specification of the objectives, review existing materials, develop first draft, review and critique by others, revision, field testing, revision, etc.); your rating should reflect the degree to which the essential steps were followed (note: essential practicality, not academic theory, is the main criterion). Moreover, even though all of the essential steps may have been done, if they were done mechanically and did not or are not likely to result in a high quality product, this question should not be rated high.

2. **Does evidence exist that the project was responding to a priority area of need or weakness within the DD service system which meets one of the Council priorities for FY86?**

P.L. 98-527, the public law under which federal monies are granted to the DD Council to fund projects, lists four priority service areas. Utah has chosen two areas to focus on in FY86 and defined them as follows:

   a. Case Management Services: services which

      (1) assist DD persons to gain access to and utilize effectively needed social, medical, educational, and other services;

      (2) assist providers of services to adapt methods of service delivery to meet the highly individualized needs of DD persons; and

      (3) enable administrators to share responsibility for negotiating, coordinating and obtaining the appropriate mix of needed services.

   b. Alternative Community Living Services: services which assist DD persons in maintaining suitable residential arrangements in the community, including in-house services (such as personal aides and attendants and other domestic and supportive services), family support services, foster care services, group living services, respite care, and staff training, placement and maintenance services.

Each project, as a part of its proposal, was to write a **Statement of Need** describing the rationale for the program and relating it to a priority need. This section of the proposal can be reviewed and the project staff interviewed to determine if a systematic and comprehensive process was used to identify the particular area of need, and if the need so identified can reasonably be related to one of the DD Council's priorities.

A judgment of whether a particular project was responding to a DD Council priority need was already made by the review panel at the time the project was approved for funding. The same question is considered again during the onsite evaluation for two reasons. First, the issue of priority need is the foundation upon which DD Council funding rests. Second, it is often the case that an onsite evaluator will have additional and/or different information available to make this judgment.

3. **Are evaluation activities being properly implemented which will provide valid information about project effectiveness or impact?**

Each project, as a part of its proposal, was to develop an **Evaluation Plan** that would describe how it would determine the extent to which it accomplished each of its objectives. In addition, those projects that requested it were provided with technical assistance in developing a more comprehensive evaluation plan that may provide more detailed information. These and any other appropriate documents can be reviewed and the project asked to provide evidence that it met its objectives.

In addition, your rating on this question should reflect whether or not a systematic process has been identified through which appropriate data can be collected regarding the effectiveness of the project in meeting its objectives and the desirability of continuation. Evaluation plans need not be highly sophisticated or highly technical, but they should be capable of yielding useful and valid information about the effectiveness of the project. Remember that the extensiveness of the evaluation component will often have to be balanced with the overall project resources. A $10,000 project should not be expected to use $8,000 in evaluation.

In addition to the above requirements for all projects, the following is required for direct service project (If your project is an **indirect service** the remainder of this paragraph should be disregarded). Each direct service project, as part of its proposal, was to develop an Evaluation Plan that would employ objective measure of developmental progress (i.e., standardized tests or other objective measures) to determine gains made by clients. Such measures were also to be coordinated with each client's Individual Habilitation Plan (IHP). In addition, those projects that requested it were provided with technical assistance in developing an evaluation plan which may provide more detailed information regarding this aspect of program evaluation. These and any other appropriate documents can be reviewed and the project asked to provide evidence that (1) objective measures of clients' developmental gains were made, (2) the measure coordinated with clients' IHPs, and (3) the gains demonstrated were clinically significant.

4. **If the project is effective, is there evidence that the contractor plans to continue the project after DD funding is completed? Are appropriate plans currently being made to identify and secure continuation funding?**

DD Council funds are granted to projects as seed monies, that is, funds are provided for a maximum of three years so that projects can develop and demonstrate innovative approaches to meeting the needs of the developmentally disabled. It is expected that each project, as it demonstrates its effectiveness, will also seek financial support so that it can be continued after DD funds are no longer available. The project staff may be asked to provide evidence of its efforts to secure continuation funding. Appropriate types of evidence include but are not limited to, copies of proposals or contracts submitted and/or funded, evidence of meetings held or correspondence with funding agencies, and evidence of lobbying efforts.

5. **Are appropriate Individual Habilitation Plans properly maintained for each client being served?**

The DD Council requires each **direct service** project to develop an Individualized Habilitation Plan (IHP) for each client, and to review that plan at least annually. P.L. 98-527, part of which follows, outlines the content to be included in IHPs and procedures for their review.

(1)   The Secretary shall require as a condition to a State's receiving an allotment under Part C that the State provide the Secretary satisfactory assurances that each program. . .(1) has in effect for each developmentally disabled person who receives services from or under the program a habilitation plan meeting the requirements of subsection (b), and (2) provides for an annual review, in accordance with subsection (c) of each such plan.

(b)   A habilitation plan for a person with developmental disabilities shall meet the following requirements:

(1) The plan shall be in writing.

(2) The plan shall be developed jointly by (A) a representative or representatives of the program primarily responsible for delivering or coordinating the delivery of services to the person for whom the plan is established, (B) such person, and (C) where appropriate, such person's parents or guardian or other representative.

(3) The plan shall contain a statement of the long-term habilitation goals for the person and the intermediate habilitation objectives relating to the attainments of such goals. Such objectives shall be stated specifically and in sequence and shall be expressed in behavioral or other terms that provide measurable indices of progress.

The plan shall (A) describe how the objectives will be achieved and the barriers that might interfere with the achievement of them, (B) state objective criteria and an evaluation procedure and schedule for determining whether such objectives and goals are being achieved, and (C) provide for a program coordinator who will be responsible for the implementation of the plan.

(4) The plan shall contain a statement (in readily understandable form) of specific habilitation services to be provided, shall identify each agency which will deliver such services, shall describe the personnel (and their qualifications) necessary for the provision of such services, and shall specify the date of the initiation of each service to be provided and the anticipated duration of each such service.

(5) The plan shall specify the role and objectives of all parties to the implementation of the plan.

(c) Each habilitation plan shall be reviewed at least annually by the agency primarily responsible for the delivery of services to the person for whom the plan was established or responsible for the coordination of the delivery of services to such person. In the course of the review, such person and the person's parents or guardian or other representative shall be given an opportunity to review such plan and to participate in its revision.

Attached to your summary rating sheet is a copy of a checklist the evaluation team should use in determining the extent to which a project is complying with DD standards for developing IHPs. To use it the team should randomly select a number of IHPs to be reviewed, check off where each is and is not in compliance with DD standards, and compute the percent of IHPs in compliance with each standard. A blank copy of the checklist is attached to your summary rating sheet.

6. **Is an effective system being used to protect the confidentiality of records and information describing DD persons served by the project?**

P.L. 98-527 requires that the DD Council evaluate the procedures of the projects it funds for assuring client confidentiality. Some points the evaluation team may wish to focus on in determining if a project has effective procedures for protecting confidentiality include:

* Does the project have a written policy regarding confidentiality?

* Does the project have appropriate forms for requesting information from other agencies?

* Does the project have appropriate forms for releasing information to other agencies?

* Are confidential records kept in locked files or in a locked room?

* Is there a procedure staff members are to use in checking out confidential information?

* Is there a staff member assigned responsibility for monitoring who has confidential information checked out?

7. **Do project expenditures and financial accounting procedures conform with state and federal requirements?**

Each project funded with DD Council monies is required to maintain a clear "audit trail" of their project expenditures. In other words, there should be an official project ledger showing each project expenditure of DD Council funds with appropriate back-up documentation for each expenditure (e.g., Purchase Orders, Receipts or Invoices, Cancelled checks).

As a part of your visit, you should ask to examine the ledger sheets and accompanying financial records to determine if funds have been spent appropriately. In most instances, it will be sufficient to peruse ledger sheets fairly carefully and then pull a random sample of entries for further examination of the associated requisitions or purchase orders. If any of the entries in the ledger sheet seem questionable, you should also examine supporting paper work for those entries in more detail. The worksheet attached to your summary rating sheet should be used to document information gathered about the budget. All major budget modifications (more than 10% of any line item) should be approved in writing by the DD Council. The original budget and any approved modifications submitted with the project application will be critical in answering this question. Minor clerical errors which you believe to be unintentional should be noted and will lower your rating in this category to some degree, but not dramatically if the project agrees to correct them promptly.

SUMMARY

This section is one of the most critical in the onsite evaluation report, since it is likely to be the only section perused by many readers. The intent obviously is not to repeat all of the content presented earlier in the report, but rather to summarize succinctly the major observations, judgments, and recommendations which the evaluation team believes are of most importance. Specifically, the summary should contain the following subsections:

1. Strengths

This section should contain a listing or brief discussion of each of the major strengths the evaluation team perceives in the project (e.g., its conception, operation, adherence to DD Council guidelines and purposes, outcomes, etc.). At the end of this section, you should discuss briefly and **specifically** the **contributing factors** which seem to be most responsible for the strengths presented in this section.

2. Weaknesses

This section should contain a listing or brief discussion of each of the major weaknesses the evaluation team perceives in the project (e.g., weaknesses in conception or operation, failure to adhere to various DD Council guidelines and purposes, unclear outcomes, etc.). At the end of this section, you should discuss briefly and **specifically** the **contributing factors** which seem to be most responsible for the weaknesses presented in this section.

3. Recommendations

In this section, the evaluation team should present their overall recommendations concerning the project, (i.e., given the strengths and weaknesses reflected in the two previous sections, what should be done?) If the project is applying for continued funding, would the team recommend that the project be continued unconditionally, continued if specified conditions are met, or discontinued? If a project is in its final year of DD Council funding, does the team recommend that it be promoted for use in other areas? In reaching these recommendations, it should be stressed that they are **not** merely the "flip side" of weaknesses, but should draw on the listed strengths as well. Recommendations might include suggestions for continuing and solidifying those things seen as strengths, suggestions for how to correct the deficiencies described in the section on weaknesses, and overall recommendations concerning decisions that should be made about project support, continuation, or extensions.

EXHIBIT 6.10: PRE-VISIT MATERIALS FOR ONSITE EVALUATORS

UTAH COUNCIL for
HANDICAPPED and
DEVELOPMENTALLY
DISABLED PERSONS

Post Office Box 11356 / Salt Lake City, Utah 84147
Telephone (801) 533-6770

MEMORANDUM

To: DD Onsite Evaluators

From:

Subject: Onsite Evaluation of DD Council Projects

Date:

Thank you for your cooperation in helping to evaluate projects funded by the DD Council during FY 1985. Enclosed with this memorandum are the following documents:

- a copy of the memorandum from the DD Council Executive Director to projects regarding onsite visits

- a copy of the original proposal for the project you will be evaluating

- technical assistance reports (if any) on the project you will be evaluating

- a copy of a letter sent to DD Council members who will be participating in the evaluation process

- a copy of procedures for conducting the onsite visit

- a copy of the rating form to be used during the onsite visit

- a copy of the format to be used in writing onsite evaluation reports a list of projects funded by the DD Council during this fiscal year showing your name as   onsite evaluator, the name and phone number of the project director, and the names and phone numbers of the two members of the DD Council who will comprise the rest of the evaluation team.

These documents should provide all the information necessary for you to complete the onsite visit and write a final report; however, if you have questions, please don't hesitate to contact me.

Reimbursement for your services will be at $150/day and should include one-half day for preparation, one day for attending the mid-year review conference, one day for making the onsite visit, and one day for report writing. Please complete the enclosed consultation form and return it with your final report. Your mileage and other expenses (if any) will also be reimbursed and should be reported on the enclosed orange form. Copying and other expenses will be reimbursed if you include a statement and receipts with your report.

Thanks again for your cooperation and help.

Enclosures

PROCEDURES FOR CONDUCTING EXTERNAL ONSITE EVALUATION VISITS TO
PROJECTS FUNDED WITH DD FORMULA GRANT MONEY

1. Onsite evaluator attends review of mid-year reports conference to meet Council monitors and prepare for onsite visit - April 15, 1985.

2. Onsite evaluator contacts the Council monitors to discuss a date for the onsite visit, transportation, etc.

3. Onsite evaluator contacts the project director to:

   a. schedule the onsite visit

   b. request documentation regarding the project, i.e., revised proposal, evaluation plan, any documents the project director would like reviewed prior to the team's visit, etc. Request copies be sent to all team members.

4. Team reviews all relevant material prior to visiting the project:

   a. project proposal

   b. memo from Councils Executive Director regarding onsite visits

   c. evaluation instrument

   d. technical assistance notes

   e. documentation from director.

5. Onsite evaluator contacts Council monitors, confirms date for onsite visit, and outlines procedures for onsite visit.

6. Onsite evaluator contacts the project director and outlines procedures for onsite visit, schedules staff to be interviewed, etc.

7. Notify DCHP of scheduled visit by April 1, 1985.

8. Conduct onsite evaluation visit by April 26, 1985.

   a. introductory interview with project director (review purpose of visit; discuss summary rating sheet; review and adjust as necessary schedule for the day)

   b. collect data regarding each evaluative question

- interview, as appropriate, project director, project staff, parents, clients, etc.

- observe project operation

- examine products and developed materials

- examine financial records

- examine internal evaluation reports and documents

- examine client folders

   c. check perceptions with other team members

   d. complete summary rating sheet and outline final report

   e. conduct exit interview with project director and project staff

9. Write draft of final report and send to the DCHP and the project director by May 3, 1985.

10. Obtain feedback from DCHP and the project director by May 8, 1985.

11. Revise report and send final copy to the DCHP and the project director by May 10, 1985.

Checklist for Onsite Evaluation Visits

1. Notify DCHP of date for onsite visit   April 1 _____

2. Attend mid-year review conference   April 15 _____

3. Conduct onsite visit by   April 26 _____

4. Draft report to DCHP and project director   May 3 _____

5. Obtain feedback from DCHP and project director   May 8 _____

6. Final report to DCHP   May 10 _____

7. DCHP must have reports to DD Council by   May 13 _____

EXHIBIT 6.11: MODEL ONSITE EVALUATION REPORT

EXTERNAL ONSITE EVALUATION REPORT

for

SCHOOL VOLUNTEER DEVELOPMENT PROJECT

Clearview School District

by

Harrison Jones

David Bushell

April 22, 19xx

MODEL REPORT

Note: Although based on an actual site visit, names have been changed throughout this sample to protect confidentiality.

EXTERNAL ONSITE EVALUATION REPORT

SCHOOL VOLUNTEER DEVELOPMENT PROJECT

Clearview School District

PROCEDURES

Prior to Onsite Visit

The evaluators met after reading the external onsite evaluator training package and the proposal by the Clearview School District to conduct a school volunteer program. During this meeting, decisions were made about the particular people who should be interviewed during the onsite visit, and specific questions which should be answered were noted. Telephone contact was made with Dr. Vern Carlson and Ms. Linda Hanes to schedule the onsite visit and to review the activities which would occur during the visit. A tentative agenda for the onsite visit was outlined and questions were answered concerning the external onsite evaluation form and the procedures for the visit. Arrangements were also made with Ms. Gonzales, member of the Title IV State Advisory Council who teaches in the Clearview School District, to serve as a member of the external onsite evaluation team. A brief visit was held immediately preceding the onsite evaluation visit between Dr. White, Mr. Bush, and Ms. Gonzales to further clarify the purpose and procedures of the visit.

During Onsite Visit

The visit commenced at 9:00 a.m. on April 22, with members of the evaluation team meeting with Ms. Hanes who has been the coordinator for the project. Ms. Hanes reviewed the project's activities for the year and responded to questions from the onsite evaluation team members concerning the project. The team leader outlined the agenda for the day's activities and minor adjustments were made in the schedule. This initial meeting with Ms. Hanes lasted approximately one hour.

Following the meeting with Ms. Hanes, members of the evaluation team met with Mr. Tom Smith, the chairperson of the School Volunteer Advisory Board, Dr. Vern Carlson of Clearview School District, the project director, and Ms. Hanes. The discussion during this meeting focused on the role of the advisory committee and Mr. Smith's perceptions of the project, its strengths and weaknesses, and what he would like to see as its future direction. Dr. Carlson also participated extensively in this discussion.

Following this meeting, Mr. Bush and Ms. Gonzales conducted telephone interviews with four adult volunteers who had participated in the project and Dr. White continued his discussion with Ms. Hanes concerning various components of the program. Following these interviews, the team went to lunch with Ms. Hanes, Ms. Linda Okley (the district's Title I coordinator who has participated in the volunteer program) and Ms. Marge Kildon (the volunteer coordinator for the northern half of the district).

Following their discussion at lunch, the team traveled with Ms. Hanes to Bonneville Elementary School and Highland Middle School where the Cross-age Tutoring Program has been operated during the 1985-86 year. At these schools the team met with principals (Allen Fester at Bonneville Elementary, and Alton Cange and Gary Hayes, assistant principals at Highland Middle School), teachers (Ms. Hill, Roydeu, and Andrews at Bonneville School) and two students who had participated in the tutoring as tutors at Highland School and one student who had been tutored at Bonneville Elementary School.

Following the visit to the schools the team returned to the district office where they reviewed the financial records and then met together as a team to summarize their observations and ratings. The team then met together with Ms. Hanes and Dr. Carlson to summarize their conclusions in an exit interview. The exit interview was completed approximately 5:00 p.m.

PROCEDURE DESCRIPTION

The current School Volunteer Program is an extension of an adoptable project which was previously conducted by the Clearview School District. The programs in each year were different but related and both came from the same developer in Dade County, Florida. The first year's program focused on getting community people involved in volunteer efforts in the schools. Volunteers included the parents, retired persons, college students, and community business persons. Through these efforts more than 20,000 hours of volunteer time was donated to the district during the previous school year.

The current project continued this thrust but expanded the volunteer program of the district into a cross-age tutoring program referred to as Training for Turnabout Volunteers (TTV). This cross-age tutoring component was recently approved as an additional component of the Dade County volunteer program which had been adopted the previous year. The TTV program consists of a series of video tapes and written instructional modules for teaching older children (in the case of Clearview School District, children at Bonneville Elementary School) in reading and mathematics.

The first instructional module teaches the tutors tutoring skills and consisted of a 30-minute session taught by Ms. Hanes every day for two weeks. Remaining modules focused on specific content to be tutored. Thirty children from Highland Middle School participated in the program during the current school year. Each of these children tutors 4 times a week for 45 minutes. Tutors were selected based on their volunteering and then being screened by school administrators as well as receiving parental permission. Following the training sessions which started in February, the tutors have gone to Bonneville Elementary School (which is adjacent to Highland Middle School) four times each week for 45 minutes a day. On the fifth day of the week tutors met with Ms. Hanes in a class which provides them additional instruction in tutoring content for reading and math. This instruction is provided via video tapes and written materials and provides the tutors specific instructional sequences which can be used in the classroom.

In addition to the TTV program, the district has continued the adult volunteer program. Much of this program is coordinated through the district's PTA, although volunteers come from many other areas as well. Volunteers are solicited via a mailing which goes to the total population of Clearview, through advertisements in newspapers and radio announcements, and at the schools' grandparents day. Through March of the current school year adult volunteers had contributed approximately 11,000 hours which had been recorded and it appeared that substantial data for this time period were still coming in.

Both components of the volunteer program (adult volunteering and the cross-age TTV tutoring) have continued to be supported by the Dade County developer through onsite workshops and correspondence via letters and telephone.

OBSERVATIONS REGARDING EVALUATIVE QUESTIONS

Based on interviews with the district's staff, observations and interviews at the schools participating in the TTV program, and telephone interviews with adult volunteers, the following observations were made regarding each of the evaluative questions.

1. **Did project activities conform with the approved plan or approved modifications?** (Points assigned: 50/60)

The project has experienced some minor problems in terms of implementing the activities proposed but none of them was serious enough to jeopardize the success of the project. Generally the team felt this was a good project which was making a substantial contribution to the quality of education in the Clearview School District.

The Cross-age Tutoring Program has been implemented in two schools although it was somewhat late getting started and has only involved 30 tutors instead of the 50 originally proposed. The fact that the project was late getting started meant that the tutor training had to be compressed more than would have been ideal, but from our observations and conversations with students, this does not seem to have been a serious problem.

The organization for enlisting and managing the community volunteer program is still in place and actively recruiting volunteers. Some parts of this community volunteer program discussed in the proposal have not been implemented (e.g., the transportation for the elderly, the focus on how to improve the project's retention rate, and the concerned effort to reach out to business and church groups). Another concern of the team was that community volunteers receive little training in how to function as volunteers. In addition, some of the volunteers interviewed felt that the lack of training and the lack of preparation of teachers resulted in volunteers being used inappropriately in the classrooms on some occasions.

Nonetheless, it was clear that substantial amounts of tutoring and volunteer work are being contributed to the district. Teachers pointed out that tutoring programs and volunteer programs have come and gone in the district over the years but that this program is better because it is more systematic, has organized follow-up, and has strong district support. Indeed, teachers suggested that the program would never have been as successful as it has without the strong central support of the district.

One of the biggest problems with both components of the volunteer program seems to be instructing teachers how to use the volunteers appropriately. This is not a serious weakness with the project at this point because it will understandably take time for teachers to recognize the program as a permanent addition to the district's educational efforts, and for them to incorporate volunteers and tutoring into their teaching strategies. However, if the program is to be as effective as it could be, it is important for future efforts to focus on helping teachers take advantage of both community and cross-age volunteers. For example, the instructional packages in which the cross-age tutors are trained for reading and math are well conceptualized and appear to provide useful activities that could be incorporated directly into the teaching curriculum. However, based on our interviews with teachers, students, and administrators, these instructional packages are utilized very seldom by the teachers. In most cases when cross-age tutors come to the classroom, they serve as untrained aides, assisting in drilling students on word lists or helping them with workbook exercises.

The district has also implemented a program this year whereby each of the district-level administrators participate in tutoring by offering one hour of their services each week as a tutor. This has been an excellent program and appears to have communicated to other people in the district that district administrators are firmly committed to the concept of volunteerism. In the opinion of the onsite evaluation team, these types of activities have made a very positive contribution to the volunteer efforts of the district.

The only major activities described in the proposal which have not been substantially addressed are the evaluation activities. The original proposal described a comprehensive evaluation plan involving experimental and control groups and multiple outcome measures. At the time of the visit, little effort had been made in evaluation beyond recording of volunteer hours. Although the team agreed that the evaluation plan outlined in the proposal was overly ambitious and probably not necessary, it would have been better if the project staff had made this decision earlier in the project, designed a more appropriate evaluation plan, and requested permission for the change from the State Office of Education.

The Clearview School District was obviously adopting the key components of the originally validated project. The video tape and written training materials were being used by Ms. Hanes in training the tutors, and interviews with teachers and students supported the conclusion that the project was being appropriately implemented in the school district.

Everybody interviewed by members of the evaluation team had positive comments about the project. Administrators at both the district and building level were supportive of the project and felt that it was making a valuable contribution. Parents who had participated as volunteers in the project were enthusiastic. Teachers particularly emphasized the value of getting parents into the classroom so that they could see what was going on in the schools. The presence of parents in the classes also communicated to the schools and to children that parents and adults really do care about what's happening in the schools. Children who had participated as tutors were also very positive about the program. All children said they would do it again next year if they could and felt that it was improving their own performance as well as that of the tutees. Building level administrators pointed out that the program seemed to be having a positive impact on the behavior of many of the tutors as well as an academic impact.

2. **Was the project responding to a priority area of need or weakness within the LEA?** (Points assigned: 8/10)

The rationale for using both community volunteers and cross-age tutors to respond to some of the district's priority needs is clear. In a time of tight budgets, both volunteering and tutoring can have substantial impact at little or no cost. Tight budgets also tend to increase class size, and tutoring and volunteers can ameliorate some of the disadvantages of larger classes. In addition, districts are feeling a need to get more community involvement in education. The community volunteering program provides an excellent vehicle in accomplishing this purpose by getting parents involved in schools in productive ways, communicating to parents what's happening in the school, and communicating to the children that parents really care about the education process.

In their proposal for the current year's project, Clearview District emphasized the importance of these needs among their inter-city population where there were major areas of disadvantaged or educationally deprived families. This inter-city population was identified as the segment of the district which had the most urgent need for a project of this nature. A minor concern of the evaluation team was that after the district had argued so convincingly in the proposal that the inner-city population was who needed the cross-age tutoring program the most, the district then proceeded to implement the project in Bonneville and Highland schools which, although they draw from the inter-city areas to some degree, are clearly not inner-city schools. Furthermore, in spite of the fact that the project has received such overwhelming support from all levels of the district during this first year, no definite plans were under way for rapid expansion of the program to the inner-city schools where supposedly the most urgent needs existed. This concern is relatively minor however, given the fact that the project is clearly responding to important education needs which can be addressed by community volunteers and cross-age tutors.

3. **Did the project evaluation provide valid information about project effectiveness or impact? Did evaluation yield information which can assist the district in decisions about project continuation?** (Points assigned: 9/30)

The project proposal described a comprehensive evaluation plan with subjects randomly assigned to experimental and control groups and assessments on multiple outcome measures (including achievement test scores and measures of attitude towards the program). In addition, the program proposed to follow-up on the community volunteer program by collecting data about retention of community volunteers and reasons for dropping out.

At the time of the onsite visit, there was no clear plan for collecting project evaluation data. The project staff had decided that an evaluation as comprehensive as that outlined in the proposal was inappropriate (a conclusion with which the onsite evaluation team agrees), but had not developed a new evaluation plan that would be more reasonable. The rather informal data collection which had occurred via the project monitoring and through feedback from teachers has been overwhelmingly positive and there was little doubt in the minds of project staff or participating teachers about whether the project should be continued. However, this approach to evaluation leaves out two extremely important concerns which should be addressed.

First, in a time of tight budgets, summative evaluation about a project's effectiveness could be particularly important in convincing the district administration that this program is worthy of continued support and expansion. Although the level of summative evaluation would need to be matched with the available resources for conducting evaluation, the onsite team felt it would be unfortunate if more extensive efforts were not made to collect summative evaluation data regarding the effectiveness of the project. Much of this data could be collected reasonably and inexpensively by forming experimental and control groups and looking at children's scores (both tutors and tutees) on end-of-year district standardized achievement tests. In addition, by structuring the way that volunteers' hours are contributed to the district, experimental and comparison groups could be utilized to obtain an estimate of the impact of adult tutors on children's academic growth. A number of teachers and building-level administrators mentioned that the cross-age tutoring program was having a beneficial impact on children's behavior. Data about improved behavior could also be recorded using a data-based system rather than relying solely on testimonial data. Objective data gathered from teachers, participating volunteers, tutors, and tutees would be more convincing to district administrators than the testimonial data that is now available. Summative data of the type described above could be very persuasive in arguing for the continuation and expansion of the program.

Secondly, the project has made little effort to systematically collect formative evaluation data which could assist them in revising and improving the project in the future. The types of questions which could by answered from such evaluation data might include:

Should parents from community volunteers programs assist in their own child's classroom?

Are people hesitant to volunteer because they think they do not have the necessary skills?

How do teachers feel about the volunteer program and what types of action would make them feel better?

From where do people come who volunteer -- i.e., which recruitment efforts are most productive?

How do principals feel about volunteers and what problems have they encountered?

In what kinds of tasks do volunteers generally engage?

Would more systematic training make people more skillful volunteers or at least make them less fearful about volunteering?

Would training teachers result in better use of volunteers and tutors?

Do parents of children who are being tutored have concerns about the tutoring or volunteer program?

Why do people volunteer as community volunteers or as cross-age tutors?

Answers to questions such as these would be a great benefit to the program as it continues to be refined and expanded.

One resource that the project can take advantage of in structuring an evaluation thrust is the advisory council. Based on our discussions with the chairperson of that advisory council, the council would be very willing to assist with evaluation activities. With a limited amount of technical assistance, members of the advisory council could do much of the leg work necessary to collect and analyze high quality evaluation data.

It should be noted that the project is continuing to track hours of community volunteers and tutors and was planning to look at achievement test scores at the end of the year for those children who have participated in the program. Although these data will provide some information about project evaluation, it was felt that additional data were necessary for an acceptable evaluation.

4. **If the project is effective, is there evidence that the LEA plans to continue the project after Title IV - C funding is completed?**   (Points assigned: 26/30)

Many people in the district are clearly supportive of the volunteer program. During the past two years, the district has contributed substantial support to the project beyond what has been received from Title IV funding. The project coordinator has been released from other responsibilities to devote a major share of her time to the project. In addition, teachers, principals, and other district administrators have been willing to contribute time to the success of the project. Project staff have been successful in winning the support of the district's board of education. Indeed, the chairperson of the board of education has been heavily involved in different aspects of the project and has traveled to a number of national meetings with members of the project staff to make presentations about the project. The chairperson of the board appears to be heavily committed to the concept of volunteer programs and the board has officially recommended that the district establish a volunteer office. Project staff have also been successful in adding a new course to the district's curriculum to accommodate the cross-age tutoring program in the middle and elementary schools. In discussions with the district staff, such an addition to the curriculum is a major accomplishment given current attitude of the district. The advisory board appears to be willing to do all that they can to assist in continuing the project. Although they have not done so in the past, this willingness includes efforts to raise money to help support the project's operating expenses. Finally, the district's PTA organization is heavily committed to the concept of volunteerism whether or not the district pursues this type of program. Indeed the PTA has operated volunteers programs prior to the program and would continue to do so in the future. If the district were to drop this program, the PTA would probably pick up much of it because of their heavy involvement in it during the past two years and their recognition of the program's strengths.

There are, however, some weaknesses in terms of whether the project will be continued after Title IV - C funding is completed. District administrators are not currently committed to continuation because of the tightness of money. In conversations with the superintendent, it appears that this program is viewed as an important program but still a fringe benefit. If faced with further budget reductions, the volunteer program would probably not be one of the programs protected. Furthermore, the district's commitment to continuation of the program is questioned somewhat on the basis of their plans for expanding the program during the coming year. Although some expansion of the program will take place, this expansion does not appear to be as extensive or as rapid as members of the team would have expected if district administrators were strongly committed to the concept.

In summary, the program appears to have very strong backing from some segments of the educational community. Continuation, however, is somewhat dependent on next year's budget. Current prospects for the project are reasonably good. (Points assigned: 26/30)

5. **Were appropriate and sufficient efforts made to include private schools?**
   (Points assigned: 10/10)

The project director wrote a letter to each of the private schools within the Clearview School District's boundaries who are eligible to participate in Title IV - C Programs. Because she received no response from these letters, she also had telephone follow-up with each of the schools and later also invited them to the workshop conducted by the staff member from the developer site. In spite of these contacts, none of the private schools are participating in the program. However, it does appear that project staff did all that could reasonably be expected from them to inform private schools of their opportunity to participate.

6. **Are relevant LEA personnel sufficiently aware of and do they understand the purpose of Title IV - C; and are they aware of the expectations and requirements associated with accepting a Title IV - C grant?** (Points assigned: 10/10)

Based on our discussions with project staff members it does appear that they are completely aware of the purposes of Title IV - C and the expectations and requirements associated with accepting the Title IV - C grant. Key concepts discussed included the need for project continuation, the need for internal evaluation of the project's success, the concept of seed money, and the various requirements associated with financial accountability, onsite evaluations and project recordkeeping.

7. **In selecting an adoptable program to meet their identified need, did the LEA sufficiently consider other options besides the one ultimately selected?** (Points assigned: 9/10)

Project staff did review the **Educational Programs That Work,** a book distributed by the National Diffusion Network. However, they stated that they had pretty much made up their mind about which program to use prior to reviewing this book because of their previously successful experience with the Dade County program. Having worked the previous year with the same project and having been very pleased with the services that they had received, the systematic way in which the program was structured and supported, and the content of the program, district staff were excited about continuing to work with the Dade County schools in this new component of the program which they felt would complement their existing program. Given this set of circumstances, it is understandable that they chose to go with the Dade County program again without a great deal of further searching.

8. **Did the project have sufficient contact with the original developer or with certified second-generation trainers?** (Points assigned: 10/10)

A staff member from the original developer (John Bullen) spent two days with the project in December and did a workshop for Bonneville Elementary School teachers, a workshop for parents involved in volunteering through the PTA, and a workshop for eighth grade teachers at Highland who would have students participating as tutors. Representatives from each of the other elementary schools that might have an interest in cross-age tutoring were also invited to the workshop with the Bonneville teachers. Participation from invited teachers was 100% while participation from parents was quite low. In addition to these workshops, Mr. Bullen has had extensive telephone contact with the project and has been very responsive to their requests. The project has also used all of the Dade County training materials including video tapes and teachers' guides. Ms. Hanes commented on the excellent quality of these materials and particularly praised the way in which the materials are organized. In summary, the amount of contact which Clearview School District had with the developer seems to have been appropriate and extremely beneficial in implementing the project.

9. Did project expenditures and financial accounting procedures conform with state and federal requirement? (Points assigned: 27/30)

The project's financial accounting was done appropriately. A random sample of ledger entries were checked and appropriate documentation and supporting information was found for each of the expenditures. A couple of minor problems or concerns were discovered during the financial review. First, the State overpaid the district several months ago which meant that some figures in the accounting system did not add up appropriately. This problem will be worked out before the project is closed. Although it was a minor concern that the district had not yet discovered this overpayment, it was not a serious problem, could easily be corrected, and would have been noted eventually.

Secondly, the district has changed the line-item amounts in the original proposal. Significantly more money has been spent on travel than was projected. Although all of the money was spent on appropriate activities that were described in the original proposal, it would have been good to have written approval since the changes were fairly large and a substantial amount of convention travel was done. Part of this travel supported the board of education chairperson to make presentations about the volunteer program in different parts of the country. In terms of the project's continuation and support from key people, this money was probably very well spent.

Finally, a similar type of situation arose with the money originally budgeted for contracted services. The district had proposed in their application that this contracted-services money would go to the Council on Aging to assist the project in advertising and promotion. Because the project had a substantial amount of money to be carried over from the previous year, however, they were able to use the carry-over money for these purposes and to use the money in this project for other project-related purposes. Their rationale for where the money was used was very appealing and it is clear that the money has been well spent and appropriately managed. However, the fact remains that money was spent differently than originally intended, and no written approval was given.

SUMMARY

Strengths

On balance, the School Volunteer Program is a strong program that is responding to important needs within the Clearview School District. The way the district has coordinated the two different components of the project is admirable and will likely lead to increased benefits. The needs to which the project is responding are persistent needs that have been present for sometime. Based on our observations, this project has the capability of making substantial impact on those needs. Also, the quality of the materials and the support received from the Dade County program was impressive. Clearly, this is a well-developed program that can be effectively implemented by districts who have similar needs. A major strength of the program has been the local support from the PTA, teachers, district administrators, and the school board. Support has enabled the project to overcome obstacles and be successful in accomplishing its major objectives of getting a volunteer and cross-age tutoring program up and running. Factors which have been important in the success of the program include the project coordinator who has enthusiastically pursued the project objectives. She has been a major motivator behind much of what the project has been able to accomplish. Also the level of district commitment both in terms of money and attitude has been an important part in bringing the project as far as it is. The interest of parents and their willingness to volunteer their time for the program, as well as the interest and support of the advisory board have also been important contributors to the success of the program. As can be seen, the project coordinator has been able to gather support of the program from a broad base. This base of support will likely be important as the project completes the Title IV - C funding and looks for alternative ways to support what they have begun.

Areas in which improvement is needed

Although the project was generally successful, there were a number of important areas which could be addressed to make the project even better. As mentioned earlier in this report, both formative and summative evaluation were lacking from the project. Evaluation data could have been important in improving the current operation of the project and in enlisting support for continuation and expansion of the project in the years to come. A second area in need of improvement was in training teachers to utilize community volunteers and cross-age tutors, training community volunteers in developing the skills needed to effectively participate in the classroom, and integrating the training students were receiving in specific tutoring strategies into the program. This weakness stemmed in part from a project coordinator who was already overextended in trying to keep the other parts of the project operating. Indeed, given that this is the first year of the project, it probably would have been unrealistic to expect the level of training referred to above to have really been implemented. Given her many other responsibilities, it is impressive that the project coordinator was able to accomplish as much as she did. Consequently, training teachers is not so much an area of weakness, as an area which should be emphasized in the coming years.

Recommendations

The onsite evaluation team is unanimous in recommending that both components of the School Volunteer Program be continued and expanded in the Clearview School District. We would like to see even more rapid expansion than is presently being planned by the district. Based on our observations, the program appears to be enthusiastically supported by all who have had contact with it. Such enthusiastic support, coupled with the important needs to which the project responds, make it a natural for further expansion. However, such expansion must be accompanied by continued district support for coordination and assistance. A number of teachers with whom we talked said that this project would not have been as successful as it has without the consistent and strong central office support which came through Ms. Hanes in providing the coordination for much of the project. Without someone to fill this position and to keep the project objectives clearly in focus, it is probable that much of the potential impact would be diluted. In continuing the project and looking for ways to expand it, it is also important that the district look for ways to train teachers better in how to utilize community volunteers and cross-age tutors so that they can be more effective in working with teachers. The project is clearly capable, when properly implemented, of repaying its costs many times in terms of the services provided and the benefits derived.

CHAPTER 7: CONDUCTING, REPORTING AND EVALUATING ONSITE EVALUATION ACTIVITIES

Procedures and considerations important to assure an effective, efficient, and objective onsite evaluation are discussed briefly in this chapter.

CONDUCTING ONSITE EVALUATIONS

Even if team members have been selected and trained appropriately, there are a number of important issues about how the visit is conducted which must be attended to if the evaluation is to yield useful and timely information. As described below, it is particularly important for the team to thoughtfully allocate their time among the many possible activities so that the onsite visit can be as productive as possible. The remainder of this section provides guidelines which can be used in planning the conduct of an onsite evaluation.

Amount of Time On Site

As noted in the previous chapter, the amount of time allotted for onsite visits varies greatly. Many onsite evaluation systems depend on one- day visits, or one full day preceded by an evening for orientation and an initial team meeting. For larger or more complex projects, however, neither of these variations of the one-day onsite visit may suffice, and it may be necessary to schedule two or more days onsite. For such projects, shorter visits run a risk that the onsite evaluation process will fail to provide the kind of discriminative information necessary to differentiate among worthwhile projects and procedures. Several of the procedures and recommendations included in this chapter are proposed to correct this deficiency and simply cannot be completed in less than two days.

The issue of how long a visit should last is related to the issue of how often such visits should occur. In an earlier evaluation of Colorado's administration of Title III, new (first year) and old project directors were asked their opinions on seven questions relating to the length and frequency of onsite evaluations. The data in Table 4 are drawn from these responses [17 p. 43]. In this study, directors of both old and new projects felt that individual onsite evaluation visits should be made at least once a year (or in some cases more frequently). Perhaps more important, a sizeable majority suggested that onsite evaluation visits should last at least two days (although the preferred duration tended to be longer for directors of old projects than for directors of new projects). This finding parallels our experience in interacting with numerous administrators in planning their onsite evaluations. More experienced project directors seem to feel that sufficient formative evaluation help is derived from an onsite evaluation team visit to warrant spending more time on such activities than the one-day visit typically allotted.

Table 4

TITLE III PROJECT DIRECTORS' VIEWS ABOUT FREQUENCY
AND DURATION OF ONSITE EVALUATIONS

QUESTION	CATEGORY	RESPONSES			
		Every 2 years (%)	Every year (%)	Every 6 months (%)	
How often should an onsite evaluations be?	Director of Old Projects	0	56.6	43.5	
	Director of New Projects	9.1	63.6	27.3	
		1 Day (%)	2 Days (%)	3 Days (%)	3 Days (%)
How long should an onsite evaluation be?	Director of Old Projects	17.4	43.5	34.8	4.3
	Director of New Projects	45.5	36.4	18.2	0

In the following discussion, the onsite agenda and activities presume a two-day period on site to conduct the evaluation. If onsite visits of a different duration are planned, appropriate adjustments would have to be made. If a two-day period is assumed, it does not necessarily follow that the period will cover two consecutive full days. It may be more desirable to distribute the two-day time block differently. For example, it might be advisable to begin at noon on one day, using the remainder of that day and the second day to collect data. Then the evening of the second day could be used by the team to complete their rating of the project and agree on important points to discuss with project staff. This would allow the morning of the third day to be used for the exit interviews, completing the site visit by noon of the third day.

Also, allowances may need to be made in some instances for distributing the two-day period somewhat differently to accommodate very unique scheduling problems (mountain driving conditions, long distances, etc.). Since it is often difficult to block out three days for team leaders and members, however, the actual scheduling of the two days should be negotiable between the team leader and the project director.

Onsite Agenda and Activities

To assist in planning for onsite evaluations, an example of the activities which would occur during a two-day visit are outlined below. Each of several essential activities and considerations dealing with the actual conduct of the onsite evaluation are discussed briefly. Suggested time allotments are also given for each activity; obviously, these can only serve as general guidelines and will vary widely in practice.

Brief team meeting (first day: 30 minutes). This will typically be the first onsite meeting of the evaluation team and should be attended by the onsite team only. Assuming that training (see previous chapter) has already occurred, this can be a short meeting designed to re-orient team members to the purpose of the evaluation and to their specific tasks. If training is to be included in this session, then the time will need to be extended appropriately. In this initial session, the following activities should be accomplished:

1. The team leader should re-emphasize the purpose of the site visit and the expected products.

2. The team leader should point out that the success of the visit is directly dependent on the collection and interpretation of as much accurate, pertinent, and objective information as it is possible to obtain in two days.

3. The team leader should be certain that each member has sufficient numbers of ratings scales, interview forms, and other necessary material.

4. Agreement should be reached on interview assignments, locations, and times, including the time at which the team will reconvene to assess its progress.

Although it is generally advantageous for all team members to be present at pivotal events, such as initial briefing of the team by the project director, exit interviews, and the like, there is seldom a need for multiple team members to be present at very many of the individual interviews. If simultaneous interviews are scheduled and the onsite team splits up to cover those interviews, considerably more data can be collected during the period of the onsite visit. If such a procedure is used, it is wise to have multiple team members participate in a small sample of interviews to assess the reliability of their perceptions and ratings.

Team briefing by project/program staff (first day: 60 minutes maximum). It is inevitable that project or program directors and staff members will want to spend as much time as possible orienting the onsite team to that which is to be evaluated. Indeed, if unrestrained, many local administrators and staff members will commandeer the agenda, with the result that the evaluation team will have little time left for data collection after the orientation session is completed.

During this initial orientation session, the following activities should be accomplished:

1. The briefing should include only important information about the program's operation not otherwise or previously available to the onsite evaluation team. This is not generally the time for a slide show or for ". . . general comments about our project," other than as requested by team members. Lengthy and repetitive orientation sessions can be avoided if the team leader has previously asked the project director to use it for only a quick general overview and an opportunity to allow for clarification. If this request is forgotten, it may be necessary to tactfully guide the project/program administrators or staff back on track by reminding them that the team has received and carefully read all advance materials describing the project. Of course, if advance materials were not available, then appropriate modification in the initial briefing session will be necessary.

2. It is suggested that efficient interview procedures be used to enable each team member to interview as many persons as possible, maximizing the total number of persons from whom data can be collected during the site visit. As noted earlier, it is generally ineffective, inefficient, and unproductive to conduct many interviews with either the team or interviewees in groups. Some general interview guidelines include the following:

   • Have team members conduct interviews individually or, at the most, in two interviewer pairs. The one-on-one interview is obviously the ideal. Avoid extended "interview sessions" where the whole team is invited to meet with the advisory board or project staff at great length; rather, meet briefly together and then split up for one- on-one interviews.

   • Conduct as many intensive, in-depth interviews as possible within the two days.

- Make interview procedures more efficient by thoughtful use of telephone calls to facilitate wide geographic contacts (e.g., random sample of parents in the community).

3. Although procedures and categories will, of necessity, vary somewhat with each onsite visit, a number of general suggestions for interview procedures for each of several possible categories of interviewees can be given:

Staff

- Interview all project staff. (Staff in most cases can be considered those persons with at least 20 percent of their fulltime equivalent salary on the project payroll.)

- Project staff should be interviewed apart from authorities (e.g., principals, clinic directors, project director, superintendent, members of advisory boards).

- Project staff should be assured that their anonymity will be preserved, except in cases where that assurance cannot be given because of small staff size or other factors that might preclude anonymity.

Cooperating Personnel

- A wide sample of project cooperating personnel (such as other non-project staff within the agency and advisory or policy boards) should be interviewed. Their anonymity should be preserved also.

Consumers

- Potential consumers or users (and proposed users) of the project and its products. Interviews with this group should be helpful in determining the extent to which the products of the project will be useful.

As a practical example, most of the above data collection activities were used in both the Title IV and DD project onsite evaluations. During the onsite evaluations, data and information were collected relative to several evaluation questions. Members of the evaluation team collected data by: (1) interviewing members of the project and agency staff; (2) examining project records and materials and previous evaluation reports (internal and external), (3) reviewing the project's financial records, and (4) conducting telephone interviews with people served by the project. Based on the data collected from these activities, the evaluators rated the project on each of the evaluation questions and criteria. The written material distributed to each of the evaluation team members contained additional information about how these ratings should be applied to each of the individual questions. In addition, during the training of evaluation team chairpersons, each question was discussed in detail and examples were given for each rating category for each question. Thus, although the ratings depended on professional judgment and consequently were to some degree subjective, the ratings could be done reasonably consistently across projects by different evaluation teams.

Team meeting two (evening of the first day). At the end of the first day, the team should assemble to compile the data collected thus far, because this may result in restructuring or targeting the second day's activities differently then initially planned. There are several items to which the team should attend at that time.

1. This is a good time to check on the progress of the data collection thus far and identify problems.

2. The agenda should be modified where necessary and the team leader should communicate this as quickly as possible to the project director.

3. In addition, the team may share general information and discuss logistical problems, changes in their interview schedule, and so on. It may be wise to avoid excessive subjective discussion concerning initial or incomplete impressions of the project at this point. Tentative observations should be identified as preliminary and subject to change as further information is collected. If preliminary observations are not **clearly identified as such,** they may become solidified out of proportion as a function of many people naturally, but prematurely, supporting and reinforcing one another's opinions in the camaraderie of the moment. In any case, possible misperceptions based on only one day of data collection (so far) could distort the data collection on the second day, resulting in an inaccurate evaluation of the project.

4. The team should be free to spend the rest of the evening as they wish, conducting further interviews if desired.

Second day data collection (morning of second day). The morning of the second day should be used to complete data collection activities. If some team members can be spared without sacrificing important information, this can also be a useful time for team members to summarize their individual ratings and perceptions prior to attempting to reach total team consensus on an evaluation of the project.

Team formulation of overall ratings and evaluative summary (second day: 4 hours). It is a sizeable step from individual team members impressions and ratings to a cohesive team report to which all team members are willing to subscribe. The steps and activities suggested to reach team consensus are outlined on the following page.

1. Toward the end of the morning (or perhaps this could be accomplished while the team eats lunch together), the team should reassemble for data sharing and begin to formulate the team response to the onsite rating forms. This rating process should be completed by shortly after lunch.

2. Between approximately 1:00 and 3:00 p.m., the team leader should assign each team member to record in writing three basic things regarding their onsite visit component responsibilities. (This assumes members may have had differential responsibility for collecting data on different aspects of the project. However, the same general procedure could be used in the absence of differentiated assignments by having each team member respond in relation to the project as a whole.) The three items are:

   • project strengths

   • project weaknesses

   • recommendations for improvement or modification.

3. Between approximately 3:00 and 4:30 p.m., the team should reassemble and have a full discussion of the written statement in order to seek consensus or note minority reports. Team members should then redraft their written statements as necessary. This process should result in each team member producing a rough-draft, written statement relating to the three points outlined above.

4. At about 4:30 p.m. each team member should give his/her written statement to the team leader, so the individual statements can be reviewed preparatory to the exit interview.

Exit interview of onsite evaluation team with project staff. Some evaluators seem to prefer to collect their data and leave the premises without revealing the slightest hint of how they view the project. Such a procedure not only extends (and often heightens) the anxiety of project staff unnecessarily, but it can also be viewed as less than courageous. It is professional, if not easy, to share face-to-face the team's perceptions of project weaknesses in need of amelioration, rather than sending later missives from afar when the project staff are unable to respond or query the rationale or data on which those perceptions are based. Furthermore, there are sometimes instances where the evaluation team reaches an incorrect and even silly conclusion based on their misunderstanding or oversight of some critical piece of information. The exit interview serves as a final check to ensure that such mistakes do not occur. In short, an exit interview should be an integral part of every onsite evaluation and should include the following activities:

1. The team leader should present an oral report of the findings of the team. It should be impressed upon the project staff that the onsite evaluation team is appreciative of the cooperation and facilitation (assuming such was provided) of its work. It should also be noted that statements made by the team leader reflect team consensus, unless minority reports are noted. It should also be pointed out that the team's reactions are based on impressions gained in a relatively brief visit and, therefore, may be over-simplified and lacking in some details. Further, the possibility of some errors in team perceptions exists. The final written report will note this and include all comments to be made during the exit interview. The team reserves the right, however, to modify points in the oral report if further reflection and consideration of the data make such modifications necessary.

2. Discussion, questions and answers, and other attempts at **Clarification** should be dealt with as appropriate.

3. The project staff should be informed that they will receive a draft of the written report and will be asked to review it for inaccuracies or inappropriate conclusions. They should be informed that their input and suggested modifications will receive careful consideration, although the evaluation team reserves the right to determine the final content of the report. Extensive rebuttals during the exit interview may be avoided by pointing out the opportunity to have such reactions put in writing and attached to the onsite report as an addendum or submitted separately, depending on the preference of the funding agency.

4. It may be useful to have the project director and onsite team members sign a sheet which certifies that the evaluation was completed on the specified date(s). This does not necessarily signal that the project director agrees with the summary provided in the exit interview but merely certifies that it has taken place. A sample of a form which might be used for that purpose appears as Exhibit 7.1.

Onsite evaluation team reimbursement. After the exit interview, the team leader should distribute the reimbursement forms to be filled out and sent to the designated individual responsible for payment of fees and travel expenses.

REPORTING THE RESULTS OF ONSITE EVALUATION VISITS

One of the most challenging tasks of the onsite evaluation team leader is to produce a written report that reflects both the diversity of individual team members' perspectives and the overall team consensus about the project or program. Similarly, it is challenging to combine the reports of separate onsite evaluations into a cohesive and coherent commentary on the "umbrella" program which contains the projects visited. Both of these tasks are made easier if standardized procedures and criteria were used by individual team members and by each onsite evaluation team. Here the wisdom of spending time to standardize evaluation instruments and deal with scaling problems becomes apparent, since information about individual evaluators or from different onsite evaluation teams can be collapsed to yield summary data about a particular project or about a larger program.

Additional considerations about the preparation and use of final reports are discussed briefly below.

Nature of Written Onsite Evaluation Reports

The written onsite evaluation report should be clear and concise and should contain a summary of the team's judgment of the project/program on each criterion or in relation to each evaluative question. The report should also contain a clear summary of the team's perceptions of the project's strengths and weaknesses, along with recommendations for modification.

The report should be intelligible, interpretable, and free of esoteric jargon and educationese (i.e., it should be unlike this sentence!). All summary rating forms should be appended as part of the report. The format of the onsite evaluation report should be specified in advance and (as described earlier) models provided wherever possible for team leaders to follow in preparing their written reports.

Distribution of Onsite Evaluation Reports

Prior to formalizing an onsite evaluation report, the written draft should be sent to all onsite team members and to the project director (and as designated, the project staff) for review and comments. It is the responsibility of the onsite leader to incorporate those comments into the final document, using minority reports and rebuttals, if appropriate, as discussed in the previous section.

Once the onsite evaluation report is finalized, copies should be sent to the project director, all team members, and to the funding agency. Any further release or distribution of that report must normally be approved by the funding agency, unless such release is granted **a priori** in the contract or agreement authorizing the onsite evaluation.

Use of Onsite Evaluation Reports

As was mentioned in the introduction to Section II, the primary purpose of onsite evaluation is to assist in the improvement of educational projects and programs. If that purpose is to be served, it will be important that the funding agency read the report and seek any necessary clarification from the team leader. The funding agency should also discuss, as appropriate, the report with the project director.

The project or program receiving the onsite visit should obviously address itself to recommendations resulting from the report. Unfortunately, this is not always the case. For example, a colleague of the authors has on two occasions inserted five-dollar bills between the pages midway in final reports submitted to a federal agency and found them still there (in the obviously unread reports) when visiting the funding agency almost two years later. Therefore, it is useful for the team leader or coordinating agency to highlight specific recommendations that require action and to take advantage of opportunities to discreetly follow up on whether any action has occurred. Furthermore, if the onsite evaluation is formative in nature and the project is judged to be unsuccessful or questionable to date, the funding agency may request a subsequent onsite evaluation team visit for summative evaluation purposes.

EVALUATION OF ONSITE EVALUATIONS

It is important to funding agencies to know who they can rely upon to perform well as onsite team leaders and members. Officials in the sponsoring agencies are often in a good position to judge the competence and professional conduct of team leaders. This is often not the case for team members, however, for it may be difficult for a funding agency to determine just what each team member contributed to a particular onsite evaluation. Insightful funding agencies, therefore, will often ask the team leader to evaluate the contribution of each member of the onsite evaluation team. A sample evaluation form for this purpose appears in Exhibit 7.2. These ratings should be forwarded to the funding agency and should prove useful in providing for the selection of subsequent onsite evaluation team members and the discontinuance of the services of onsite evaluation team members judged not helpful for this type of evaluation activity. This information may thus be stored for use in selecting future team members.

An annual review of the onsite evaluation system used by a funding agency should be conducted by that agency, with a review panel comprising appropriate agency personnel, outside evaluators, and members of any appropriate advisory or policy councils. The purposes of this review would be to:

1. Determine if evaluation procedures, both internal and external, are adequate for all projects funded under the program authorization

2. Determine if the instrument used will provide the proper criteria to make valid decisions in regard to each project

3. Establish procedures for compiling the results of all evaluations, both internal and external, in a usable form, and determining whether appropriate actions have been taken on any recommendations made

4. Develop procedures to use the results of such evaluation for funding or continued funding.

It is frequently desirable to include, as part of the evaluation of the onsite evaluation system, the perceptions of project directors who received onsite visits during the period in question. For example, in the evaluation of the Title IV onsite evaluation system, Title IV project directors were asked to rate the onsite evaluations on several dimensions. The results were very helpful in refining that onsite evaluation [19].

STIPEND AND EXPENSE CONSIDERATIONS

In view of the responsibilities and obligations connected with the onsite visit (including the time commitment of the team leader and the team members), an appropriate reimbursement schedule should be established. Honoraria, plus expenses and per diem, should be set for the team leader and for each team member. Team leaders should obviously be remunerated at a higher rate because of their additional work preparing for the onsite visit and drafting the final report.

It would be foolish to try to suggest specific fees for onsite evaluations. It is appropriate, however, to emphasize that paying for preparation and writing time (in addition to onsite time) generally results in team leaders and members taking the tasks of preparation and writing seriously. Also, as in most other walks of life, paying low stipends in hopes of obtaining "bargain basement evaluations" is usually false economy. In evaluation, as elsewhere, one normally gets what one pays for. Evaluation can be, after all, a cost-saving factor. The savings in wasted materials and resources (people, time, money) which may derive from better judgments concerning the continuation (or discontinuation) of some projects and programs is incalculable and may more than offset the cost of onsite evaluations.

EXHIBITS FOR CHAPTER 7

EXHIBIT 7.1: SIGNATURE PAGE FOR ONSITE EVALUATION REPORT

EXTERNAL ONSITE EVALUATION REPORT

Project Name _____

Project Location _____

Project Director - Name _____

                    Address_____

                    Phone _____

External Onsite Evaluation Team Members:

     Chairperson _____

                    _____
                                  (Name and Address)

     Member   _____

                    _____
                                  (Name and Address)

     Member   _____

                    _____
                                  (Name and Address)

Year of Project _____
                          (First year, second year, third year, etc.)

Date of Visit: _____
Date of Report: _____

Signatures: Project Director:_____

           Chairperson of Onsite Team:_____

           Team Member:_____

           Team Member:_____

EXHIBIT 7.2: ONSITE TEAM LEADER RATING
OF TEAM MEMBERS

Name of Team Member _____

Would you recommend this person to participate in subsequent external onsite evaluation team visits? Please check one response. If you check either 2 or 3, please explain your response.

O   1. Would definitely recommend for future onsite visits.

O   2. Might recommend if no one better was available. (Please explain)

O   3. Would not recommend under any circumstances. (Please explain)

_____   Signature of Team Leader

_____   Date

_____   Project Visited

SECTION III: TECHNICAL ASSISTANCE FOR FUNDED PROJECTS

Many agencies which fund individual projects of the type described earlier in this book have had the experience of funding a project which seemed destined for success -- it was addressing a very important need, had a plan that seemed appropriate, and had enthusiastic staff who seemed reasonably well qualified to conduct the proposed activities. Despite these positive factors, however, something went wrong and the project proved to be a miserable failure. There are a wide variety of reasons that such projects fail, but in many cases, it seems that a small amount of expert help at the right time could easily have made the difference between a poor project and a good project, or a good project and an exemplary project. Such expert help is referred to here as "technical assistance."

WHY IS TECHNICAL ASSISTANCE NEEDED?

Project staff members often have the necessary experience and expertise in most areas needed to successfully operate the project, yet either lack expertise in one specific area or are inexperienced in operating funded programs. For example, project staff may lack expertise and/or experience in setting up an internal evaluation, establishing transition services from one program to another, preventing client attrition, maintaining an "audit trail" of financial expenditures, disseminating information about the project, or securing outside funds for continuation services. In such cases, a relatively minor amount of expert assistance provided at the right time could make all the difference.

Unfortunately, many such projects are either unaware that the project has needs which are not being met, or they do not know where to obtain the help that they need. Even worse is when they recognize the need for help, but naively recruit a so-called expert who is totally unqualified to provide such assistance. In such cases, the project often suffers more than they would have without any "help," and project staff are often persuaded that using outside consultants is a poor investment of project resources.

In many cases, agencies which operate funding programs can contribute substantially to the quality and ultimate success of funded projects by organizing a way of providing short term, specifically targeted technical assistance. Not only is the funding agency in a position to recognize the types of problems which projects have historically experienced, but they can often be more successful in identifying those experts who are really capable of providing the types of assistance projects need.

Based on the experience of the Title IV and DD Council projects, the provision of such technical assistance often makes a substantial contribution to project success. Conversely, project weakness and, in some cases, rejection of proposals or discontinuation of projects often results from deficiencies that could have been readily avoided had qualified technical assistance been utilized.

What is true for Title IV and DD Council projects is probably also true for many other educational and social service funding programs, especially those operated under guidelines which are rigorous and/or technical in nature. In short, the better the availability and quality of technical assistance in areas where prospective applicants and/or project recipients lack relevant technical expertise or experience, the higher the probability that funded projects and programs will be successful.

PURPOSE AND ORGANIZATION OF TIIIS SECTION

It is the purpose of this section to present suggested steps and procedures for use by funding agencies in providing technical assistance to prospective applicants and/or project recipients. Although examples used in this manual are drawn from materials developed in relation to provision of technical assistance in the Title IV and DD Council funding programs, they should have broad applicability to technical assistance in other areas.

This section is divided into two chapters. Chapter 8 includes considerations necessary in designing and establishing a technical assistance system for the types of projects often funded by educational and social service agencies. This chapter is organized around the following topics:

- Funding of technical assistance services

- Developing guidelines for technical assistance services

- Identifying and maintaining a pool of qualified technical assistance personnel.

Chapter 9 deals with the actual operation of such a technical assistance system by addressing the following topics:

- Marketing the availability of technical assistance

- Keeping track of requests for assistance

- Technical assistance delivery.

- Another model of technical assistance: the use of "models"

- Evaluation of technical assistance services and systems.

In both chapters, materials used in either the DD Council or Title IV project are included to provide readers with concrete examples of how such a system could be organized and operated. Readers are encouraged to adapt and use these materials for their own projects, if appropriate credit is given as to their source.

CHAPTER 8: ORGANIZING A TECHNICAL ASSISTANCE SYSTEM

Although there are many ways to organize and deliver expert services to individual projects, some techniques seem to be more effective than others in identifying and matching project needs with the available expertise. Without appropriate planning and organization, technical assistance systems seldom achieve their potential. This chapter discusses the various ways in which a technical assistance system might be organized and provides guidelines for setting up such a system.

ALTERNATIVE ARRANGEMENTS FOR OBTAINING TECHNICAL ASSISTANCE SERVICES

Prospective applicants and/or project recipients might obtain needed technical assistance in a variety of ways, but the most common arrangement would be one of the following:

- assistance provided by designated individual(s) who are fulltime employees of the funding recipient (e.g., school district staff)

- assistance provided by a regional or area-wide service center supported by funds from the state or several individual units

- assistance obtained from a private consultant who is paid with project funds by the funding recipient to provide such assistance

- assistance provided or arranged by and paid for by an external agency (such as the funding agency).

The relative advantages and disadvantages of obtaining technical assistance from each of these various sources are considered hereafter.

Assistance Provided by Staff of the Funding Recipient

Each project recipient could maintain on its staff personnel who, collectively, possess all of the technical expertise needed to develop, operate, and evaluate today's increasingly sophisticated and technical educational and social service programs and systems. Realistically, however, very few individual project recipients are large enough to justify a staff with so many such technical specialists. Even in the case of large agencies, it is difficult to maintain all the important competencies on the same staff. For example, in educational programs, persons hired for their expertise in psychometrics may establish fine district testing programs but prove to be inept in the very different competencies required in curriculum evaluation or needs assessment. Few individual agencies which operate the type of projects described in this book will, therefore, be able to satisfy their needs for all relevant types of technical assistance from within their own agency. Indeed, attempts to do so by maintaining "stables" of technical experts have generally proved to be a costly if not infeasible alternative. Furthermore, even in those cases where the agency does employ people with the necessary technical expertise, such people often have other responsibilities that make them unavailable to the project at the time their help is needed.

Despite this issue of feasibility, it is often the case that some of the needs for technical assistance can be provided by regular employees of the funding recipient. Where available, such local technical assistance is often the most helpful, since the recipient's own technical specialist(s) will usually be familiar with the procedures, personalities, and politics of the agency that can so often be troublesome stumbling blocks to those who come in from outside to provide assistance. Moreover, the internal technical specialist often commands the best ground for providing follow-up services, given his or her proximity and continuing association with other agency staff.

One word of caution, however. It is sometimes difficult for educators and social service professionals who are not themselves expert in technical areas to judge accurately the qualifications of those who claim expertise in those areas. Consequently, agency administrators would be well advised prior to hiring technicians "from the inside" to seek opinions concerning the qualifications of those people from recognized experts in the field. This would help to avoid the too frequent situation where programs have foundered because of inadequate or even misleading internal technical support.

Assistance Provided by Regional Service Centers

Regional or area-wide service centers which are supported by the state or by groups of individual agencies would be expected to find it more practicable to maintain staffs with sufficient technical expertise to serve needs within their regions, thus freeing individual agencies (especially smaller ones) of the burden of trying to provide necessary technical skills within their own staffs. Reasonably close proximity to the agency in need is usually an advantage of regional service centers, as is continuity of service and at least some familiarity with the individual agency. Conversely, it can be costly for even a regional service center to employ all the important types of technical expertise needed in today's educational and social service programs, especially if the center is funded by requiring individual agencies to share costs, instead of receiving state or federal funding support.

Consequently, many, if not most, regional service centers can only offer limited technical services which can only reasonably be expected to assist in a fraction of the needs of individual agencies in the service region. And again, the same caution; employment within a regional service center is no guarantee of competence, even though it might lend an aura of credibility. It is still appropriate for individual agencies served by regional centers to seek "second opinions" from recognized experts about the capabilities of regional center staff before expending significant energy or resources in utilizing them to provide technical support.

Assistance Provided by Private Consultants

Assistance obtained from a private consultant or consultant firm has, like the other arrangements discussed above, both advantages and disadvantages. Although such services must usually be paid for by the funding recipient's project budget and, therefore, will take more of the project budget than technical assistance underwritten by external agencies (see next section), contracted services typically will cost substantially less than trying to retain fulltime staff members to provide such services. Outside consultants may be naive about important aspects of the local context, although this can often be corrected by adequate briefings. In some cases, a relatively naive external perspective may be an advantage, especially where objectivity is sought in program or curriculum evaluation.

The prime advantage in using outside consultants, however, is the opportunity for the agency to select precisely the types of expertise they need, without a continuing obligation to provide financial support beyond the specific service requested. In this fashion, some of the most qualified technical specialists can assist in a variety of projects that may be experiencing similar needs. Of course, it is also important here to be certain that would-be consultants or consultant firms indeed have the expertise they claim. Perhaps the best guide is to examine prior work samples and contact previous clients served by such independent contractors.

One of the most serious problems with depending on private consultants for the type of assistance being discussed here is the not infrequent failure to get around to hiring the consultant. Many project directors allow the pressures of day-to-day project management and service, the feeling that they are under-budgeted to do what they want to do, and the fact that they don't know where to find qualified technical expertise to prevent them from ever getting around to bringing in the outside consultant which had been planned.

Assistance Provided by an External Agency at No Cost to Recipient

If sufficient financial support from outside sources is available, technical assistance for applicants and recipients can be provided or arranged for by an external agency, at no cost to the applicant or recipient. There are numerous examples of such technical assistance efforts maintained by the federal government. For example, the network of Chapter I (formerly Title I) Technical Assistance Centers was established to provide technical assistance to state and local educational agencies in their efforts to comply with federal regulations for the evaluation of Chapter I. The federally supported Regional Resource Centers created to assist states and local districts in implementing the requirements of the Education of the Handicapped Act (Public Law 94-142) is a second example, and the Protection and Advocacy Centers funded by the U.S. Department of Health and Human Services to protect the rights and advocate for the needs of people with developmental disabilities represent a third example.

Unfortunately, even though there are numerous examples of such federally funded technical assistance centers, the number of such centers is very small, given the diverse needs of funding programs and the governmentally imposed restrictions about who is eligible to receive such services and/or the highly specialized services such centers offer. Furthermore, it is unrealistic to expect the establishment and/or operation of such a center for the hundreds of relatively small funding programs which have enormously diverse goals and needs. Therefore, the majority of funding programs do not have access to such a service center.

An alternate model is that employed in both the Title IV and DD council funding programs, which used state or federal support (instead of individual project funds) to hire short-term technical consultants to assist individual projects or agencies with technical needs. In this model, the funding agency is responsible for identifying, maintaining, and paying for the services of a pool of qualified technical assistants who can be used by funded projects on a short-term basis. This approach to providing technical assistance has several distinct advantages. For example, this approach is less costly than maintaining a staff of technical experts in a center, since there is no need to pay for "down time," staff benefits, and the like. In addition, a larger pool of qualified individuals can be available to each project, depending on specific needs and the skills required. It is thereby possible to provide a good match of needs and technical experts' competencies.

The relative advantages of the various alternatives discussed above are summarized in Table 5. In this table, **agency cost savings** refer to the financial resources required to implement each approach. Generally, this refers to whether or not the approach requires the individual agency to pay for more than the real cost of actual services delivered. **Technical expertise** refers to whether or not individual agencies can get the best qualified technical specialists to assist with each of their technical needs. **Local knowledge and access** refers to the technical assistance provider's physical and social proximity to (or in) the individual agency, local knowledge of the context, and continuity of contact with agency staff. **Objectivity** refers to impartiality and lack of bias which is especially important in providing technical assistance in evaluation and similar types of activities.

The ratings of high, medium, and low in Table 5 are estimates of what seems likely to be the case in **most** instances. Certainly there are conspicuous exceptions to several of the ratings.

The ratings on "technical expertise" for approaches 2 and 4 may need explanation. Ostensibly, such centers are staffed with experts. True as that may be, the number of staff is finite and often too small to encompass within it all the relevant and important technical

Table 5

Relative Advantages of Different Approaches
to Providing Technical Assistance

CRITERION

Approach Technical Assistance Provided By:	Funding Provided By	Agency Cost Savings	Technical Expertise	Local Knowledge & Access	Objectivity
1. Individual agency staff	Individual Agency	Low	Medium	High	Medium
2. Staff of area or regional service centers	State or Groups of Agencies or Districts (shared)	Medium	Medium	Medium	Medium
3. Consultants or consulting firms	Individual Agency	Medium	High	Low	High
4. Technical assistance center staff	State or Federal	High	Medium	Medium	Medium
5. Consultants from a "technical assistance pool" (Title IV and DD Council Model)	Funding Program Sponsor	High	High	Low	High

skills. This deficit is not shared by approaches 3 or 5. On "objectivity," approaches 2 and 4 fail to receive high ratings simply because the continual association and "repeat business" such center staff members have with a particular agency often makes it very difficult to retain the impartial and non-partisan posture so necessary in evaluation and related activities.

Overall, Which is the Best Approach to Providing Technical Assistance to Individual Agencies?

There is obviously no single answer to this question. If one accepts the analysis presented above, however, the best choice would seem to be the externally funded "technical assistance pool" such as that provided in the Title IV and DD Council projects. If external funding were not available, the best choice, on balance, would seem to be the use of external consultants, especially since the only low rating on this approach could be largely rectified by adequate briefings of outside experts brought in to provide technical assistance. It would be rather more difficult to remedy inherent problems in the remaining approaches.

Given the superiority and broader availability of the "technical assistance pool," for the types of funded projects of concern in this book, the remainder of this section will focus primarily on suggestions for establishing and operating that type of technical assistance delivery system. Many of these suggestions are relevant to the other approaches as well, however. Consequently, the materials in each chapter can be used selectively by those implementing the various approaches.

DEVELOPING GUIDELINES FOR TECHNICAL ASSISTANCE SERVICES

One of the potential difficulties in using a pool of short-term technical assistants is that the agency providing the funding and the project receiving the services do not have an ongoing contractual arrangement with the person providing the assistance. Consequently, it is essential that clear guidelines and procedures be established to maintain control and ensure that the technical assistance is both consistent with the guidelines of the funding agencies as well as being appropriately focused on identified needs.

When are Technical Assistance Guidelines Necessary?

Whenever there are boundaries as to what type of technical assistance can be requested and provided, some type of guidelines are necessary. For example, in the Title IV funding program, technical assistance providers were required to operate within carefully prescribed guidelines. Those guidelines were made available to all persons selected to serve as technical assistants and they were required to adhere to the guidelines in the provision of services to Local Education Agencies (LEAs). LEA project directors who requested technical assistance were also provided copies of the guidelines to help them determine the range and scope of specific services they might request.

Are Different Types of Guidelines Required for Those Who Deliver and Those Who Receive Technical Assistance?

Yes, obviously so. Different sets of guidelines are needed for those who deliver and those who receive technical assistance. It would be as sensible to think that physicians and clients could use the same set of guidelines in performing their independent but unique roles as to assume the same set of guidelines would serve both the service provider and the recipient of such services.

What Should Be Included in Technical Assistance Guidelines for Service Providers?

Adequate technical assistance guidelines for service providers should contain, as a minimum, the following:

- a description of the basic purpose the technical assistance is expected to serve

- the range and scope of specific services that can be legitimately provided under the particular technical assistance authorization

- a description of any extant processes which will be used to request technical assistance from them

- a description of legal and professional considerations in delivering technical assistance services, including conditions under which such assistance would be appropriate or inappropriate

- any relevant suggestions concerning the process of consultation which may help improve service delivery.

What Should Be Included in Technical Assistance Guidelines for Service Recipients?

Adequate technical assistance guidelines for service recipients should include, as a minimum, the following:

- a description of the basic purpose the technical assistance is expected to serve

- the range and scope of specific services that can be legitimately requested under the particular technical assistance authorization

- a description of any existing processes which service recipients should use in requesting technical assistance

- conditions under which technical assistance should and should not be requested

- names of approved individuals who are qualified to provide technical assistance

- any timelines or budget information relevant to the requesting of such technical services.

An example of the technical assistance guidelines sent to Title IV project directors appears as Exhibit 8.1 at the end of this chapter.

IDENTIFYING AND MAINTAINING A POOL OF QUALIFIED TECHNICAL ASSISTANCE PERSONNEL

The need for technical assistance arises primarily from three factors. First, educational systems and other social service endeavors are becoming increasingly complex enterprises, because of new technology, sophisticated methodology, and social and legal mandates. Second, these new considerations that must be dealt with by practitioners in education, social services, and related fields often require new configurations of competencies rather different from those possessed by most education and social service agency employees. Third, agencies operating projects of the type of interest here often need quick but **temporary** access to competent assistance in technical areas such as evaluation, computer technology, needs assessment, opinion surveys, and the like.

Technical assistance providers (consultants) are individuals with special knowledge and skill that comes from specialized training and/or experience. If the need for technical assistance is to be satisfied, it is apparent that the key lies in identifying and making available to clients those persons whose specialized training or experience has given them special knowledge or skill that makes them particularly qualified to render the assistance needed.

What Attributes Must a Technical Assistance Provider Possess?

According to Trohanis, Woodard, and Cox [23], consultants who are most successful possess the following characteristics:

- specific knowledge and expertise

- communication skills

- systematic procedures

- interpersonal skills.

The rationale for these seems patently clear. Without specific knowledge of relevant research and methods, the consultant could not speak with authority, and his or her credibility would be low. Poor skills in listening, speaking and writing interfere seriously with efforts to assist others, however astute the consultant might be in the technical content or process involved. Haphazard, disorganized suggestions and procedures are unlikely to prove useful to even the haphazard and disorganized who need help, not emulation. Finally, interpersonal trust and attributes such as sensitivity and flexibility are the very foundation of good relationships between service provider and recipient.

How Can Qualified Assistance Personnel Be Identified?

Perhaps the best way is to contact those who have a history of intelligent use of technical assistance to identify those individual consultants with whom they are well pleased. Reactions to services provided by former service providers is a good, though not foolproof, guide. A good supplement would be to contact known experts in the geographical area to be served and ask them for nominations of persons whom they know to have the requisite blend of technical and interpersonal characteristics to make good technical consultants. There is no substitute for compulsively careful efforts to identify the very best personnel for inclusion in technical assistance personnel "pools." Parochialism, "cronyism," and lack of information can be nowhere more harmful than in the choice of consultants.

Examples of the types of letter that could be used in soliciting nominations for a technical assistance pool are included as Exhibit 8.2. This exhibit contains an example letter sent to a previous user of technical assistance as well as a letter to an "expert."

Once Identified, How Can Qualified Technical Assistance Personnel Be Retained in a Technical Assistance Pool?

Although it may appear to be overly simplistic, the key to retaining a qualified pool of technical assistance personnel is, generally, to pay qualified individuals a reasonable fee, depending on their training and experience. It is ironic that many administrators think nothing of paying a physician or lawyer at a rate equivalent to $80-100 per hour, but balk at paying more than 20% of that hourly rate to technical consultants whose training may have been just as intensive and long. It is interesting to note that business and industry have increasingly recognized the worth of technical experts in education and allied fields and have begun to "pirate" top-flight specialists from many educational and human service agencies by offering enormously better remuneration than that typically offered by state and local agencies. As in other walks of life, one generally gets the quality of technical assistance for which one pays.

Although some limited technical assistance for projects can be obtained from experts even without appropriate remuneration, such assistance is generally short lived and undependable. For example, many universities and colleges maintain "Speakers' Bureaus" which serve as brokerage houses for community groups and civic clubs who seek individuals to speak on selected topics, usually on an unpaid basis. Although some qualified individuals continue to provide this service over long periods, the more typical speaker extinguishes and withdraws after two or three years, resulting in continual turn-over (and sometimes under-qualification) on the part of nominated speakers. It is similarly difficult to depend on volunteers for long-term technical assistance needs.

Prompt and courteous payment of fees and expenses is another important consideration in maintaining the services (and good will) of technical assistance providers. Consultants are unappreciative of the not infrequent situation where not only fees continue unpaid, but reimbursement of hundreds of dollars of travel and other expenses remain unpaid for months, while VISA continues to charge 18% on the unpaid balance!

What Information About the Qualifications of Technical Assistance Personnel Should Be Made Available to Potential Users of Their Services?

Although others may often serve as brokers in arranging technical assistance or other forms of consultation, it is generally desirable and appropriate for consumers to select consultants directly from among those judged to be qualified for the task. To assist in this selection, information about the qualifications of each individual consultant should be maintained in a "talent bank" that can be perused by consumers. Information about consultants' prior training, experience, substantive and methodological specialization, interests, and availability should all be included in such a bank. Talent bank information may take the form of individual resumes or vitae, standardized consultant profiles filled out by individual consultants, and references and evaluations of work provided by the consultants' former clients.

For example, in the Utah Title IV program, all individuals who agreed to serve as technical assistants were asked to provide brief resumes for inclusion in a file made available to any LEA who wished to examine backgrounds of potential technical assistants. In addition, personal knowledge of the particular strengths of each potential technical assistant was used to supplement the written information. An example of the type of information that could be collected for each potential technical assistant is shown in Exhibit 8.3

Whatever system is used, it is of paramount importance that those who use technical assistance services are provided with sufficient information to assure them that the individual(s) providing such services is well- qualified to do so. Such assurance is generally greater if the client has had some involvement in the selection of the technical assistance provider. In the absence of such involvement, it is far too easy for perfectly competent consultants to find that their credibility may be called in question by clients who feel that these particular individuals were "foisted off" upon them. Appropriately used, a talent bank can be a very helpful mechanism for recruiting qualified people and maintaining their credibility among users.

EXHIBITS FOR CHAPTER 8

EXHIBIT 8.1: TECHNICAL ASSISTANCE GUIDELINES FOR TITLE IV PROJECTS

250 EAST 500 SOUTH STREET · SALT LAKE CITY, UTAH 84111 · TELEPHONE (801) 533-5431

UTAH STATE OFFICE OF EDUCATION

TO: All Title IV - Part C Project Director

FROM: Bill Cowan

RE: Availability of Technical Assistance (TA) Services

As each of you proceed toward completion of the objectives of your Title IV - Part C project for this year, I thought it might be helpful to remind you that technical assistance is available to you to assist you in complying with various technical requirements of Title IV guidelines. For example, you will recall that you are required, as a condition of receiving a Title IV - Part C Grant, to do the following:

1. conduct an internal evaluation of your project to determine if the stated objectives have been accomplished (this is separate from the external onsite evaluation which may also be conducted);

2. provide documentation of all project expenditures so as to leave a clear "audit trail" of all financial transactions, including authorization for any shifts in budget categories, etc.;

3. cooperate with external onsite evaluators in their evaluation of your project; and

4. submit a final report.

Although some districts have staff available who possess expertise in the above areas and also have time to help with these activities, that is not so in all districts. To assist those projects which would benefit from additional expert help in any of the areas listed above, we have identified a number of highly qualified technical assistance (TA) consultants. These individuals have agreed to help LEAs with their projects upon request. **Costs of TA services, including honorarium, travel, and per diem, are borne by our office and will not be charged to your project.**

Guidelines for the provision and use of TA assistance are enclosed. If you wish to avail yourself of this source of assistance, please contact me and I will be pleased to identify several qualified TAs, from whom you can select the individual you would like to have serve you.

I hope you will seriously consider using this resource wherever it would assist you in complying with Title IV regulations and improving the overall quality of your project effort. If you have any questions, please feel free to call me.

250 EAST 500 SOUTH STREET · SALT LAKE CITY, UTAH 84111 · TELEPHONE (801) 533-5431

UTAH STATE OFFICE OF EDUCATION

GUIDELINES FOR TITLE IV TECHNICAL ASSISTANCE SERVICES

The primary role of the Technical Assistant (TA) is to serve as an internal evaluation consultant (a technical assistant) to assist the administration and staff of funded Title IV - Part C projects with the formulation and execution of the project's internal evaluation and other technical areas required by Title IV regulations.

Local Education Agencies (LEAs) who receive Title IV - Part C monies have the opportunity of involving TAs as part of their grants. Once funded, the LEA requests assistance from the State Education Agency (SEA) in securing the services of the TA. The SEA responds by sending to the LEA a list of persons who are qualified to serve as TAs. In conjunction with staff from the SEA, the LEA selects a TA from the list and directly requests that person's services. Once a TA agrees to serve, the arrangements for service are handled directly between the LEA and the TA, although the identity of the TA is to be made know to the SEA.

The costs of TA services, including honorarium, travel, per diem, and other expenses are borne by the SEA. It is the LEA's responsibility to contact the SEA to arrange for the money.

Although it is anticipated that most TA activities will focus on the internal evaluation activities of the project, a number of other activities are also possible. Listed below are brief descriptions of the types of assistance you may want to request from a TA.

1. Proposal Preparation

Particularly as it relates to the preparation of continuation proposals, the TA is in a position to assist the agency prepare a proposal that meets the technical standards of the SEA and that will compete well for funding support.

Although responsibility for the submitted proposal is assumed by the LEA, the TA can provide valuable technical assistance in proposal preparation. To assure the TAs that they are adequately prepared to render such a service, it is imperative that they thoroughly familiarize themselves with the guidelines, models, directions, and descriptive literature related to proposal preparation. The following relevant documents are available from Bill Cowan, Utah State Office of Education, 250 E. 500 S., Salt Lake City, UT 84111, phone number (801) 533-5061.

- Request for Title IV - Part C Proposals for FY 1982

- Model Proposals for Title IV - Part C

- Purposes of Title IV - Part C

2. Proposal Revision

Proposals for Title IV - Part C funds are sometimes funded with the provision that certain changes recommended by the reviewers be incorporated in the final project plan. For example, reviewers might say that the objectives of the project are poorly stated (not measurable or imprecise) or inadequate (overly process-oriented rather than outcome-oriented), the evaluation design might need refinement, the budget may need clarification, there may be a need for a clearer delineation of project activities and timelines, etc. In such instances, the role of the TA would be to assist the project correct the noted weaknesses.

Since such assistance requires considerable technical skill on the part of the TA, the TA should be prepared to be of genuine assistance in all these areas. Very literally, the project people expect the TA to be "the expert," and every effort should be made to meet that expectation.

3. Internal Evaluation

All Title IV - Part C funded projects are required to include in their project proposals an evaluation plan that is related to the objectives of the project. Although, as noted in item 5 below, the end-of-year evaluation (the summative evaluation) is conducted by an external onsite evaluation team, it is the responsibility of the project to monitor its day-to-day activities to assure that it is on task and congruent with the terms of the proposal, with particular emphasis on the accomplishment of the project's objectives.

Unless the formative evaluation process is given adequate attention, however, it can be forgotten entirely and the consequences can be severe. It is not unusual, in fact, to find that during the entire year of a project, no attention whatsoever is given to monitoring progress toward the accomplishment of the objectives. Occasionally, after the proposal is written and funded, it is filed and its contents essentially forgotten.

To assure that this does not happen, the TA may be asked to work with the project administrator and staff in the conduct of internal evaluation activities. In this role, the TA can draw attention to project timelines, assist in the development/selection/adaptation of evaluation instruments, assist in the development and execution of the project's evaluation design, and suggest modifications that should be made based on experiences and data that are generated by the project. It must be remembered that a project's objectives represent before-the- fact attempts at making reasonable projections of what the project hopes to accomplish. Once the project is initiated, it may be found that one or more of its objectives is, in fact, not reasonable. Without an adequate internal evaluation being conducted, this fact can be missed and the project severely affected.

The absence of adequate internal evaluation procedures generally means that claims of project success or effectiveness cannot be defended -- even in those cases where the project director and staff are totally convinced of the project's success. Such an unfortunate circumstance can usually be avoided by appropriate assistance from a well-qualified TA, thus providing an invaluable service to the project.

4. Budget Preparation and the Establishment of an Audit Trail

A major concern of Title IV is that its support monies be appropriately accounted for and managed. To assure that such is the case, TA services can be made available to the LEA to assist with budget preparation and to suggest accounting procedures that will establish a clear and precise audit trail of all project expenditures. Recommendations can also be made regarding the identification, use, and assignment of equipment and supplies purchased by the grant so that the onsite evaluation team can easily document project expenditures.

5. Preparation for Onsite Evaluation Team Visit

Many projects are included in the sample of projects to be thoroughly reviewed annually by an external onsite evaluation team. It is the responsibility of this team to objectively assess particular aspects of the project to determine if it is complying with the terms of the proposal, expending its funds as proposed, and generally performing in a manner consistent with the intent of Title IV.

Since the onsite evaluation may raise questions in technical areas, the TA can be of substantial assistance is preparing for such a visit. Such preparations could include, but need not be limited to: (1) a clear analysis and reporting of project data; (2) a thorough accounting and documentation of project expenditures; (3) where appropriate, the arrangement of interviews with parents, teachers, students, and school administrators; and, (4) the review of products produced by the project.

Before a TA can adequately prepare the project for the onsite visit, he or she needs to be thoroughly familiar with the onsite evaluation process. To gain this familiarity, the TA is strongly advised to obtain a copy of "External Onsite Evaluation of Title IV - Part C Projects," available from Bill Cowan at the address referred to earlier.

6. Preparation of Project Reports

All projects are required to submit end-of-month final reports. Although the LEA must assume final responsibility for such reports, the TA can provide the project with a valuable service by assisting it with the preparation of such reports. Such assistance can help assure that the reports are technically adequate, well-written, and sufficiently complete.

7. General Assistance

Although most technical assistance provided by a TA might typically be expected to fall within the areas noted above, other types of general or technical assistance to the project are permissable. For example, TAs might aid in curriculum development, conducting specialized training workshops, assisting with management plans, and the like.

EXHIBIT 8.2: EXAMPLES OF LETTERS USED FOR RECRUITING TECHNICAL ASSISTANTS

 WASATCH INSTITUTE FOR RESEARCH AND EVALUATION

Andy Richman, Ph.D.
619 Oakdale Drive
Riverdale, Utah 84391

Dear Andy:

As you may know, the Wasatch Institute for Research and Evaluation is again responsible for organizing the provision of Technical Assistance Services to Title IV projects for the coming year. As you know from your past experience, Technical Assistants serve on a short-term basis to provide consultation to projects in such areas as proposal preparation, development of project reports, conducting internal evaluations, program development and operation, and inservice training. Because of your recognized expertise in this area and past successful experience in providing technical assistance to Title IV projects, I would like to request your involvement during the coming year. In addition, I am interested in learning of other people within the state who you think would function successfully in this capacity.

As was the case last year, the specific assignment for each Technical Assistant will be negotiated based on the expertise in the pool of available assistants as well as the needs of the project. Technical assistants will be paid $150.00 per day plus expenses. Timelines for providing assistance will be individually negotiated with the projects.

I would appreciate it if you could complete the attached form and return it to me as soon as possible, whether or not you plan to participate during this coming year. I have enjoyed working with you in the past and hope we will be able to do so in the future.

Sincerely,

Blaine Worthen, Director
Wasatch Institute for Research and Evaluation

BW:ed

Enclosure

<u>   Andy Richman   </u>
Name

1. Please indicate your availability for Technical Assistance work in conjuction with Title IV Projects during the 84-85 year.

    O I would like to be included in the Technical Assistance pool during the 84-85 year.

    O I do not want to be included in the Technical Assistance pool during the 84-85 year.

2. Please indicate in the space below any people within the state who you think would be appropriate for providing Technical Assistance Services to Title IV Programs during the 84-85 year.

WASATCH   INSTITUTE
FOR RESEARCH AND EVALUATION

Carol Ann Wuthrop, Ph.D.
Project Director
Project Lift
Mountain View Elementary School
Mountain View, Utah 89741

Dear Dr. Wuthrop:

As a project director of Project LIFT last year, you received Technical Assistance help through the State Office of Education in conjuction with the operation of your project. We are currently developing a list of people to use as Technical Assistants for next year's projects. I have attached the names of the people who have been tentatively included on that list and would like to invite you to add the names of any other people whom you believe would be particularly appropriate for providing such technical assistance.

Based on your experience with the project last year, I assume you have a fairly good understanding of the kinds of skills that people would need to function effectively in this role. To refresh your memory, I am attaching a copy of the Guidelines for Technical Assistance that you received last year. I would appreciate it if you could fill out the attached form and return it to me at your earliest convenience.

Sincerely,

Blaine Worthen, Director
Wasatch Institute for Research and Evaluation

BW:ed

Enclosure

<u>   Carol Ann Wuthrop, Ph.D.   </u>
Name

1. The following people are currently included in our Technical Assistance pool for the coming year.

_____	_____
_____	_____
_____	_____
_____	_____
_____	_____
_____	_____
_____	_____
_____	_____
_____	_____
_____	_____
_____	_____
_____	_____
_____	_____
_____	_____
_____	_____

2. Please indicate in the space below any people within the state whom you think would be appropriate for providing Technical Assistance Services to Title IV Programs during the coming year.

EXHIBIT 8.3: INFORMATION ABOUT AVAILABLE TECHNICAL ASSISTANTS

Name: _____   Preferred address for contact:

Title/Position: _____   _____

Agency:_____   _____

Social Security #: _____   _____

                                                              Preferred Telephone:

                                                              _____

Please check the areas in which you have consultation expertise (check as many as apply).

Type of Children	**Content Areas**
_ early childhood	_ reading
_ elementary	_ language arts
_ secondary	_ math
_ post secondary	_ arts
_ gifted	_ career/vocational education
_ bilingual	_ physical education/health
_ special education	_ parent involvement

Methodological Expertise

_ statistics/experimental design	_ program management
_ proposal preparation	_ inservice training
_ program evaluation	

Please indicate availability.
I am available to accept assignments:

WHEN	**WHERE**	**HOW OFTEN**
_ business days	_ within 50 miles	_ less than 5 days/year
_ weekends	_ within 100 miles	_ 6-10 days/year
_ school year	_ anywhere in the state	_ more than 10 days/year
_ summer		
_ any of the above		

Please indicate minimum fee requirements: $_____/day

Is your current resume on file with WIRE: ___ yes ___ no. If no checked, please send us a copy of your resume along with this form.

I understand that this registration is for information only and does not obligate me to accept any assignment and does not constitute an obligation by WIRE to offer assignments. Also, this profile will not be duplicated and shared.

_____   _____
Date   Signature

CHAPTER 9: PROVIDING TECHNICAL ASSISTANCE

Recognizing the areas which would benefit from technical assistance and establishing and organizing an appropriate system is an essential first step, but it is only the beginning. Many such systems that should have been effective have failed to achieve their potential because of problems with getting clients to use the system, retaining the participation of qualified consultants, effectively managing the system, or providing appropriate materials and support. This chapter explains what can be done to make sure that the system works properly once it has been established. Guidelines and materials (which readers are welcome to adapt and use for their own purposes, if appropriate credit is given), are provided in the following five areas.

- Encouraging the Use of Available Technical Assistance

- Keeping Track of Requests for Assistance

- Delivery of Technical Assistance

- Using Model Materials to Support Technical Assistance

- Evaluation of Technical Assistance Services and Systems

ENCOURAGING THE USE OF AVAILABLE TECHNICAL ASSISTANCE

The often laudable "I'd rather do it myself" attitude is alive and well in many of today's educational and social service agencies which apply for or receive funds for the type of projects described in this book. Unfortunately, such an attitude is sometimes more pervasive than appropriate. Too frequently, individuals who are long on enthusiasm but short on preparation attempt to perform -- sometimes with disastrous results -- technical tasks for which they are qualified by neither training nor experience.

Strangely, such actions have sometimes come in a context where qualified technical assistance was readily available, sometimes free for the asking. For example, in both the DD Council and Title IV programs, several individual agencies performed poorly in technical areas in which the funding program sponsor had offered repeatedly to provide, free of charge to the agency, qualified consultants to assist as needed. It is not a rhetorical question, therefore, to ask how best to motivate potential clients to make appropriate use of technical assistance services.

How Can Potential Consumers Be Encouraged to Use Technical Assistance Services?

The first step in motivating individual agencies to use technical assistance is to aggressively advertise the availability and benefits of such services. Interestingly, most professionals in the field of education and human services are reluctant to engage in any specific promotional activity. Although this "shrinking violet syndrome" may have the merit of modesty, it also has resulted in educators and human service professionals often being required to expend considerable energy attempting to identify and locate high-quality programs or well-qualified individuals who could provide needed services. Because some agencies and individual consultants' excellence is exceeded only by their furtiveness and unwillingness to appear to be "pushing their products," projects needing help often end up obtaining services from less qualified (and less retiring) consultants or agencies.

In this context, the procedures used in the Title IV and DD Council projects provide some useful models. For example, in the Title IV project, the following steps were taken to maximize the availability and utility of technical assistance to LEAs.

1. All district superintendents were informed of the availability and nature of technical assistance in a letter from the State Office of Education which invited districts to submit Title IV proposals for each fiscal year. A "tear-out, sign, and return" page was attached for districts to use to inform the state officials that technical assistance was desired.

2. All Title IV project directors were provided with a set of guidelines for technical assistance services, along with an appropriate cover memorandum which outlined the existence, purpose, and availability of technical assistance for any Title IV project which required it (see Exhibit 8.1). In addition, the technical assistance guidelines were distributed at each Title IV project directors' meeting, along with reminders of the availability of technical assistance at no cost to districts.

In addition to using similar procedures with prospective applicants, the DD Council project used an additional technique to ensure that recipients of funded projects made appropriate use of the available technical assistance. Specifically, all project recipients were required to attend a post-funding conference. At that post-funding conference, staff from the funding agency, the chairperson of the proposal review process, and the person in charge of organizing and maintaining the technical assistance pool met with each project director to review the results of the proposal review process, agree on necessary modifications to the project's proposed activities, and identify and arrange to address the technical assistance needs of the project. In cases where proposal reviewers had identified serious weaknesses in the proposed activities or agency capability, the provision of such technical assistance was, in fact, a requirement of funding. In such a face-to-face meeting, it has been found that the initial "false modesty" of technical assistance providers and reluctance of the project to accept technical assistance can almost always be overcome. Furthermore, the needs of the project can be more appropriately matched with the capabilities of individuals available from the technical assistance pool.

A final, and perhaps most important, way of encouraging the use of technical assistance, is to operate a high quality, responsive technical assistance program that satisfies its customers. In most relatively small funding programs that are likely to make use of a technical assistance system such as described here, the prospective applicants and recipients of project funding will either be "repeat customers" or else will be well acquainted with people who have participated in the system. Once the initial reluctance to use such a system is overcome, and people begin seeing the benefits, the most powerful motivator (or serious obstacle) to continued use of the system will be past performance and "word of mouth" advertising. Therefore, it is essential that the agency or contractor responsible for managing the system make sure that (1) the guidelines in the remainder of this chapter are followed, and (2) the system is able to respond efficiently and appropriately to the changing needs of individual projects.

What Incentives Might Prompt Better Use of Technical Assistance?

It would seem reasonable to conclude that no incentive would be necessary to prompt better use of technical assistance beyond the improvement that results to the project. In both the Title IV and DD Council projects, for example, it was apparent that technical assistance provided to prospective applicants and project recipients markedly improved the quality and relevance of the funded projects. Projects conducted after such technical assistance was available were found to be better, compared to those conducted before the technical assistance systems were operational. It is also clear that the funding program sponsors (the State Education Agency and the State Social Services Agency) were willing -- even eager -- to provide technical assistance at no cost to individual projects to encourage them to obtain and use relevant technical assistance as necessary in their projects. These funding agencies recognized that the relatively small amount of money required to set up a technical assistance system to service all funded projects was one of the most cost effective techniques they could use to enhance the degree to which the goals of the funding program were accomplished. Yet it remained a fact that many agencies that demonstrably would have benefitted from help with the technical aspects of their projects, failed to request or obtain such technical assistance.

To ensure that individual agencies that participate in such funding programs obtain needed technical assistance, **it is recommended that technical assistance, as appropriate, be mandated by the funding agency at the time that specific proposals are**

approved. Whenever outside funds are involved, making the receipt of necessary technical assistance a condition of funding for particular projects greatly enhances the quality and effectiveness of individual agency efforts to mount projects where outside technical expertise would be paramount.

KEEPING TRACK OF REQUESTS FOR ASSISTANCE

Nothing is more discouraging to someone who needs technical assistance than to reach the point of asking, only to find that submitting the request had no more observable results than dropping rocks into a bottomless well. Bureaucratic inefficiency or tardiness in arranging for requested help can be one of the greatest deterrents to effective technical assistance delivery.

How Might Requests For Technical Assistance Be Recorded and Processed?

It is said that an important military campaign in World War II was lost because a beleaguered quartermaster, preoccupied with supplying requests for munitions, failed to record or forward requests for salt tablets. At the risk of belaboring the obvious and presenting what some may see as pedestrian details, there are a number of routine things that must be remembered if the system is to operate smoothly.

1. As in the case of the "tear-out, sign and return" page mentioned earlier, it is useful to provide potential recipients with a form to use in requesting technical assistance. This form might well contain identifying information about the applicant agency, a description of the specific program or project on which assistance is needed, the precise nature of the required technical assistance, the time schedule and conditions under which technical assistance might be provided, and (if appropriate) financial considerations which may be relevant. Addresses and telephone numbers for use in further contacts to discuss the technical assistance delivery should also be included. A sample of such a form is shown in Exhibit 9.1 at the end of this chapter.

2. A log should be developed for use by technical assistance providers (or brokers) to record the number and nature of requests for technical assistance, along with information concerning the actual assistance provided. An example of such a log appears as Exhibit 9.2.

3. All requests for assistance should be directed to an individual who has responsibility for arranging for the service to be provided.

4. A process should be agreed upon and implemented for matching the requests for assistance with the qualifications of the individual consultants who might render such assistance. For example, information from the "talent bank" may be used by the funding recipients to identify their own consultants. In such cases, the funding recipient could be directed to identify and contact consultants directly and make

necessary arrangements to receive the assistance. This may result, however, in some consultants being overworked and other qualified consultants being under-utilized. In other situations, the funding recipient may rely on the technical service agency or on some intermediate broker (either internal or external to the funding recipient's own agency) to nominate one or more consultants. In such cases, those who arrange for consultation services should consider variables such as the geographic proximity of consultant and funding recipient; compatibility of professional philosophy of the selected consultant and the service recipients; interpersonal and ethnic idiosyncrasies and sensitivities; the consultant's experience working in similar programs; and any conflict of interest situations which may exist (e.g., asking a funding recipient to receive technical assistance from a consultant from a competing program).

5. In cases where the funding recipient chooses not to contact a consultant directly, it is necessary for the technical assistance agency and/or consultant to make arrangements for appropriate services, as requested, to be provided. In the Utah Title IV system, form letters were developed and used by the State Office of Education officials to communicate with Title IV project directors who requested technical assistance and the consultants assigned to provide those services. Copies of those letters, which might serve as models, appear in Exhibit 9.3.

TECHNICAL ASSISTANCE DELIVERY

Although essential precursors, everything discussed to this point about the provision of technical assistance is really only preamble. It is the actual assistance of a technical expert that is the central focus of any technical assistance delivery system. Everything up to and including the scheduling of the first session between funding recipient and consultant should by now have been arranged. Attention must now turn to the actual consultation.

Are There Different Ways to Deliver Technical Assistance?

Yes. Although face-to-face consultation between funding recipient and consultant at the funding recipient's home base is the most frequent pattern of technical assistance delivery, it is not the only format. In the previously cited Technical Assistance Development System (TADS) document, Trohanis and his colleagues [23] discuss mail and telephone interchanges, funding recipient visits to consultants' sites, consultations at workshops and conferences, and increasing use of electronic consultations with the help of computers and new telecommunications equipment.

Trohanis, et al., also point out that there are a variety of methods for delivering assistance to clients. Figure 4 is a modified summary of the information presented by Trohanis and colleagues.

On-site Consultations:	Technical Assistant is sent to client's location.
Program Visit:	Client is sent to another program to observe its operation and/or receive instruction.
Small-Group Consultations:	Technical Assistant works with small gathering of several clients on topic of mutual concern.
Micro-Computer Transactions:	Clients with terminals may tie into a TA agency data system via phone.
Networking:	TA agency arranges for several clients to meet or talk with each other to resolve specific concerns or mutual problems.
Instructional Materials:	Slidetapes, videocassettes, bibliographies, awareness materials, and/or self-instruction packets are provided to clients.

Figure 4: Some Common Methods of Delivering Technical
Assistance (TA) to Clients

What Professional Standards Should Be Maintained by Technical Assistance Providers?

The recently developed **Standards for Evaluation of Educational Programs, Projects, and Materials** [24] that took half a decade or more in their development provide all necessary guidelines for the professional conduct of technical assistance activities. In addition, a set of evaluation standards developed by the Evaluation Research Society [25] have been widely promulgated among evaluators in the social sciences and health professions and are also directly applicable here.

USING MODEL MATERIALS TO SUPPORT TECHNICAL ASSISTANCE

One of the most effective ways to assist others in improving their performance of technical tasks is to provide them with a clearcut model -- an example that is easy to understand and possible to emulate. Such indirect technical assistance, through the development and dissemination of models, may be among the most effective and least expensive forms of technical assistance. Such model materials can be used independently or in conjunction with personal assistance from qualified experts.

What Type of Model Might Be Useful As a Type of Indirect Technical Assistance?

Perhaps the most useful type of indirect technical assistance is the instructional package-- a "do-it-yourself" kit -- which enables a consumer to perform technical tasks at an improved and acceptable level. Such packets might be little more than the too-frequently disdained, but often useful, "cookbooks" which provide detailed, step-by-step descriptions of how to perform certain technical tasks. Alternately, they may take the form of model products, such as model proposals or model reports that provide examples to be emulated. Such models are particularly effective if they contain both examples of what is good and examples of what is bad, to help the neophyte differentiate between the two.

For example, as one part of the Title IV and DD Council technical assistance process, an effort was made to give "technical assistance" to project directors in the preparation of their final reports. This assistance came in the form of a "Model Final Report" developed by the technical assistance contractor and sent by the appropriate state official to all project directors.

An example of the model report used in the Title IV project is included as Exhibit 9.4. This model report was designed as an instructional packet, with annotated comments inserted to explain the rationale and/or preferred content for specific sections of the report. In addition to an acceptable report, contrasting segments of an "unacceptable report" were included to illustrate how the report should **not** be written. Acceptable and unacceptable versions of each report section were presented on facing pages so that project directors could compare and contrast adequate and inadequate handling of content for each section.

Similar models could be developed to meet a wide variety of needs. In most cases such models are most feasible in areas where multiple projects all have the same or similar needs. For example, in the DD Council program all projects were required to submit a mid-year report in preparation for the external onsite evaluation visit. The model developed by the technical assistance coordinating contractor helped projects understand both the content and the level of detail desirable in this report.

EVALUATION OF TECHNICAL ASSISTANCE SERVICES AND SYSTEMS

As with most services and systems in education and social services, technical assistance activities far too often escape the helpful scrutiny of either formative or summative evaluation. It is simply presumed that such services, since they are delivered by experts, must be helpful. A reasonable assumption, perhaps, but not necessarily an accurate one. Evaluation is as essential to the improvement of technical assistance services as it is to any other area in our education and social service systems.

The delivery of technical assistance services should be evaluated the same way one would evaluate any other service or system -- by thoughtful use of: (1) description of what is to be evaluated, (2) explication of criteria for judging effectiveness, (3) collection of trustworthy data, (4) analysis of information and application of the criteria to determine effectiveness or utility, and (5) reporting the evaluation results to those who should receive the information. It is beyond the scope of this chapter to outline in detail evaluation methods and procedures. Readers are referred to the following publications, both of which contain information relevant to evaluation of technical assistance programs and other education programs.

- Worthen, B. R., & Sanders, J. R. (in press). **Education Evaluation: Alternative Approaches and Practical Guidelines.** [26].

- Brandt, R. S. (1981). **Applied Strategies for Curriculum Evaluation.** [27].

Obviously, evaluation of technical assistance programs can occur at several levels. At the very minimum, the contractor responsible for coordinating the technical assistance system, or the agency responsible for the overall funding program, should request that the recipient of technical assistance services complete a brief evaluation of each discrete technical assistance activity that requires a previously determined minimum amount of resources (e.g., very small technical assistance activities such as an occasional phone call would be excluded). An example of the type of form that could be used in such evaluations on a regular basis is shown in Exhibit 9.5.

Information from such evaluations, if collected on a regular basis, can be used to (1) provide feedback to expert consultants on the way their assistance is being received, (2) plan future TA activities, and (3) where necessary, provide corrective feedback or drop ineffective consultants from the pool. Such ongoing feedback, planning, and adjustment is critical if any technical assistance system is to have the benefit it should.

EXHIBITS FOR CHAPTER 9

EXHIBIT 9.1: EXAMPLE OF FORM FOR REQUESTING TECHNICAL ASSISTANCE

REQUEST FOR TECHNICAL ASSISTANCE

To facilitate the delivery of technical assistance (TA) to your project, certain kinds of information would be helpful. Please respond to each of the items on this form. **DO NOT SKIP ANY ITEMS.**

Name of program/project receiving TA: _____

_____

Parent   organization   (e.g.,   school   district,   agency   of   government, university/college/department):_____

_____

Address:_____

_____

Contact person(s), title(s), relationship to the project/program, telephone number, and address (if different than above):

Name	Title	Relationship To Project/Program	Phone No. and address

Please rate the availability of local resources to assist with delivery of TA (NOTE: "availability" means that the resources exist locally and can be used, as contrasted with resources that exist but are beyond the geographic or financial reach of the program/project):

	Not Available	Not Likely to Be	Somewhat Available	Likely to Be	Readily Available
Expertise	1	2	3	4	5

If your rating is 3, 4, or 5, describe: _____

_____

_____

Fiscal Support	1	2	3	4	5

If your rating is 3, 4, or 5, describe: _____

_____

_____

Cooperative Attitude of Relevant Personnel	1	2	3	4	5

If your rating is 1, 2, or 3, please describe: _____

_____

_____

Briefly describe your project:_____

_____

_____

Precisely, what is the nature of your technical assistance needs?:_____

_____

_____

_____

_____

_____

During what period of time will you need the assistance? Please be specific by identifying beginning and ending dates, describing absolute deadlines and periods of time between the beginning and ending when work could not be performed, etc.:_____

_____

_____

_____

_____

What local conditions exist that would impact on the delivery of TA, (e.g., distances to be traveled and road conditions, availability of lodging, . . .)?_____

_____

_____

_____

If you know of a particular consultant that you would especially prefer, please name that person here, and provide his/her address, phone number, and present position:

Name   Address   Phone No.   Present Position

_____

_____

If there is anything else that you can tell about your program/project that will facilitate the delivery of TA, please add that here: _____

_____

_____

_____

_____

_____

_____

_____

Thank You

Return to:

_____

_____

_____

_____

**EXHIBIT 9.2: EXAMPLE OF LOG OF USE OF TECHNICAL
ASSISTANCE SERVICES**

Request from: _____

Date of Request	District	Project	TA Assigned	Number of Days of Service Assigned

**EXHIBIT 9.3: EXAMPLE OF LETTERS ARRANGING
TECHNICAL ASSISTANCE**

250 EAST 500 SOUTH STREET · SALT LAKE CITY, UTAH 84111 · TELEPHONE (801) 533-5431

UTAH STATE OFFICE
OF EDUCATION

TO: Dr. James Mote

FROM: Bill Cowan

DATE:

RE: TA Services

Thank you for your willingness to serve as a Technical Assistant (TA) to the South St. John School District.

You should contact the person listed below within the next few days to arrange a mutually agreeable time for you to meet and provide whatever technical assistance seems appropriate.

Val D. Edgert, Superintendent   787-2119

To help you determine what services are appropriate for a TA to provide, **please read the enclosed "Guidelines for the TA Services" before you begin to provide such services.** This is important to make certain the services provided are within the scope of activities permitted under Title IV funding. A copy of these guidelines is also being sent to the project director listed above.

Reimbursement for your services will be at the rate of $135 per day, with total reimbursement for your honorarium, travel and other expenses you incur not to exceed a total of $500. Please submit receipts and a reimbursement claim to me at the completion of your services to the district.

I appreciate very much your contributing your expertise to help us improve our Title IV projects here in Utah.

If you have any questions, please feel free to call me at 533-5061.

WC/gm

250 EAST 500 SOUTH STREET · SALT LAKE CITY, UTAH 84111 · TELEPHONE (801) 533-5431

UTAH STATE OFFICE OF EDUCATION

TO: Val D. Edgert

FROM: Bill Cowan

DATE:

RE: Assignment of a Technical Assistant (TA) to Your Project

In response to your recent request for technical assistance on your Title IV - C project, I have assigned the following person to assist you.

Dr. James Mote   750-2003

The TA should be in contact with you in the next few days to arrange a mutually agreeable time to meet. Or, you may wish to contact him at your convenience at the above telephone number.

To help you know what type(s) of technical assistance can be provided, I have enclosed a copy of our "Guidelines for TA Services" which has also been provided to each TA. I hope this might help you identify the full range of technical assistance which we intend this assignment to make available to you.

Reimbursement to your TA will be at the rate of $135 per day, with payment for his time and all travel-related expenses not to exceed a total of $500. This should help you plan how much assistance you might be able to obtain. Should you wish to receive additional help from the TA beyond the $500 limit USOE will pay, you will need to cover those costs from other funds at your disposal.

If you have any questions, please call me at 533-5061.

WC/gm

EXHIBIT 9.4: MODEL FINAL REPORT FOR TITLE IV PROJECT

PROJECT LIFT

Final Report of Title IV - C Project

Mountain View School District

July 1, 1985

*NOTE: This document contains annotated **acceptable** and **unacceptable** versions of the type of final report that must be submitted by each Title IV Project Directors by July 1, 1986. Any questions about the format or contents of the report chould be directed to the State Office of Education Title IV Coordinator. To save space, figures and tables are referenced in the text, but have been deleted from these examples.*

UNACCEPTABLE VERSION

Problems with this Version

1. *The nature of the program and the intervention is not clearly described.*

2. *The age of the target group is not specified.*

3. *The relationship between parents, teachers, and children is not clear.*

4. *The origin of the project is not specified.*

5. *Objectives are not stated clearly. One objective was omitted.*

6. *The nature of the evaluation procedure and design is very unclear, and most of the information given is irrelevant.*

ABSTRACT

Project LIFT is a program designed to help handicapped children. Parents and teachers are trained by project staff to work with the children using a special procedure called CAMS.

The main purpose of the project is to help handicapped children improve their verbal and visual motor skills.

The project was evaluated through the use of pre- and posttests which indicated that the children participating in LIFT improved more than non-participants. Although it is recognized that such an evaluation procedure is not perfect, it should be pointed out that similar procedures have been used by many other projects that have found positive results for early intervention programs. Therefore, it seemed like an appropriate evaluation for this project. Futhermore, the fact that resources for evaluation were limited made it difficult to implement the type of evaluation that was desirable.

ACCEPTABLE VERSION

ABSTRACT

Project LIFT is a home- and community-based intervention program for handicapped children living in rural areas. The program has been developed, implemented, and evaluated by the Mountain View School District during the last three years. Parents and preschool teachers of identified handicapped children are utilized as the primary intervention agents in working with the handicapped children. Training is provided to the parents and teachers in the use of the Curriculum and Management System (CAMS) developed by the project. CAMS provides intervention procedures and techniques to promote the child's growth in receptive and expressive language, motor development, self-help skills, and social-emotional adjustment. Parents and teachers are trained in the correct procedures for using CAMS and are then monitored by project staff on a regular basis. Representatives from the two private schools in the area have participated in an advisory committee which has reviewed and critiqued the project materials and plans. Two children from private schools participated in the project.

Objectives for the project include:

1. During the nine-month intervention period, three- to five-year-old handicapped children participating in Project LIFT will, on the average, increase their relative standing on empirically established norms for their age group by 20% on the Peabody Picture Vocabulary Test (PPVT), the Visual Motor Integration Test (VMI), and the Sequenced Inventory of Communicaation Development (SICD).

2. The parents of preschool handicapped children will demonstrate satisfaction with the project by (1) utilizing the programs to teach their child and (2) through positive responses on an attitudinal questionnaire.

Suggestions to Writer

The abstract is a brief condensation of the larger report. It should contain a brief summary of each of the major parts of the report except for the Budget Section. For example, this abstract describes the purpose of the project, how it functions, the involvement of private schools, specific objectives, evaluation data, and plans for continuation.

Note that the objectives are stated in specific measurable terms.

UNACCEPTABLE VERSION

Problems with this Version

7. *Unwarranted and unsubstantiated conclusions are made.*

8. *Future plans are not stated.*

Based on the project evaluation data, it can be concluded that Project LIFT develops participants in verbal and visual motor skills, enabling them to compete with their non-handicapped peers. Furthermore, this is done in a cost effective manner which can be adopted easily by programs in different geographical areas and serving a wide variety of children.

ACCCEPTABLE VERSION

Thirty-four children were selected to participate in the operational field test of Project LIFT because they scored below the tenth percentile on the Denver Developmental Screening Test. Pre- and posttest data were collected for each of these children on the PPVT, VMI, and SICD at the beginning and the end of the nine-month intervention program. These data demonstrated that children enrolled in the program made 21% greater gains than similar children not enrolled in the program. Gains of this magnitude represent approximately three-quarters of a standard deviation gain and are statistically significant at the .01 level.

Evaluation data collected from the parents of partici- pating handicapped children indicate that parents believe the program is valuable, are satisfied with the training and monitoring provided by project staff, and most parents participated extensively in the program.

Based on the project evaluation data, it can be confidently concluded that participation in Project LIFT enables preschool handicapped children to make substantially greater gains than would have been made had they not participated in the program. Mountain View School District has concluded that the program is a successful intervention technique for preschool handicapped children living in rural areas and intends to continue operating the program now that Title IV - C funding has ended.

Suggestions to Writer

The report of the evaluation activities of the project is the heart of the abstract. It should contain a concise description of what can be concluded, based on the evaluation data about the success of the project in meeting the objectives of Title IV.

*Because the abstract is a condensation of the entire report, it should generally be written **after** the larger proposal is completed.*

UNACCEPTABLE VERSION

Problems with this Version

9. *Too specific. At this rate, the report will be a 300 page book.*

10. *Some dates are important, but only enough to give the reader a sense of the projects' general time lines.*

PROJECT DESCRIPTION

Beginning March 1, 1981, two teachers (Jean Kelly and Bob Dixon) met with the principal of Wilson Elementary (Rosa Wilson), to discuss the problems they were having with their kindergartners.

During the summer of 1981, they talked to several parents and early childhood specialists to try to understand why some of the children were so far behind the others. Finally, they realized that their children had special handicaps that impeded their progress.

In September, 1981, these teachers and the principal approached Mrs. Hansen, the Director of Special Education Programs for the Mountain View School District. Together, they began to plan a way to develop a program that would help handicapped children. This began a series of activities that would eventually lead to the submission of a Title IV - C grant and the development and implementation . . . *(Note to reader: Because of space constraints, this version will not be continued at this level of specificity)*

ACCEPTABLE VERSION

PROJECT DESCRIPTION[1]

Suggestions to Writer

Developed over the past three years by the Mountain View School District, Project LIFT is a home- and community-based intervention program for handicapped children (aged 3 to 5) living in rural remote areas. The program utilizes:

1. The parents of preschool and kindergarten handicapped children as intervention agents by providing them with a detailed and specific curriculum for their young handicapped children, training them in its use, and providing weekly monitoring; and

2. Existing preschool and community day care agencies to deliver additional services to young handicapped children by providing the current staff with curriculum materials that are coordinated with and supplement the programs and techniques being used by parents in the home.

Need to Which Project was Responding

During the last five years, the Mountain View School District has been committed to completely fulfilling the mandates of Public Law 94-142 regarding the provision of a free and appropriate education to all handicapped children. In November, 1982, a special task force consisting of special education teachers, regular classroom teachers, central office administration, and representatives of Brigham Young University reported on their three-month-long evaluation of the status of special education with the district. Although

The project description section should be written so that a completely naive reader can understand in a few minutes basically what the project was designed to do and what approach was used.

The section describing the need to which the project was responding will generally be a brief summarization of the needs statement included in the original project application. However, any "new" needs that have surfaced during the operation of the project and further strengthen the necessity of having such a project should be described briefly.

---

[1]Although certain elements have been changed, this model report is based substantially on an actual project operated by the Developmental Center for Handicapped Persons at Utah State University. This project is entitled the Multi-Agency Project for Preschoolers (MAPPS).

UNACCEPTABLE VERSION

Problems with this Version

11. *The nature of the needs assessment survey and the parent survey is not clear.*

12. *The rationale which led to the decision to develop a new program is incomplete and not accurate.*

During February, 1983, parents were polled to see how they felt about pre-school children's handicaps. They indicated strong support for a program to alleviate the problem and said that they would be willing to participate in such a program. In fact, a few parents were so enthusiastic about the program that they offered to assist with teaching, transportation and materials development.

After taking this survey and polling the teachers' interests, the Director of Special Education Programs decided there weren't any existing programs that would meet our need. So she applied for and was granted Title IV - C funds to develop a program.

ACCEPTABLE VERSION

they found that special education programs within the district were as good as most other programs throughout the state, they recommended that much additional progress could be made by moderately handicapped children if interventions were begun earlier. Since one of the top district priorities is the additional involvement of parents in school programs, and since previous research literature indicates that parents can be used effectively in providing services to young children, a decision was made to pursue the identification or development of a program which could be used in conjunction with parents in the Mountain View District to provide an early intervention program for moderately handicapped children living within the district.

During February, 1983, a survey was conducted to ascertain parents' interest in participating in such a program as well as their perceptions of the quality of services which were now being received by their handicapped children. This survey included parents of older handicapped children who were enrolled in district programs to determine whether they would have been receptive to participating in an early intervention program had such a program existed. The results of the survey indicated that although parents were generally satisfied with the services that their child had received, they would be or would have been willing to become much more involved in the educational programs of their child.

Following the survey, an exhaustive literature search by district staff identified a few programs which had used parents as intervention agents with their handicapped children. However, most of these programs dealt only with a specific handicapping condition (most frequently in the area of deafness) or were not appropriate for the rural setting of the Mountain View District. Although parts of these programs would have been appropriate for the Mountain View School District, it was decided that no existing total program was appropriate. Consequently, recommendation was made by the special education staff of the district and ratified by the Board of Education in March, 1982, to pursue Title IV - C funding for the development of a home and community based program for early intervention with handicapped children ages 3 to 5.

Suggestions to Writer

A brief explanation of the rationale that led to the selection of the specific program or approach will help the reader understand the contxt in which the program was developed or operated.

UNACCEPTABLE VERSION

Problems with this Version

13. There is not enough detail to give the reader an accurate picture of the project materials and activities. Care must be taken to be brief, yet specific enough to help the reader understand what the program entailed.

Project Materials and Objectives

The final curriculum package addressed several objectives in receptive language, expressive language, motor skills, self-help skills, and socio/ emotional adjustment.

The final CAMS includes a manual, placement tests, a slide/tape presentation, and five sequenced curriculum programs. Based on the reactions of parents and teachers who have used the materials, it appears that they are easy to use and can be used without unnecessarily extensive training.

ACCEPTABLE VERSION

Project Materials and Activities

Materials. The foundation of the intervention program is the Curriculum and Management System (CAMS) developed by the project in five developmental areas:

a. Receptive language
b. Expressive language
c. Motor skills
d. Self-help skills
e. Social/emotional adjustment

Behavioral principles, particularly those implicit in the areas of program instruction, guided the design and development of the project materials. The critical skills in each curriculum area were identified through an exhaustive literature search and then critically reviewed by curriculum experts who were knowledgeable in the specific skill areas. Next, the skills were stated as behavioral objectives and were ordered hierarchically. Comprehensive placement tests were developed for the specific skills identified in each curriculum area.

The final CAMS system includes:

1. A manual which provides an overview of the CAMS model and explains the procedures for using the five curriculum programs.

2. Placement tests for locating each child at the appropriate level in each program.

3. A slide-tape presentation which introduces the curriculum programs(a total of 374 objectives), provides instruction in the appropriate techniques for

The section describing the materials and activities utilized by the project will often simply be a condensation of what was described in the original proposal. However, in many cases, specific activities and materials for a project are altered to some degree during the project and that should be noted. This section should also describe any additional activities which were not originally proposed.

It is helpful to describe how the program is organized and implemented.

UNACCEPTABLE VERSION

Problems   with   this   Version

14. *The nature of the data sheets to be*   The curriculum programs are bound in a
    used in monitoring student progress   special notebook for easy reference. Individual
    is not clear.   data sheets are also provided for monitoring each
                                               child's progress through the programs. In this
                                               way, parents can tell exactly lhow much progress
                                               their children are making and can easily determine
                                               what part of the program should be taught next.

ACCEPTABLE VERSION

using the program, and explains the simple system for scoring the child's responses.

4. Five sequenced curriculum programs (with detailed teaching instructions) which can be utilized by persons with varied backgrounds and little or no formal training in teaching handicapped children.

Each of the curriculum programs is printed in an easy-to-use block style design and bound in a notebook. This format was selected to allow photocopying of individual pages for use by the parents or trainers working directly with each child. The information provided on the individual data sheet is essential to the appropriate use of CAMS. As shown in Figure 1 (*Note to reader: figures which would have been in an actual report are omitted from this model report in the interest of brevity*), each program has printed at the top of the sheet the name of the program, the objective number and name, and a list of materials needed in teaching that objective. There is also a space for entering the student's name and the date on which the activities on the form were begun.

It is helpfuf to give brief examples of the types of materials developed by the project. However, such examples should be extremely brief. Appendices should generally be avoided and in no case should more than ten pages of appendices be attached.

Each sheet is divided into the following four sections or steps:

1. The Step Statement describes what skill the student will learn at this step of the program.

2. The Teaching Procedure explains what the teacher must do to teach the skills described in the step statement as well as what to do if the student makes a mistake.

3. The Trial Criterion explains what the student must do to receive "yes" on any trial.

4. The Step Criterion tells how many correct responses a student must get before going to the next step of the objective.

Although not exhaustive, this information gives the reader a basic understanding of how instruction is delivered to an individual child.

UNACCEPTABLE VERSION

Problems with this Version

15. Many important activities were omitted from this description.

Activities. Participants in the program were nominated by several sources and then screened using the DDST.

Selected children were given placement tests in the skill areas of CAMS, the individualized programs were developed for each child.

After training parents to use the CAMS programs and manual, the project staff visited homes and schools to monitor the teaching of the children.

ACCEPTABLE VERSION

Suggestions to Writer

Data about each child's performance on the program (including the percentage of correct responses, the response rate, the total number of trials, and the total number of sessions) are recorded by the teacher or parent on the data summary sheet which is used to determine when the child should progress to the next skill. As the child moves from skill to skill through the developmental sequence, it is always possible to know exactly which task is being taught and what progress is being made.

Activities. Participants for the program were solicited via a public information and awareness campaign directed toward parents, public health nurses, and physicians. Referred children were screened using the Denver Developmental Screening Test (DDST) and those scoring below the tenth percentile of the DDST were included in the project.

Selected children were given the criterion placement tests in the five skill areas of CAMS. At least one parent of each child observed the assessment process and participated with the classroom teacher from the preschool where the child would be enrolled as well as with staff from the district special education office in the development of an individualized program for each child. Parents and preschool teachers were then trained by project staff in the use of the intervention programs and provided with the manual which included the general information necessary to use the CAMS program.

A good idea in writing the description of the project is to sit down and outline carefully all of the tasks and activities which you accomplished in developing and implementing the project. Although all of this information may not be used in the final report, it will frequently save you from forgetting important factors in the descripltion of the project.

Following the training period, parents were monitored during monthly home visits by project staff or visits to the school. Preschool teachers were visited monthly by the staff. Parents and teachers participated in monthly work- shops which addressed topics such as growth and development of handicapped children, managing a child's behavior, and counseling and supportive services. In addition, parents were contacted weekly by telephone to check on the child's progress.

UNACCEPTABLE VERSION

Problems with this Version

Project Objectives

16. The project objectives appear to be in constant flux. That may be so; but at the end of a three-year period, the reader would expect to find some fairly stable terminal objectives.

17. The specific tests used to measure the children's progress are not described or even named properly.

1. When the project first began, we intended to help pre-schoolers with handicaps "catch-up" to their non-handicapped counterparts. As the realities of the severe restraints placed on the children by their handicaps became apparent, we adjusted our expectations. We decided that we would try to raise the children's relative standing on empirically established norms for their age group by 20% on several tests.

Now that the project is almost completed, it does not appear that 20% improvement was a realistic goal. However, these gains accomplished by the children, 10% increase on the PPVT and 5% increase on the VMI, do seem to be an important indication of what the project is accomplishing.

ACCEPTABLE VERSION

During 1985-86, 34 children (19 boys and 15 girls) participated in Project LIFT. These children all suffered from moderate to severe handicapping conditions including mental retardation, cerebral palsy, sensory motor impairments and/or emotional handicaps. Two of the children were Native Americans, one Chicano, and the remainder, Caucasian.

Project Objectives

The project objectives were:

1. During the nine-month intervention period, 3-5 year old handicapped children participating in Project LIFT will, on the average, increase their relative standing on empirically established norms for their age group by 20% as measured by the Peabody Picture Vocabulary Test (PPVT), the Visual Motor Integration Scale (VMI), and the Sequenced Inventory of Communication Development (SICD).[2]

2. The parents of preschool handicapped children will demonstrate satisfaction with the project by (1) utilizing the programs to teach their child and (2) demonstrating positive attitudes in their responses on an attitudinal questionnaire.

An evaluation of the effectiveness of the project focused upon both of these objectives.

Project objectives will also be generally taken from the original project application. Objectives may change or be refined during the course of the project development and implementation. The objectives in the final report should be the final project objectives.

---

[2]For example, if a group of 36 year-old children scored, on the average, at the 30th percentile for their age group at the beginning of the program, this objective would be met if nine months later the average score of these children was the 36th percentile for their age group (now 45 months old).

UNACCEPTABLE VERSION

Problems with this Version

*18. Involvement of private schools in the
project is not explained. Because this is
a requirement that must be met by all
Title IV projects, it must be included in
the final report. It is absolutely essential
that the guidelines for the final report be
carefully followed. In other words, you
should carefully review the guidelines
and make sure that the report addresses
all of the information requested.*

ACCEPTABLE VERSION

Suggestions to Writer

Historical Background

1985-86 represents the third year of funding for this project. During the first year of the project, curriculum materials were developed, critiqued by experts in the field, modified, and finalized into a draft form that could be used in implementing the project. During the second year of the project, these materials were used on a pilot basis with 10 handicapped children. The emphasis of the project during the second year was on formative evaluation and data were collected that assisted in the revision and refinement of materials for the third year. The third and current year of the project focused on an operational field test of the materials summative evaluation whether the project was effective in meeting its goals and should be continued by the district.

A brief section on historical background may be helpful for some projects in enabling the reader to understand the context in which the project was developed. Particularly for multi-year projects, it is frequently important to see how the final report for the current year ties into other activities which the project has undertaken or will be undertaking.

Involvement of Private Schools

Two private schools are located within the Mountain View School District. Both of these schools include preschool, elementary, and secondary programs. From the beginning of the Title IV - C funding for the project, representatives of these schools have been included on the project's advisory committee. The responsibilities of the advisory committee have included bimonthly meetings at which the progress of the project was reported; review and critique of project materials and plans; and occasional participation in project workshops and activities. Two of the 34 children enrolled in the operational field test of the project come from families whose other children are enrolled in these private schools. As this information demonstrates, the project has had extensive involvement of private school children and their families during its development and implementation.

A brief summary of the efforts to provide opportunities for private schools to be involved in the Title IV - C project should be given. Sometimes there will be no private school involvement because the private schools choose not to participate. This should also be reported.

UNACCEPTABLE VERSION

Problems with this Version

**EVALUATION DESIGN AND
RESULTS**

Evaluation Questions

19. Evaluation questions are so general that is is impossible to know whether or not they have been answered.

The evaluation was designed to determine whether an early intervention program such as this one would help handicapped children and their families to improve. It was also important to collect information which would be helpful in improving the operation of the project so that it could be managed efficiently.

Evaluation Procedures

20. Inadequate rationale is given for using these particular tests.

The tests for evaluating students' progress included the CAMS Criterion Referenced Tests, the PPVT, VMI, and SICD. These tests are used by many similar programs and had been used previously by project staff.

21. No explanation is given for why these standardized tests are the "best" for this particular situation or why standardized tests were used in the first place.

These tests were selected for the evaluation because they are some of the least standardized tests available. The results are presented in Figure 2 below (*Note to readers: Figures which would have been in an actual report are omitted from this model report in the interest of brevity*).

ACCEPTABLE VERSION

EVALUATION DESIGN AND RESULTS

Suggestions to Writer

Evaluation Questions

The summative evaluation of Project LIFT was designed to determine:

a. Whether children enrolled in the program made more gains in receptive and expressive language skills, motor development, self-help skills, and social/emotional adjustment than would have been expected if they had not been enrolled in the program; and

The evaluation section should usually begin by stating the specific questions you expect to answer. These questions should be tied closely to the objectives stated earlier.

b. Whether parents of children in the program were satisfied with the project as demonstrated by their participation in the program and their responses on the attitudinal questionnaire.

Evaluation Procedures

After being referred to the program and screened using the DDST, 34 children were selected for participation in the program. Each child was assessed using the CAMS criterion referenced test, placed on one or more of the CAMS programs, and monitored weekly during the nine months of program operation. Standardized and CAMS criterion referenced test data were collected on a pre-posttest basis. All tests were administered by licensed psychologists or certified educational diagnosticians hired by the project. The tests included:

The evaluation design should match the project. Not all evaluation designs will be as sophisticated as the one reported here. Obviously, it would be unwise for a $5000 project to spend $4000 on evaluation. The important thing is that the evaluation design provides valid information which can be used in assisting the district and the State Office of Education in deciding if the project has been successful.

a. The CAMS Criterion Reference Tests in receptive and expressive language, motor skills, self-help skills, and social/emotional adjustment.

b. The Peabody Picture Vocabulary Test (Dunn, 1965).

c. The Sequenced Inventory of Communication Development (Hedrick, Prather, & Tobin, 1984).

d. The Visual Motor Integration Scale (Berry, 1969).

UNACCEPTABLE VERSION

Problems with this Version

22. *Discussion of the results is inadequate and there is insufficient rationale for the conclusions.   There is too much emphasis on statistical significance with no reference to the educational importance of their results.*

As the results in Figure 2 indicate, children in the intervention scored significantly better (p < .01) than they would have without the program. In other words, there is less than one chance in 100 that children would have done this well without the program.

ACCEPTABLE VERSION

Suggestions to Writer

Following the questions, you should describe as clearly as possible the techniques you plan to use in order to obtain answers to the questions stated above.

Each of the standardized tests provides empirically established norms at three-month intervals which can be used in determining where the child is scoring in relationship to other children of the same age. Evidence of project effectiveness depended on whether children scored higher at the end of the project than they had at the beginning of the project in relation to other children in their same age group who were not in the program. In other words, if the project was **not** effective, a 36-month-old child who scored at the 10th percentile in relation to other 36-month-old children on the Peabody Picture Vocabulary Test at the beginning of the project, would score at the 10th percentile or lower of 45-month-old children at the end of the project. If, however, the children scored at the 20th percentile of 45-month-old children at the end of the project, this would be evidence that the child had made greater gains than would have been made had they not participated in the project.[3]

The standardized tests used in the evaluation were chosen because they sampled the same domain of items upon which the intervention focused and because past research has demonstrated their validity for use with handicapped populations. In addition, each of these tests had appropriate empirically established norms that could be used in implementing the "norm referenced" evaluation. Finally, it was deemed inappropriate to use the same tests in measuring growth for the children that had been used in selecting the children for the program (the DDST) or placing the children in

Because so many different educational tests are now available, it is usually helpful to briefly explain the rationale for selecting the particular outcome measures used in the project evaluation. This discussion should assist the reader in understanding how these specific measures relate to the project objectives.

Tables and Figures often provide a wealth of information which can be presented much more succintly than information in the text. Do repeat information in the text which is already contained in the Figure or Table.

---

[3]The evaluation model used in this project closely parallels the evaluation model designed for Chapter I evaluation referred to as the Model A or the "norm referenced" evaluation model. Extensive use of this model has demonstrated that it is an effective way of estimating whether children have made greater growth than would have been expected had they not participated in the program.

Problems with this Version

23. *This conclusion is not supported by the data collected. Not only is there no report of data about program costs, but there is no report of any efforts to value the benefits or to determine whether the results of this project are likely to be applicable elsewhere. Report writers should be sure that conclusions can be adequatelly supported by the data.*

Because children who participated in the program demonstrated such remarkable improvement, it is obvious that project LIFT is cost beneficial. Other schools interested in long term cost savings should implement similar programs.

ACCEPTABLE VERSION

a particular curriculum (CAMS Criterion Reference Placement Tests) because of the problems associated with statistical regression towards the mean. Since the standardized tests cited above had not been used in either selection or curriculum placement, it was decided that they would be the best indicator of whether children had made more gains than would have been anticipated had they not participated in the program.

Pre- and posttest data collected during the program of each of the three standard tests are presented in Figure 2. For ease of interpretability, scores in figure 2 have been standardized so that the scores on each test have a mean of 100 and a standard deviation of 16. As noted in Figure 2, children's mean standard scores increased 9 standard score points on the PPVT, 11 standard score points on the VMI, and 15 standard score points on the SICD. Since pre- and posttest standard scores have been adjusted for age, these data indicate that children in the intervention program were, on the average, 21% higher in relation to their age group peers than they were at the beginning of the program. Not only are gains of this magnitude statistically significant at the .01 level, but they are educationally important as well.

To be more confident that the intervention program was really responsible for the observed gains, two primary alternative explanations were considered. The first was that maturation alone could have accounted for much of the average gain made by children enrolled in the program. However, the use of standard scores in relation to empirically established norms eliminates any effect of maturation from the observed growth. The second was that since the children were selected for participation in the program on the basis of having scored in the lowest ten percentile of the DDST, statistical regression towards the mean could have accounted for some of the average gain made by children. However, the fact that intervention gains are based on standardized assessment measures other than the test which was used for selecting children into the program eliminates most, if not all, of any regression toward the mean.

Before concluding that the project has been responsible for the observed gains, it is often beneficial to consider alternative explanations for why such gains might have been observed. When no plausible alternative explanations are identified, one can be more confident that the program is indeed responsible for the gains.

UNACCEPTABLE VERSION

Problems with this Version

24. It would have been helpful to mention that parents actively participated in the program, thereby demonstr ting their interest in it.

25. This is "boiled down" a bit too much. More specifics are needed to provide the reader with sufficient understanding of the parents'   reactions. The "Acceptable Version" of the report may have too many numbers for some readers, but it is certainly preferable to this uninformative summary.

Satisfaction of Parents

In addition to the tests administered to the children, questionnaires were sent to parents served by the project to obtain evaluative feedback. These questionnaires were designed to determine whether or not parents were satisfied with the program their children were receiving.

Parents responses to the questionnaire were very positive. These data suggest that parents of children in the program liked it and think their children gained a lot from it. Since parents are most familiar with their own children, they are probably in the best position to know whether or not the children have benefitted from the program.

ACCEPTABLE VERSION

Satisfaction and Participation of Parents

Suggestions to Writer

The second major objective of the program was that the parents of preschool handicapped children enrolled in the program would demonstrate their satisfaction with the project by utilizing the program to teach their child and by their responses on an attitudinal questionnaire. Some data regarding the successful accomplishment of this objective have been presented above in the sense that most parents must have participated in the program if they were able to increase their child's performance by approximately 21% over a nine-month period. In addition, questionnaires were sent to parents served by the project to obtain evaluative feedback. A summary of the most important data from those questionnaires is given below. The complete report is available upon request.

Not all evaluation activities need to be statistical in nature. Opinions can provide very powerful data about the effectiveness of the project. The important thing is to gather the best type of data for your project which will provide information about whether or not it has been successful.

	Dis-Satisfied	Satisfied	Very Satisfied
1. Satisfaction with the interventions provided by the Project.	0%	8%	92%
2. Satisfaction with training and materials to carry out educational interventions at home.	0%	6%	94%

3. Family members participating in the program:

Mother	79%
Father	79%
Siblings	70%
Grandparents	17%

4. Specific benefits of participating in the program:

(a) Knowledge of child's problem and needs	71%
(b) Better feelings of acceptance of child	38%
(c) Better knowledge of child's abilities	67%
(d) Better understanding of child's behavior	54%
(e) Specific skills for working with child	92%
(f) Knowledge of services available for child	67%
(g) Better ability to cope emotionally with child	42%

These data highlight the most relevant information from the questionnaires collected from parents, but are not a complete report. Although complete data should be available upon request, it is often not necessary to include everything in the project's final report. The information included in the final report should be a "boiled down" synthesis of what is most relevant.

UNACCEPTABLE VERSION

Problems with this Version

CONCLUSIONS

26. The conclusions are seriously overstated.

Since the program is **completely** exportable, efficiently utilizes parents as the primary intervention agents, is judged by them to be the best program they have seen, and causes the handicapped students in Mountain View District to improve in ways they could not have done otherwise, we recommend that this program be used in Mountain View and be disseminated to other programs. In fact, we feel this program would prevent many children from being classified as handicapped when they reach school age and would consequently save much more than it costs to implement.

27. One of the most critical parts of a Title IV - C proposal is a description of the district's plans to continue the project, should it prove effective. Such a description is unfortunately omitted from this report.

ACCEPTABLE VERSION

CONCLUSIONS

Suggestions to Writer

As noted previously, project evaluation data indicate that children make significantly greater gains as a result of the program than they would have made had they not been enrolled in the program. These gains represent approximately 2/3 of a standard deviation more growth than is made by the same age peers of these children on similar standardized tests. Gains of this magnitude are clearly not only statistically significant, but educationally significant as well.

The Conclusions Section of the report should contain a summary statement of whether or not the project has been successful in meeting the objectives of Title IV. These conclusions should follow directly from the evaluation data. Be careful not to overstate conclusions (i.e., draw conclusions for which you have no real data).

In sparsely populated areas, effective intervention programs for preschool handicapped children are particularly difficult to implement because of a lack of trained personnel. Project LIFT represents a partial answer to this problem. During the three years in which it has been developed, implemented, and evaluated, Project LIFT has demonstrated that parents can be trained to deliver interventions to handicapped 3-5 year-old children in rthe areas of receptive and expressive language, motor, self-help, and social/emotional development. Parents are enthusiastic about the program, participate extensively in its implementation, and feel that the program is valuable for their child. Since the program is exportable; continued use and further dissemination of the program appearss to be warranted.

FUTURE PLANS

Based on the evaluation data collected by Project LIFT, as well as the feedback from administration and teachers in the district, the Board of Education has granted approval for the project to be continued during the coming year even though Title IV - C funds will not be available. The project director will continue working with the project by devoting 25% of his time to the operation. Staff members who have been responsible for working with parents and community service providers will continue to be employed by the project, and it is anticipated that the number of children participating in the project will be expanded during the coming year.

A critical part of Title IV -C funding is that districts will continue to fund those projects which demonstrate their effectiveness after Title IV - C funding is completed. In this section you should state briefly your percep-tions of the district's plans in this regard and what basis you have for such perceptions.

UNACCEPTABLE VERSION

Problems with this Version

BUDGET

28. *No budget narrative is included to explain the budget outlined.*

    Reported on the following page are the project budget and actual project expenditures in each of the budget categories.

ACCEPTABLE VERSION

Suggestions to Writer

The district's continued support of the program is based primarily on the belief that early intervention programs, particularly those which have demonstrated effectiveness such as Project LIFT, although requiring substantial funds to implement and operate, more than make up for the expenditures in terms of the number of handicapped children who are provided early enough help that their handicapping conditions do not become serious disabling factors at a later point. Further research on the validity of this belief is needed however.

BUDGET

Reported on the following page are the original project budget for 1985-86, the adjusted budget which was modified with approval from the Utah State Office of Education, and the final expenditures of the project in each of the budget categories.

Budget Narrative

The first column on the following page entitled "Original Budget" describes the budget categories as detailed in the originally approved grant proposal. The second column entitled "Modified Budget" delineates the adjusted line item amounts as described in a memo from the Mountain View School District to the State Office of Education dated March 21, 1986, and approved by the State Office of Education in a letter dated March 28, 1986. As explained in the letter, the primary budget modification was made to enable the project to hire a faculty member from Brigham Young University to assist in the data analysis, interpretation, and report writing. To enable the hiring of this consultant, Dr. Heber Johnson, Bob Morrow was reduced to 33% commitment to the project instead of 50%. Also, minor alterations were made in the fringe benefits, travel, and consumable supplies line items of the budget. The final expenditures of the project are listed for each line item in the third column of the following budget. Further documentation regarding project expenditures can be obtained from the Mountain View District Office.

The Budget Section should include a summary statement of the original projected budget, any approved alterations in that budget, and a final report (based on the district's financial records) of line item expenditures. It is important to remember that any line item which deviates more than 10% from the originally proposed line item must be approved in writing by the Utah State Office of Education.

It is important to note any budget modifications that have occurred since the original proposal. These appear on the next (right-hand) page of this report in the form of a simple one-column addition to the original budget.

UNACCEPTABLE

1985 - 86 BUDGET

		Orginal Budget	Actual Expenditures
PERSONNEL: Project Director: Anne Areson (50%)	11,750	33,733	32,142
Project Staff:			
Gary Long (25% - instructional/media specialist)	4,358		
Susan Frischt (25% - physical therapist)	4,550		
Sue Vost (25% - speech therapist)	4,235		
Linda Peterson (50% - staff assistant)	4,160		
Bob Morrow (50% - secretary)*	4,680		
FRINGE BENEFITS (19% of salaries and wages)		6,409	6,107
TRAVEL: Mileage @ 18 cents/mile, average 250 miles/week	2,340	3,240	3,412
Per Diem @ $37.50/day, average 2 days/month	900		
CONSUMABLE SUPPLIES		1,860	2,114
COMMUNICATIONS: Postage	180	1,020	987
Phone (3 phones @ $15/month + $25/month toll charges)	840		
COMPUTER ANALYSIS (Keypunching & Computer Time)		450	450
CONSULTANTS (assist in computer analysis & interpretation, 15 days @ $100/day)			1,500
TOTAL		46,712	46,712

*Reduced to 33% after project was initiated

ACCEPTABLE

1985 - 86 BUDGET

		Orginal Budget	Modified Budget	Actual Expenditures
PERSONNEL: Project Director: Anne Areson (50%)	11,750	33,733	32,142	32,142
Project Staff:				
Gary Long (25% - instructional/media specialist)	4,358			
Susan Frischt (25% - physical therapist)	4,550			
Sue Vost (25% - speech therapist)	4,235			
Linda Peterson (50% - staff assistant)	4,160			
Bob Morrow (50% - secretary)*	4,680			
FRINGE BENEFITS (19% of salaries and wages)		6,409	6,107	6,107
TRAVEL: Mileage @ 18 cents/mile, average 250 miles/week	2,340	3,240	3,331	3,412
Per Diem @ $37.50/day, average 2 days/month	900			
CONSUMABLE SUPPLIES		1,860	2,162	2,114
COMMUNICATIONS: Postage	180	1,020	1,020	987
Phone (3 phones @ $15/month + $25/month toll charges)	840			
COMPUTER ANALYSIS (Keypunching & Computer Time)		450	450	450
CONSULTANTS (assist in computer analysis & interpretation, 15 days @ $100/day)		1,500	1,500	1,500
TOTAL		46,712	46,712	46,712

*Reduced to 33% after project was initiated

EXHIBIT 9.5: EXAMPLE OF FORM FOR EVALUATING TECHNICAL ASSISTANCE

EVALUATION OF TECHNICAL ASSISTANCE

Recently you received some technical assistance from _____ as a part of your project funded by the _____. Because we are responsible for organizing future technical assistance efforts for projects like yours, we would like to have your appraisal of that activity. Your individual comments will be kept completely confidential and will only be shared as a part of a larger group summary with the official(s) responsible for this program. The results of your evaluation will assist us in making future assignments and planning to meet future needs in the technical assistance system.

1. Please describe briefly what type of technical assistance you received and the approximate dates it was delivered.

_____

_____

_____

_____

_____

_____

_____

2. Had your project previously received technical assistance from this person?

_____ Yes   _____ No

3. Please indicate, using the following scale, the degree to which you agree or disagree with each of the statements listed below.

SA = Strongly Agree   D = Disagree
A = Agree   SD = Strongly Disagree
U = Undecided

Circle the most appropriate answer for each statement

a. The consultant was well qualified   SA   A   U   D   SD
    to provide assistance in this area.

b. The consultant was interested and   SA   A   U   D   SD
    enthusiastic about helping the project.

c. The consultant followed through on   SA   A   U   D   SD
    what he/she committed to do.

d. The project is a better project because SA   A   U   D   SD
    of this technical assistance.

e. The consultant was well organized   SA   A   U   D   SD
    and used our time efficiently.

f. The consultant was an effective   SA   A   U   D   SD
    communicator.

g. The consultant provided us with   SA   A   U   D   SD
    necessary expertise that was unavailable
    from our own project staff.

h. Without the technical assistance system, SA   A   U   D   SD
    it is unlikely that we would have gotten
    help in this area.

i. We would use this consultant again if we SA   A   U   D   SD
    had similar needs

4. Please summarize in the space below any suggestions you have to improve the delivery of technical assistance services. _____

_____

_____

SECTION IV: ESTABLISHING EVALUATION AGREEMENTS AND CONTRACTS

There are many potential problems in the conduct of evaluation studies that would seem to be best (if not exclusively) solved by establishing firm shared understandings and agreements between client and evaluator. Guba and Lincoln [28] put it well:

> Evaluations are done for clients who commission the evaluation, provide for its legitimation, and pay for it. Since he who pays the piper calls the tune, the evaluator must have a firm understanding with the client about what the evaluation is to accomplish, for whom, and by what methods. The evaluator also needs to be protected against certain arbitrary and possibly harmful or unethical actions by the client, just as the client needs to be protected against an unscrupulous evaluator. The means for achieving these understandings and establishing these safeguards is the evaluation contract (pp. 270-271).

Anderson and Ball [29], quoting Samuel Goldwyn's wry comment that "... oral agreements aren't worth the paper they're written on," add the following:

> For major evaluation efforts, a formal, legal contract should be negotiated; not to have one would be foolish for both parties.   In smaller evaluation efforts, a formal contract might be unnecessary, but even then a letter of agreement ... makes excellent sense. In either case, the agreement should spell out not only the financial arrangements but also the main elements and requirements of the planned evaluation (p. 155).

Precursors to an Evaluation Contract or Agreement[2]

When a client and/or evaluator contemplate(s) entering into a contract to evaluate an educational or social program or project, it can be presumed that several prior decisions have been made.

---

[2]We shall not try to be precise in our use of the terms **contract** and **ageement** in this section. We recognize that a contract is only one type of agreement that might exist, and that some agreements are less formal than contracts, but we shall use the terms nearly interchangeably to avoid the tedium of repetition. Where we use both terms together, it is to remind the reader of the spectrum from precise legal contracts to less formal memos of agreement. But in all cases, our reference is to formalized written agreements, not informal verbal understandings.

First, it evidently has been decided that an evaluation of the program or project is appropriate. Someone apparently has decided that there are relevant decisions to be made for which evaluative data would be important, or that evaluative feedback to program staff would help to improve the program. Or perhaps there is a legal requirement that the program be evaluated. Whatever the rationale for the decision, an intent to evaluate is patently a necessary precursor to an evaluation contract.

Second, it evidently has been decided that the evaluation should be conducted by an individual or agency external to the institution responsible for the program or project. Someone apparently has realized that certain types of evaluation studies (e.g., end-of-project evaluations designed to tell funding agencies if the project met its goals) are less suspect if conducted by external personnel. Concern for credibility and objectivity of the evaluation results likely have prompted the decision to seek external assistance. Whatever the motivation, contemplation of an evaluation contract would seem to suggest the notion of involvement of an external party, since only the most pessimistic are likely to require contracts when the evaluation is to be conducted by individuals employed within the same institution.[3]

Third, it evidently has been decided that the evaluation should be conducted under a contract or some similar formalized agreement, rather than having the external evaluator proceed to carry out the evaluation with guidance only from whatever informal verbal or written dialogue may have occurred. Someone apparently has decided that clear, written understandings of the conditions under which the evaluation will be carried out and of the expectations of all parties will help avoid later misunderstandings and disagreements concerning the conduct or results of the evaluation. For example, an administrator who has never received an evaluation report on time may wish to require delivery by a specified date as a requirement for full payment for the evaluator's services. Or, an evaluator whose last evaluation report was rewritten by the client (with removal of all negative findings) before presentation to the funding agency may wish to stipulate in a formal contract that no changes can be made in the evaluation report without express consent of the authors.

Consequences of Not Having a Formal Agreement

Not long ago, one of the present authors was asked to undertake an evaluation of a community center funded by state and federal funds to provide services to mentally handi-

---

[3]An exception may exist in larger institutions such as large universities where the use of an evaluation contract may be advisable when an evaluation is to be conducted by persons internal to the institution, but external to the unit or department responsible for the program being evaluated.

capped adults.[4] After some initial telephone conversations, the first meeting was held between the center's governing board (a lay group of community members) and the author, along with an experienced evaluation colleague who had agreed to co-direct the evaluation if it were undertaken. During the meeting, we[5] were able to ascertain several things.

First, the reasons the governing board gave for requesting the evaluation were two-fold: (1) to evaluate the services and activities of the center to determine how effectively it was meeting its objectives; and (2) to evaluate the management of the center by the director and administrative staff to assess how effectively and efficiently the center was being run.

Now both of us had previously seen head-hunting excursions where evaluations were proposed by sponsors as thinly disguised excuses for castigating or terminating someone whom the sponsors had already determined to be incompetent or wished to replace for other, sometimes personal reasons, so we were a bit concerned about the request to evaluate management.

Being sensitive to the possibility that we were being asked to do just such an evaluation, we tried carefully to discern whether any nefarious intent lay behind the decision to evaluate the center, whether we were being asked to evaluate the center and its management with the real hope that our findings would prove an embarrassment, or worse, to its director. We listened, we probed, and finally asked tactfully (we thought) if there were specific concerns about the director and, if so, if the board really needed the evaluation to deal with them or whether the evaluation would really change the board's perceptions.

The responses were reasonably reassuring. Yes, they had some questions about the director's management style and effectiveness, but indicated they were not at all sure their perceptions were either accurate or fair. That was why they wanted us to examine that, they said. Even though one board member confessed a personality conflict with the center director, others assured us that professional competence, not personality, was the issue, and noted that the management review was secondary to the broader issue of judging the center's worth to the community. Moreover, the board evidenced strong support for the center, its mission, and what it offered to the people. Indeed, they were all heavily involved in volunteer programs conducted under center auspices and contributed countless hours to such efforts. We even talked to the center director privately, at our request, and although he seemed normally nervous about the upcoming evaluation, we could discern nothing to suggest he thought it was a set-up or that the board was "out to get him."

---

[4] The focus of this center has been changed sufficiently here to prevent anyone identifying the actual center, to allow us to speak frankly in this example without embarrassing individuals or their agencies.

[5] "We" and "us" refer in this example to the author and colleague involved in this study, not to both present authors.

After a while, we began to feel our earlier suspicions that their motives for requesting the evaluation might be ignoble were not only unwarranted but that we should be ashamed of such nasty, suspicious thoughts. After all, these were **nice** people, so we chastised ourselves for having been warped by years of evaluation experience, and agreed to undertake the study. The board passed a resolution committing generous financial support for the study, and we agreed to draft an evaluation plan that would inform them of how we proposed to proceed and how much of the budget would be consumed by each evaluation activity. They were to review the plan and suggest any desired modifications, and if they should not approve it for any reason, they agreed they would pay for our time in preparing it. We shook hands all around as a "contract," somehow not feeling comfortable suggesting a more formal written agreement as we routinely do with most agency clients -- after all, these were such nice folks.

So we proceeded, still feeling vaguely uneasy, but unsure just why. We had covered all the bases, or so we thought. Their reasons for requesting the evaluation seemed sincere and reasonable. The audiences for the evaluation (the board, the center director and staff, the funding agencies, and the community) were clear-cut and appropriate. There was no ambiguity about what was to be evaluated; the center and its services were neither complex nor difficult to understand. The fiscal resources and time allowed for us to complete the study were ample to enable us to conduct a thorough, high-quality evaluation of all aspects of the center and its operation. The political climate in the community seemed calm; the center was not under attack; those we had spoken to who were aware of its services were generally supportive. We could sense no particularly pervasive political undercurrents to warrant concern. Everything seemed to point to the fact that an evaluation could or should be useful. So we proceeded.

The evaluation plan was drafted and sent to the board for review. After the next board meeting, the board chairperson called to inform us that the plan was excellent, and that we should proceed as proposed in the plan. We did so, drafting instruments for a community survey (and sending them to the board for review and approval), drawing survey samples, conducting initial interviews with the center director and key staff, and so on. Days passed. So did the time we were to have received promised feedback and approval of our instruments by the board. So we telephoned the board chair, seeking feedback or the green light to print our questionnaires, but could never find him. Messages we left were never returned.

Ten days passed before the mailman brought us a perplexing letter from the board chair. No need to conduct the survey, he said, since they had decided that our evaluation plan was inadequate, unsuitable for their needs, and our services no longer needed. Besides, they had been forced to fire the director and it would be inappropriate to evaluate the center until things there could be normalized, at which time it may no longer be necessary. Nothing was said about reimbursement for our time or expenses for the travel or work done to date.

We were bright enough to sense something was not quite right, and that the contents of the letter were at odds with the earlier verbal rave reviews the board had given to our evaluation plan. So we called for an explanation. And called, and called. Finally, we drove the 150 miles to the community to ferret out the facts. It didn't take long to learn that the director had been fired because he had fired a black secretary, which the board had taken as proof of racial discrimination and grounds for the director's dismissal, although no investigation of the secretary's competence or the reason she was fired was conducted. Our growing suspicion that this was an excuse for the director's demise was confirmed by a program officer in the state agency funding the center (why didn't we think to talk to him before?) who told us that all of the board members disliked the director because he refused to allow them to go beyond setting policy to make the day-to-day administrative decisions that he felt were his perogative. In his opinion, the board had absolutely no interest in evaluating the center, but could think of no other way to get information that might give them an excuse to replace the director with a more tractable push-over to serve as the center's administrator. And too bad, our contact said, that the evaluation wouldn't be continuing, for the board had shared a copy with him, along with glowing accolades, and he thought it would have been useful indeed.

We finally cornered the board chair and requested an explanation, to no avail. All we received were denials that there had been any agreement, denials that they had ever requested us to proceed beyond the first discussion, denials that they had ever verbally approved or praised our evaluation plan, and insistence that their decision to terminate further involvement was because our work was unsuitable. Once it became patently clear that scruples or ethics were not of real concern to the board chair, we left, fearing that to stay longer might result in ensuing headlines, "OUT-OF-TOWN HOODLUMS BEAT UP LOCAL MERCHANT."

To conclude the story, we never were paid for our efforts. The center was never evaluated. The board has since terminated other directors, never finding one malleable enough to play puppet. But we are wiser, having learned that we're not as wise or discerning as we thought about spotting evil intentions in advance, and determining that in the future we will insist on formal written agreements, even with "nice" people.

PURPOSE AND ORGANIZATION OF THIS SECTION

It's easier to decide to establish an evaluation agreement than to know how to go about implementing that decision. The purpose of this section is to propose explicit standards and procedures for use in evaluation contracting.[6]

Chapter 10 provides guidelines and procedures for use in establishing an evaluation agreement or contract. Chapter 11 includes suggestions and procedures for use in negotiating, monitoring, or terminating an evaluation agreement or contract.

---

[6]The remainder of this section, as well as parts of Chapter 2 earlier, draws heavily on a comprehensive treatment of this topic which was supported by the Alaska Department of Education (Wright and Worthen, [30]).

CHAPTER 10: BASIC CONSIDERATIONS IN ESTABLISHING EVALUATION CONTRACTS AND AGREEMENTS

There are at least two major reasons why it seems useful to discuss how to negotiate and draw up evaluation contracts.

First, neither evaluators nor clients of evaluators have accumulated much experience in drafting (or complying with) evaluation contracts beyond those situations where funding guidelines automatically specified the nature of the formal agreement. In the latter case, the inadequacies in such guidelines have led to markedly inadequate evaluation studies, making it clear that better contract specifications are necessary. In the majority of cases, however, no guidelines have been imposed and evaluation contracts have either been non-existent or inadequate. Although the authors have perused a few very good evaluation contracts or "agreements of understanding" between the parties involved, most seem to be characterized by numerous omissions of important points, lack of specificity or ambiguity, or internal conflicts among the contract specifications. These conditions most likely are attributable to the fact that developing evaluation contracts is new to most evaluators and clients. Efforts to begin to outline at least the parameters of evaluation contracts should be well received by both groups.

Second, evaluators and clients often have very different expectations of the evaluation, making it imperative that clarity be established about evaluative questions to be addressed, procedures to be used in the study, what products will be produced and on what schedule, who has rights to release the data, and so forth. Failure to achieve clarity on these and related matters often leads to disappointment or disenchantment (or worse) on the part of one or both parties. Most of the disputes surrounding evaluation studies are traceable to failure to be sufficiently precise and to achieve shared understandings and agreements that guide the activities of the evaluator in conducting the study and the client in its use. Brickell [31] has provided excellent examples of difficulties in client-evaluator relationships that could have been avoided in most instances by clear-cut contractual agreements. Of course, even the existence of well-written contracts cannot prevent every possible problem, as evidenced by the well-publicized instance when an evaluation of the Michigan Accountability System erupted in controversy, despite the existence of a carefully written evaluation agreement [32]. But it seems safe to say written agreements help. It is reasonable to hope that efforts to specify procedures and standards for evaluation contracts, coupled with feedback from those who attempt to use them, would lead to greater clarity in these areas in the future.

Considerations such as the above suggest that discussion of standards and procedures for developing and implementing evaluation contracts has considerable utility, if only to raise the awareness of evaluators and clients about important aspects of contracting that presently seem to escape the attention of many who attempt to initiate formal evaluation agreements.

An additional point implicit in the above discussion should be made more explicit. Neither evaluators nor evaluation clients are typically well trained in contracting procedures. Further, there is no reason to expect that either party will be well-versed in the area of specialization of the other; it is as unreasonable to expect the evaluator to be knowledgeable about the intricacies of school finance as it is to expect the school administrator to be trained in evaluation methodology. Therefore, the contract can act as a point of communication to facilitate mutual understanding and avoid either party expecting (through naivete') more than is feasible of the other party. Thus, consideration of all aspects of contracting can serve to protect both parties and to improve the process of evaluation and, through it, the quality of educational and social programs.

BENEFICIARIES OF EVALUATION CONTRACTS AND AGREEMENTS

Evaluation contracts and agreements can be of benefit to almost everyone associated with an evaluation study, but the primary beneficiaries of such formal undertakings are: evaluators, evaluation clients, and the sponsor(s) of the study.

Evaluation sponsors. Funding agency personnel (e.g., personnel in a state social services department, a federal education agency, or a private foundation) are increasingly finding evaluation agreements useful as they discharge their comprehensive evaluation responsibilities. Such agreements are useful in cases where funding agency personnel become involved in establishing the evaluation contracts directly, as well as cases where they assist in arranging evaluations mandated under funding guidelines or awards but left to the discretion of the clients to arrange.

Evaluation clients. Administrators of social or educational programs (e.g., school superintendent or principal, dean of a college of education, or state family services director) would find formal evaluation agreements useful in a manner parallel to that described above for evaluation sponsors. In short, evaluation contracts should prove useful to any administrator responsible for identifying the best evaluation help possible to carry out the evaluation.

Evaluators. The importance of evaluation contracts to evaluators should be patently clear from the foregoing discussion. Having clear understandings among evaluator, client and sponsor in planning and conducting the evaluation is enormously useful in facilitating good evaluation.

The remainder of this chapter will deal with two major topics: (1) different types of evaluation agreements and how to select which is best for your purpose, and (2) issues that should be addressed in the evaluation agreement.

CHOOSING AMONG DIFFERENT TYPES OF EVALUATION AGREEMENTS

There are three general alternative procedural frameworks for letting an evaluation contract. Although there are specific variations of these three approaches, this chapter deals only with the essential characteristics.

In the first, one or more potential contractors are considered, using appropriate criteria such as those suggested by Worthen and Sanders [26], and a single contractor is then selected as the person or agency with whom contract negotiations are initiated. Negotiations with the single individual or corporation continue until a mutually satisfactory arrangement is reached or negotiations are broken off and another contractor is selected (again, use of criteria would be appropriate). This approach is known as **sole source contracting**.

In the second approach, one solicits proposals from multiple parties and evaluates the proposals against specific, tailored criteria to identify the one best able to fulfill the contract. Here general criteria for selecting evaluators would be relevant, along with criteria for judging the specific quality of the proposals. When one contractor has been selected (on the basis of which proposal and contractor qualifications best meet the prespecified criteria), serious negotiations are then initiated. This approach is what was referred to in Chapter 2 as the **request for proposals** (or RFP) approach.

The third approach is often the most feasible option for local school districts or social service agencies. In this approach, prospective evaluators submit a brief statement of how they would proceed, given the particular evaluation situation. In addition, each supplies his or her credentials and qualifications. Applying general criteria for selecting evaluators and examining the proposed style of evaluation, the client selects a particular party with whom to negotiate. This approach has been described in Chapter 2 as the **prospectus approach**.

The RFP and prospectus approaches have been described at some length in Chapter 2, in the discussion of competitive proposals, and will not be repeated here. But brief consideration of sole course contracting, which did not fit the earlier discussion of competitive proposals, is directly relevant here.

Sole Source contracting

Sole source contracting is by and large the simplest technique and least costly in terms of time and resources required of the evaluation client or sponsor in initiating the contract. All one need do is to identify the evaluator (using appropriate criteria), and negotiate. It is particularly appropriate where there is clearly one contractor who is known to be especially capable and responsible, who will do the work at a price within the budget available, and who can complete the work by the time the information is needed. In such cases, there is seldom any reason to look further, unless there is a legal restriction that mandates the use of an alternative approach.

If no such paragon emerges, however, there are several ways to identify a pool of potentially qualified evaluators from which to choose. An individual or corporation who has performed other evaluations of a high quality for your agency is a prime candidate. So also is the evaluator who has done similar work elsewhere and received approbation from his or her clients (i.e., word-of-mouth advertising). A third approach would be to use a panel of advisors whose job it would be to recommend the best evaluator.

Legal restraints against sole source contracting are becoming more common, especially for federally funded endeavors in the United States. The presumed intent is to reduce the bias in contracting procedures, whether that bias is deliberate or unwitting. Where this constraint exists, a prospectus or RFP approach should be adopted.

Checklist of Steps for Selecting Among Procedural Options for Awarding Evaluation Contracts

The checklist in Figure 5 is proposed for use in deciding which of the three options discussed previously is best for a particular evaluation.

	Check One for Each Item	
	Yes	No
1. Is there a legal constraint against sole source contracting? (If yes, skip to Item 4 below; if no, go on to Item 2.)		
2. Is there a qualified evaluation contractor who is interested in this evaluation, and whose services are desired by the client? (If yes, go to Item 3; if no, go to Item 4.)		
3. Have such a large number of contracts been let to this same contractor that "cronyism" may be a danger? (If yes, reconsider Item 2 above for a new contractor; if no, begin negotiations.)		
4. Are the financial resources available for this evaluation sufficient to warrant the cost of an RFP? (If yes, prepare an RFP; if no, use prospectus approach to find a suitable contractor.)		

Summary

Based on questions 1-4 above, which of the following procedural options do you select for letting the evaluation contract?

a. ☐ Sole Source Contract

b. ☐ Request for Proposals

c. ☐ Prospectus Approach

Figure 5: Checklist for Selecting Among Procedural Options
for Awarding Evaluation Contracts

SELECTING THE ISSUES AND ITEMS TO BE INCLUDED IN AN
EVALUATION AGREEMENT OR CONTRACT

Once the evaluation client has selected an evaluator to do the work (whether by sole source, RFP, or prospectus review), attention can be turned to drafting an evaluation agreement. Prior to drafting the agreement, however, it is essential to decide on its essential ingredients -- those items and issues which are important to provide a firm basis for understanding between evaluator and client and prevent possibly serious misunderstandings.

There is no universally accepted list of items and issues to be included in an evaluation contract.[7] The following is an effort to organize in an understandable manner, under eight general categories, some of the most important items that should be considered for inclusion in all but the most informal evaluation agreement.

1. General Descriptive Information to be Included

Every evaluation should include essential descriptive information of the following types.

Identification of evaluation client/sponsor. The client to be served by the evaluation (and, if different, the sponsor funding the study) must be identified clearly.

Identification of evaluation contractor. The evaluator who will conduct the evaluation (or, if a team or agency effort, direct the study), must be identified clearly.

Description of the evaluation object. That which is to be evaluated should be clearly described and delineated, with appropriate explanations of what is to be included and excluded. It is also wise to have both client and evaluator formally approve this description of the program or product to be evaluated to avoid any possible later misunderstandings.

General purpose of the evaluation. The charge given to the evaluator must be set forth in clear enough terms that all can agree on the general purpose to be accomplished by the study. This general purpose will be further specified in other items proposed for inclusion in later sections of the evaluation contract.

---

[7]Several authors [e.g., 28,30, 33-36] have written variously about ingredients in evaluation contracts. In this chapter we follow primarily Wright and Worthen's [30] notions, although we draw a smattering of ideas from our colleagues as well.

Intended audiences for the evaluation information. The audiences to be served by the evaluation should be identified, as they will influence greatly how reporting will take place, who should have access to the data, and other similar concerns discussed later in this section. Of course, not every potential audience for the evaluation can be identified at the outset, but that should not deter one from listing all those which can be identified at that point, for those are likely to include the primary audiences at least.

Authorization to conduct the study. No evaluation study can be conducted effectively and professionally in the absence of an appropriate authorization of the study itself. No agency or group of professionals is likely to welcome into its bosom some self-appointed gadfly who declares his or her role as that of judging the quality of the endeavors in which that agency or group is engaged. And the group or agency is no more likely to cooperate with or provide necessary financial or other support for such unauthorized evaluations than a country infested by enemy spies is likely to provide cheerfully for their room, board, and camera equipment. It is essential to each evaluation study that the sanction and/or sponsorship of the evaluation by agencies which have the right to initiate the study and request the cooperation of all participants and audiences be made clear. Of course, not every relevant audience or participant may feel bound by such a general sanction, and wise evaluators will proceed throughout the study to secure approval of specific audiences and participants. But without this general authorization, individual efforts of the evaluator to secure cooperation are unlikely to yield sufficient results.

2. Information to be Produced by the Study

It is important in each proposed evaluation study to identify the needed information which the evaluation is intended to provide. This is what has been referred to previously as "focusing" the evaluation study [37]. Focusing can take many forms; what is important here is not the form, but rather that whatever form is used to focus the study, it results in clearly identified information that the evaluation is to provide. The needed information may be reflected in a list of evaluative questions the study will answer (insofar as answers can be found), or in some other form.

3. Work and Resource Specifications

It is essential that an evaluation agreement include specification of the work to be accomplished and the resources that will be committed to accomplish that work. This section of the evaluation contract would include the following types of information.

The overall plan for the evaluation. A summary of the evaluation design or plan should be included in every evaluation agreement to provide clarity about items such as: (1) the general design and methods of inquiry to be used in the study; (2) sources of information for the evaluation; (3) data-collection instruments and methods for analyzing and interpreting the information; and (4) general reporting strategies.

The scope of work. Perhaps the most important topic for negotiation is the scope of work for the evaluation. The scope of work is really the operational statement of the evaluation plan or design. Within it one stipulates the specific procedures to be employed, the products (instruments, reports, etc.) that can be expected from the evaluation, the time schedule for performance as well as the deadlines for delivery. It is in the light of this scope of work that one monitors the performance of the evaluator in meeting the contract.

Resources to be used in the evaluation. It is essential that the evaluation contract specify the human, financial, material, and time resources that will be devoted to accomplish the work outlined in the workscope. Listing of key personnel who will conduct particular evaluation activities is also important. Of course, it is not always possible to have a complete evaluation plan and workscope, in the level of detail that would be desirable, as part of the initial contract, for two reasons. First, many issues which will influence the conduct of the evaluation, and hence its design, cannot be foreseen prior to beginning the study. Consequently, some details of the design will need to be fleshed out as the evaluation proceeds. Second, developing a comprehensive and detailed evaluation design is a challenging and time-consuming task that few evaluators are likely to do (at least as thoroughly as they are able) until **after** they are assured it is a worthwhile expenditure of their time -- i.e., until after they have secured the evaluation contract. It is largely for this reason that very few competitive evaluation proposals (except for extremely attractive or lucrative evaluation opportunities which make the gamble, if won, worth the cost) contain adequate evaluation plans and workscopes. This is unfortunate, because all else in an evaluation is dependent, at least in part, on the logical consistency, comprehensiveness, and clarity of the design of the study.

There are ways to compensate for this problem, however. For example, insightful clients who wish to have a thorough evaluation plan at the outset sometimes offer to pay the evaluator to produce such a plan. In such instances, the evaluator is "employed" for the number of hours or days it takes to produce a detailed design which can be reviewed by the client and modified as circumstances and mutual satisfaction dictate. The design work would take place prior to the contract negotiations, and the resultant design would then be part of the contractual arrangement agreed to by both parties.

A fee should be established for preparing a detailed design, and this fee should not be contingent upon whether or not the design is accepted. In the detailed plan, the evaluator may insist on certain conditions for data collection or access to certain data, to assure that the results will be credible. The client, for valid political reasons, may not agree to those conditions. Hopefully, discussion might lead to compromise and creative alternatives, but if not, a mutual decision may be reached that the client should seek a new evaluator. Even though the first evaluator's design was rejected, compensation for time spent on its preparation is in order.

By adhering to this practice, the client is ultimately benefitted. With the knowledge that the fee is secure, the evaluator will design the study that, in his or her professional judgment, is best, within the resource limitation. Under this arrangement, there is no motive for trying to shortcut the design stage. In short, the design fee is excellent protection against shoddy performance in this critical area.

An alternative way to assure an adequate evaluation plan is to write the contract without a detailed design, and then make that design the first product required of the evaluator once the evaluation is underway. This process results in essentially the same benefits as that described above in the fee situation, since the evaluator is paid to provide a detailed design that is used as a basis for deciding whether the contract should be continued beyond the first phase. Judgment that a design was unacceptable (and could not be salvaged with minor changes) would require the termination of a contract, rather than breaking off of negotiations as in the previous case. This distinction should not be a problem, however, as long as provisions are built into the contract to terminate it, if the design is unacceptable to the client.

A third alternative is to award an independent contract for the design phase. At the conclusion of that phase a decision about the adequacy of the design is reached. The second contract for the conduct of the evaluation is thus contingent upon satisfactory performance in the first contract period. If the project is very large (for example, a three year evaluation at $150,000 a year), it may be sensible to award two or three design contracts with the understanding that the party whose evaluation plan is judged most superior will receive the contract for the evaluation itself.

The need for flexible evaluation agreements. Because a priori designs will not usually be able to anticipate all the issues that will emerge during an evaluation, there is a need to increase awareness on the part of evaluators and clients alike of the necessity for specified procedures designed to provide necessary flexibility in evaluation contracts. The concept of specifying procedures for flexibility may appear to be a non sequitur, but on close examination that appearance is belied. Evaluation contracts should carry within them specified points at which decisions can be made by one or both of the parties about how the remainder of the evaluation will be conducted. In other words, the contract should contain specific decision points at which the contract can be terminated if dissatisfaction arises on the part of either party, just so payment for time spent and work completed to that point is assured. It is senseless to lock both parties into a contract that requires them to continue from one phase to the next after it has become clear that there is dissatisfaction of one or both parties with the activities or performance involved. Yet far too often failure to think about the need for flexible phasing in contracts leads to precisely this type of unhappy situation.

A type of flexibility often neglected in evaluation contracts is provision for mutual alterations in the design, procedures, or reporting of results. Despite the best efforts of a contractor to include in the design of the study provision for all possible contingencies, something will inevitably go awry. The ironic "laws" ("if something can go wrong, it will" and "things take longer than they do") seem always in effect. Unanticipated events and problems often force alterations in procedures if the evaluation data are to be useful. Contracts must contain flexibility for mutual negotiation and decisions to accommodate such changes. Here is one area where the competence of the evaluator is most essential (and noticeable), for it takes a real "pro" to make the type of creative adjustments necessary to salvage an evaluation threatened by emergent problems or events that make it impossible to carry out the original design. This does not mean that every evaluation can be salvaged. Sometimes the evaluation can be so compromised by events that there is no chance whatsoever of producing usable or believable data. In such instances it is incumbent on the evaluator to acknowledge this fact and terminate the evaluation (which again should be possible within a well-written contract) rather than to continue to expend the client's resources in a hopeless activity.

4. Responsibilities of Client and Evaluator

There are several issues that, if left unresolved during contract negotiations, can later prove to be sources of great consternation. Perhaps the most nettlesome is identifying the respective responsibilities of the client and evaluator with respect to activities such as those outlined below.

Scope of the inquiry. In some cases the evaluator becomes aware that an important objective was overlooked in the preparation of the contract. Brickell [31] provides an excellent example of this kind of problem in evaluating a project that involved the employment of paraprofessionals. The evaluator's charge in a contract issued by the central administration of a major American city was to examine the impact of the program on student learning. But the paraprofessionals were directly employed by area superintendents who had a very different view of the purpose of the program. Brickell describes a meeting with these individuals:

> While meeting with area superintendents to explain the study, one of their spokesmen opened up with something like this: "Okay, you evaluators. Let's get one thing straight from the start. We have these paraprofessionals here in these schools not only to help kids learn but to link us to the community. That's why we have them. That's why we're going to keep them. We're not looking for a report about test results that will cause any trouble with the board of education downtown. They've got their reasons for giving us the money to hire paraprofessionals; we've got our reasons for taking the money. So no matter what you find out about kids' achievement, we're going to keep our paraprofessionals. Don't make it difficult." (p. 95)

In these circumstances the evaluator has the responsibility to identify the "hidden objective." The evaluator is not, however, required to investigate the efficacy of the project in cementing community relations. That investigation would require new resources and a new or revised contract. Indeed, this example illustrates the importance of the issue of who is involved in negotiation, a topic to which we will return shortly. At any rate, it is the client's responsibility, not the evaluator's, to ensure that the contract covers all of the salient areas of inquiry. The evaluator's role is only that of being certain that failure to address relevant objectives or efforts of a project are duly noted.

Access to data and records. It is also the client's responsibility to insure access to the data that the contract requires the evaluator to collect and/or analyze. For example, if the teachers in a given school simply refuse to respond to the questionnaire prepared by the evaluator, and the sponsoring school system cannot obtain this cooperation, the sponsor must bear responsibility for the inevitably flawed report that will result.

Managing or preventing disruptions. No evaluation will be completely unobtrusive. In the preparation of the contract, careful attention must be paid to identifying and dealing with potential problems of disruption that might result from evaluation activity so that, insofar as possible, both parties enter the agreement with a shared understanding of disruptions that could occur and what each is expected to do to minimize those disruptions and facilitate the inquiry.

5. Control and Use of Evaluation Information

Several crucial issues pertaining to the control and use of evaluation information must be resolved within the evaluation contract.

Editorial authority. The temptation to edit the evaluator's written findings, interpretations, and judgments is sometimes more than the evaluation client or sponsor can resist. It is important, in preparing evaluation reports, to have client, sponsor and other participants review a draft copy of the evaluation report to correct factual inaccuracies and challenge erroneous interpretations or conclusions before the report is finalized. However, final authority for what is said in the report typically resides with the evaluator whose name is to be affixed to that document. Having editorial procedures and authority spelled out clearly in the contract will prevent the tension that is created when a client selectively edits the evaluator's report in ways that alter its meaning.

Misuse or nonuse of evaluation findings or reports. It is also simplistic to assume that the evaluator's report will be used only by the client to whom it is submitted. Sometimes the client must report results directly to some other audience, for example the funding agency, and may abstract or modify the report submitted by the evaluator to accomplish this end. Occasionally an evaluator perceives such a modified report as misleading or inaccurate. The evaluator then has a professional and moral responsibility to respond to this misinterpretation or misuse of his or her work. For example, an unscrupulous project director may report a vocational training program as an unqualified success because 100 percent of the trainees were found to be employed in full-time jobs in their chosen field at the conclusion of the program. But the evaluator knows that 65 percent of the graduates were dismissed from these jobs for incompetence within two months after being hired. Since other students may be similarly victimized, since other agencies may be misled into attempting to implement the same training program, the evaluator has no alternative but to expose the fraudulent use of data. The means for rebuttal could be in the form of a letter written to the recipients of the report, an appeal to the ethics committee of some professional association, or a public press conference, depending on the seriousness (and perceived intent) of the misrepresentation.

The problem has another side to it. Sometimes the evaluator errs and includes inaccurate information in a report that is circulated to a wider audience. The client is now placed in a defensive posture. The report is wrong and must be corrected. Yet in correcting what may be minor factual errors, the client may discredit a report which is by and large favorable.

A related situation is the nonuse of evaluation findings. The evaluator has no right to insist that her findings be the sole basis for the client's decisions. Indeed rational decision making demands that all of the information and evidence available, not just that which is included in the evaluation report, be examined and weighed in the decision making process. Yet it can happen that a critical evaluation finding is ignored, either deliberately or through mischance, by those reaching a particular decision. Depending on the consequences of that nonuse, the evaluator may feel obligated to respond. For example, assume the evaluator found evidence to suggest that the use of a particular social studies curriculum exacerbated racial discord among students. But the decision is made to continue the use of the curriculum because the decision makers did not bother to read the evaluator's report. The evaluator should take steps to inform the relevant decision makers of the serious flaw in the curriculum. Subsequently, should the decision remain unaltered, and there is no evidence that continuation of that curriculum is required by ameliorating circumstances, the evaluator may feel compelled to address a more public forum.

The most unfortunate aspect of these situations is the fact that they are usually so easily avoided. In most instances the misuse or nonuse of data arises not from a lack of scruples, but from a lack of understanding.   If the contract included provisions for the review of reports by both parties prior to release, most problems of this nature would probably be eliminated. In the prior example of the unscrupulous vocational training program director, a conference with the evaluator might result in an impasse. The director sees an opportunity to make hay while the sun shines. The evaluator, one hopes, will not tolerate such fraud, but will make every effort to expose it. In the other examples used, however, it is doubtful that disagreement would persist. Reasonable individuals will usually find acceptable resolutions. Thus a provision for prior review to correct factual errors and examine differences in interpretation of the evidence would substantially ameliorate the situation.

Dissemination rights. The evaluation agreement must specify what formal and informal evaluation reports will be made to the audiences identified as appropriate to receive them. Contract negotiations should also result in the stipulation of any restrictions to be placed on the use of the evaluation reports. Who controls the release and circulation of the evaluation report(s)? Who, if anyone, has the right to release information about the findings to those who inquire but were not included as an audience for the report (e.g., the press)? Answers to such questions should be clear from the evaluation contract.

The publication rights issue goes beyond simply releasing the report. When the study is completed, the evaluator may wish to publish the results in a professional journal and would probably be willing to disguise the context of the study so as to preserve the client's confidentiality. The client, however, may wish to avoid or reserve to a later time any publication of the findings. Again, mutual agreement concerning the rights of publication arrived at during the negotiations phase would alleviate or eliminate problems at a more critical juncture. The evaluation contract should also specify who holds copyright to any published material resulting from the evaluation.

Other uses for the evaluation information. Another issue that sometimes arises in the evaluation agreement is the "piggy backing" of the evaluator's research interests on the evaluation study. For example, an evaluator may have a continuing interest in personality research and wishes to administer some new personality assessment measures to the teachers involved in an evaluation project. Is it proper to do so, if such evidence would be unrelated, or only tangentially related, to the client's evaluation concerns? Such an activity **can** be legitimate, but only if it has been mutually agreed-upon. The best time to consider such issues is during contract negotiations, so that the written agreement can stipulate such provisions and restrictions.

In the same vein, sometimes the evaluator can use instruments developed under one evaluation contract in another very similar evaluation. Is that legitimate? Yes, it is, unless the previous contract specifies otherwise (which would seem appropriate only where instruments have commercial potential or other characteristics that would be of direct benefit to the client). In the absence of such contract provisions, the evaluator is not restricted from using the instrument elsewhere.

The evaluation information can also have delayed use. For example, sometimes the evaluator can collect, for little or no extra cost, information that cannot be analyzed within the study's budget constraints but would prove useful to the client or others at a later date. It is important to include in evaluation agreements provisions for making such data available to others for reanalysis, as long as such use does not do a disservice to the client or evaluator.

6. Ethical Issues

Several ethical issues should be addressed in an evaluation agreement, including at least those discussed below.

Conflict of interest. The contract negotiations should also serve as an opportunity to explore potential conflicts of interest. Is the evaluator currently employed by an agency which is competing for funds from the same source? Is there any reward likely for the evaluator if the evaluation findings are favorable or unfavorable? The objectivity of the evaluator who has a spouse on the staff of the agency evaluated is likely to be influenced by what would be most advantageous for the spouse. Similarly, if the external evaluator is guaranteed continued employment if the evaluated program is refunded, and the evaluation report will be crucial in that decision, then the evaluator's own financial self-interest promotes favorable results. And as Cronbach and his colleagues have pointed out, philosophical conflicts are problematic when the evaluator attempts to evaluate a program" ... with whose basic aims he is not in sympathy; a pacifist agreeing to conduct an impartial evaluation of ROTC would find himself torn by conflict after conflict" [38, pp. 208-209]. Means of avoiding such conflict situations should be explored.

Confidentiality and anonymity. The evaluation contract should not only state the evaluator's intention to provide all informants the privilege of confidentiality and anonymity, but should also describe precisely how the privileged information will be protected. It is one thing to promise that informants' comments will not be identified or attributed to them in any recognizable way. It is quite another to keep that promise while finding a way to include the insights of informants who will be readily recognized by the unique perspective their views represent.

Professional autonomy. The evaluator does not enjoy the complete autonomy of inquiry possessed by the researcher, owing to the fact that the focus of the evaluation study is determined not by intellectual curiosity but by the client's need for information. But in conducting the study, the evaluator must be free to use her technical expertise and to make professional decisions about how best to carry out the evaluation activities, as long as they are conducted within accepted standards for professional conduct of the evaluator [24, 25].

7. Legal Issues

Two basic kinds of legal issues involve: (1) torts, and (2) statutes and constitutional law.

Tortuous injuries. Although only infrequently a problem, it is prudent for the evaluator to keep in mind the fact that personal injury claims can arise from evaluations, especially if thoughtlessly conducted, for we live in an increasingly litigious age. Suits for libel, defamation of character, slander, or fraud are possibilities which can occur. Evaluation agreements can stipulate how permission to quote individuals or obtain written approval to release certain information might prevent such unpleasantness.

Statutory and constitutional issues. In the United States, the constitution and subsequent statutes guarantee certain rights to individuals that the evaluator must not circumvent. For example, the review of data-collection techniques to assure protection of human subjects, informed-consent requirements, rights of privacy, and statutory limitations on access to certain types of information are all of concern to the evaluator. Again, the evaluation agreement should specify how the rights of individuals will be safeguarded in relation to these issues.

8. Other Contractual Issues

Of the numerous other contractual issues that might be discussed, two are singled out for consideration here: the adjudication process and payment provisions.

Conflict resolution and adjudication. An agreed-upon adjudication process for resolving conflicts and grievances is beneficial to include in the contract. There are many means that one can employ to achieve the resolution of disputes. A binding or a non-binding arbitration clause could be inserted in the contract. The arbiter could be a professional member of the American Arbitration Association. Alternatively, an agreement could be reached on the use of an individual arbiter or a panel of arbitrators chosen from relevant social or educational fields. The panel offers the advantage of permitting the representation of multiple perspectives, e.g., evaluation, administration, and the relevant disciplines. The panel should, however, consist of an uneven number of individuals in order to avoid tie votes. At least one member of the panel should be technically competent in the relevant evaluation methodologies (e.g., statistics, measurement, design, ethnography, observational systems). If that is not possible, the panel should have access to expert testimony.

Even in the absence of a binding arbitration clause, the contractual agreement for an adjudication process could serve a valuable purpose. In the case of conflicting interpretations of the data, for example, it could serve to legitimize or discredit particular courses of action. Take the earlier example of the social studies curriculum. If the client feels that the data on racial discord were inconclusive or unreliable and for that reason should be deleted from the report, arbitration might fail to resolve the differences of the client and the evaluator concerning the worth of the data but might suggest that both points of view ought to be included in the report.

The same approach to conflict resolution could be used in instances where the client wishes to amend the contract or terminate it, for example, on the grounds of non-performance, or the evaluator wishes to terminate on the grounds that the client has not met contract conditions concerning access to data. Contract amendment or termination procedures should also be a matter of contractual agreement.

Regardless of the means chosen, and irrespective of the perceived likelihood that it will be necessary, it is recommended that an adjudication process be negotiated and included in the contract. The mere availability of the process often serves to promote better communication and more facile resolution of disagreements between client and contractor.

Basis for payment for services. Of course the contract should also stipulate the basis of payment. Not only the total sum of the contract price, but the payment schedule needs to be clear. Some funding agencies have restrictions concerning what equipment costs can be legitimately paid, for example, or the amount that can be charged for indirect costs. It is wise to include these restrictions in the evaluation contract to avoid confusion. It is also useful to include in the contract specifications for appropriate remuneration in the event the contract is terminated.

CHAPTER 11: NEGOTIATING AND MONITORING EVALUATION CONTRACTS AND AGREEMENTS

In the previous chapter, we discussed the essential ingredients in an evaluation contract or agreement and some considerations in establishing such formal agreements. In this chapter we turn our attention to how to take the next steps -- negotiation of the contract and monitoring of formal evaluation agreements.

NEGOTIATING AN EVALUATION AGREEMENT

Once an evaluation contractor has been identified, the negotiations for a contract begin. If the RFP approach was used, the proposal constitutes the basis for negotiations, but much remains to be decided, including when to negotiate, who should be involved, and when to discontinue negotiations.

When to Initiate Negotiations

If evaluation is to have maximum impact, it must begin early in the life of the entity to be evaluated. For formative evaluation, this is obviously essential. Even for summative evaluation, it should be self-evident that the negotiation of an evaluation agreement must occur as soon as it is feasible to do so, i.e., as soon as the commitments necessary to proceed with the evaluation have been made.

Given the nature of summative evaluation, some have concluded that it is appropriate to engage an external evaluator only when the program or project to be evaluated has been operational for a considerable time. The evaluator is then expected to come in and collect impact data from participants, teachers, students, or whomever, and then prepare a final report. At first glance this approach may seem almost logical. In point of fact, it creates problems of the greatest magnitude.

There are basically two dimensions of a summative evaluation that determine when the evaluator should be engaged. The first of these is the type of inquiry involved. Is an experimental design or one of the time frame approaches (e.g., anthropological study, time series, or longitudinal case studies) most appropriate? The second critical dimension concerns the responsibility of the evaluator for the creation of new instruments or data collection procedures.

If an experimental design is to be used, for example, the evaluator must be involved **prior to the assignment of the treatment to the experimental units**. The complete justification of this statement would require an examination of experimental and quasi-experimental design that is well beyond the scope of this chapter. Suffice to state that any outcome is the consequence of the interaction of treatment and subject. The corrosive effects of acids depend to a considerable extent on the substance with which they come in contact. In much the same way, the impact of alternative approaches to reading, for example, will depend upon the status of the children taught. Unless the evaluator has an opportunity to influence which students receive what instruction, he will never be able to disentangle those effects which arise from treatment differences from those due to the characteristics of the students.

Contrary to the usual expectation, the use of a time frame evaluation approach requires an even earlier entry point. In these cases the evaluator must be engaged **in time to permit the collection of data concerning the status of those who are to participate well in advance of the introduction of the treatment.** In a naturalistic case study approach, for example, the evaluator must be on site and recording the nature of the phenomena of primary interest well prior to the implementation of the innovation so that he can be in a position to note the changes that occur as (or after) that event takes place. While there is no set standard for when observations begin, six months to a year prior to initiation of the treatment is not unreasonable for most projects.

The need for the development of new instruments imposes an additional lead time requirement. In these cases the evaluator should be engaged soon enough to permit the development, tryout, analysis, and revision of the instruments prior to their first intended use. There are few things less satisfying than reporting the results of a well conceptualized evaluation which is inconclusive because insufficient time was allocated for the preparation of valid and reliable instruments. One circumstance which qualifies as less satisfying is reading that inconclusive report when you are the client for whom it was prepared.

Who Should Be Involved in Negotiation

One common source of difficulty in the conduct of evaluations is the fact that significant individuals or groups were not included in the negotiation of the contract. An excellent case in point is Brickell's example (quoted earlier in Chapter 10) concerning the area superintendents who had different expectations of the paraprofessional project than did the central administration. Had the central administration thought to involve the area superintendents in the negotiation of the contract, it is highly probable that a more comprehensive evaluation would have occurred.   Certainly the evaluator's role would have been clearer and less fraught with conflict. As a general rule, **all who will be affected by the evaluation have the right to be involved in the negotiations -- at least by representation**. Too often, for example, we expect teachers, students, or welfare recipients to comply completely with an investigation without ever involving them in decisions about what data will be collected, from whom, in what manner, or when. It does not seem unreasonable to suggest that, at a minimum, a representative of each group could be involved in the negotiations and report back to those represented.

The preceding argument should not be taken to mean that these groups are entitled to be involved in all aspects of the negotiations. For example, since the argument is tenuous at best that the teachers, students, or welfare recipients are affected by the annual salary made by an evaluator, they are not entitled to that information or to involvement in negotiation concerning salary or budget. It may be that some day all publicly supported contracts, salaries, and budgets will be open to public view. Road contractors, public servants, and hospital employees would then all be subjected to the same scrutiny. In that case the evaluation contractor's records should also be open. Until that day arrives, however, singling out the evaluation contractor is simply discrimination.

Moreover, one must bear in mind that involvement in the negotiations does not equal veto power. The primary negotiators are usually the evaluators, the funding agency, and the direct client. Thus, if a state department of education provides money to a school system for a particular evaluation project, the state department and the legally constituted authorities of the local system are the principal negotiators with the evaluation contractor. The involvement of principals, teachers, students, and citizens is at a secondary level and limited to those aspects of the contract that directly affect them. Yet, the involvement of these groups is in keeping with the fundamental values of a democratic society. It also tends to maximize communication and reduce the threat of non-cooperation on the part of those who either don't understand what is going on or are alienated by virtue of their exclusion from the decision making process.

Procedures and Causes for Terminating Negotiations

Usually this is not an issue. Negotiations are usually over when the agreement is consummated, and for most evaluations that is neither a long nor involved process. But in large, complex, and costly evaluation studies -- especially those sponsored by agencies with numerous regulations that affect the study's conduct -- the contract can be extensive and the negotiations drawn out and difficult. The remainder of this section pertains only to such large and extensive activities.

Consider the following situation. An evaluation contractor has been selected by means of an RFP to do a $246,000 nationwide evaluative survey of opinions toward extension education efforts supported by the United States Department of Agriculture. Negotiations have been going on for two months; the survey must be implemented within the next three months. Time is getting short. Does the client break off negotiations and begin bargaining with their second choice evaluator? It all depends.

It depends on whether the negotiations are progressing smoothly and a contract can be expected soon. It depends on how much lead time before implementation the evaluation will require. It depends on how much money has been invested thus far in the process, and what it is expected to cost before a contract is consummated. It also depends on whether the evaluator and client think that it is worth the expenditure of more time and energy to pursue the negotiations.

Neither the client nor evaluator can force negotiations to a successful conclusion. If irreconcilable differences exist, the only intelligent course of action is to agree to terminate negotiations. The wisest way to proceed might be for all the parties involved to set some resource and time limitations on what they will invest in the negotiation.

Checklist for Use in Negotiating an Evaluation Agreement

The checklist in Figure 6 is proposed for use in assessing whether essential issues, items, and concerns have been included in the evaluation agreement and the negotiations intended to lead to its consummation.

To illustrate how the standards and procedures proposed previously might prove useful, three hypothetical contracts have been constructed and appear as Exhibits 11.1 - 11.3 at the end of this chapter. The first is a contract for the design of an evaluation. The second is a comprehensive contract for the conduct of that same evaluation. Each of these contracts has been formally drawn with a great many details provided in the contract to illustrate how completeness and precision might be obtained. The third contract is far less formal and complete. It illustrates the minimum content of a contract. Since many contractual areas are not dealt with, a document of this kind assumes a high degree of trust and confidence between the two parties. Each relies on the other's professional sense of responsibility.

None of the sample contracts are proposed as ideal, but rather as examples of more or less compulsive attention to the issues discussed in Chapter 10 and in the preceding sections of this chapter.

		Check One for Each Item	
		Yes	No
1.	Are negotiations initiated early enough to permit the evaluator early enough entry and sufficient lead time to use the evaluation methods and instruments judged as apropriate for the study?		
2.	Have adequate provisions been made for the development of an evaluation design through one of the following: preparation of design for set fee; preparation of design as the first phase of the contract; or preparation of design under an initial contract, with a separate contract for implementing the design.		
3.	Does the evaluation agreement contain: a. identification of evaluation client/sponsor?		
	b. identification of evaluation contractor?		
	c. description of that to be evaluated?		
	d. statement of the general purpose of the evaluation?		
	e. specification of the evaluation's intended audiences?		
	f. specification of the authorization for conducting the study?		
4.	Are the information needs for the study clearly listed?		
5.	Is there a summary of the overall evaluation plan which includes: a. the general design and methods of inquiry to be used?		
	b. sources of information for the study?		
	c. methods and techniques for data-collection, analysis, and interpretation?		
	d. general reporting strategies to be used?		
6.	Does the negotiated Scope of Work include: a. the procedures to be employed by the evaluator and a time schedule for their performance?		
	b. adequate description of the products to be expected from the evaluation and deadlines for their delivery?		
	c. criteria for judging that the contract has been fulfilled?		
7.	Does the agreement specify: a. human resources necessary to do the work?		
	b. financial resources necessary to do the work?		
	c. material resources necessary to do the work?		
	d. time necessary to complete the workscope?		

Figure 6: Checklist for Negotiating an Evaluation Agreement (continued)

	Check One for Each Item	
	Yes	No
8. Has the negotiations dealt with the respective responsibilities of the client and contractor concerning: a. the identification of the scope of the inquiry?		
b. access to data and records?		
c. managing or preventing disruptions?		
9. Does the agreement deal with: a. editorial authority? rights of prior review?		
b. misuse of nonuse of findings or reports?		
c. dissemination rights (e.g., publication and copyright)?		
d. other uses of evaluation information produced (e.g., "piggybacking" of research interests)?		
10. Does the negotiated agreement deal with: a. potential conflict of interest?		
b. provisions for maintaining informants' confidentiality and anonymity?		
c. professional autonomy of the evaluator?		
d. possible legal issues?		
11. Has an adjudication and conflict resolution procedure been established?		
12. Has a basis for payment been established?		
13. Have the primary negotiators been identified?		
14. Have those who will be affected by the evaluation been invited to participate at a secondary level in the negotiations, at least by representation?		
15. Has a time and resource limit for negotiations been set by mutual agreement?		
Summary Based on questions 1-15 above, have negotiations been sufficiently successful to warrant awarding a contract or contracts for accomplishment of the evaluation design and conduct of the evaluation?		

Figure 6: Checklist for Negotiating an Evaluation Agreement

MONITORING THE IMPLEMENTATION OF AN EVALUATION CONTRACT

Assume that the negotiations have been successfully concluded and that a contract to conduct the evaluation exists. If the negotiations have been well conducted, why does one need to monitor the contract? There are three basic reasons for monitoring. The first is to identify unanticipated events or changes that will affect the capacity of the client or evaluator to comply fully with the contract so that renegotiation, if necessary, can occur. The second reason for monitoring is to identify promptly problems or areas of dissatisfaction on the part of either the client or the contractor so that small problems do not grow into a "breach of contract" situation. The third reason is to facilitate mutual agreement to terminate the contract if that seems to be the best course of action.

The Tools of Monitoring

There are two tools that permit the client to monitor the performance of the contractor. The first is the scope of work section of the contract. The second is use of qualitative judgments about how well the work has been conducted. Development of such judgments of quality is beyond the scope of this chapter and will not be dealt with further here; readers are referred to prior sources of information about standards for use in determining the ability of evaluation studies [24, 25].

In relation to the workscope, there are four basic questions one can ask of the evaluator's performance:

1. Did the evaluator use the agreed-upon procedures?
2. Did the evaluator use the procedures within the agreed-upon time schedule ?
3. Did the evaluator deliver the agreed-upon products?
4. Were those products delivered by the agreed-upon deadlines?

Without specification of these elements in the contract, it is virtually impossible to monitor the contract, to establish contract fulfillment or breach. It is in short a "no win" situation for all concerned.

Procedures for Renegotiation of the Contract

More often than not the evaluation will not be accomplished strictly in accord with the contract. There always seems to be some unexpected event that forces modification of the original intent. If, for example, three of six teachers who are using a new math curriculum resign for one reason or another, it is clear that some change in the evaluation design is in order.

Whenever circumstances change from those anticipated in the contract, the client and the contractor need to consider whether renegotiation is required. Both parties should examine the scope of work contained in the contract and determine which elements can still be accomplished and which are no longer feasible. Adjustments can then be made. The timelines may need to be altered. More, or less, money may be appropriate, given the changed situation. In the event that the client and contractor disagree about the kind or extent of modifications required, the adjudication process stipulated in the contract should be used.

Given the constraints of the real world, flexibility is essential for both parties. One also must on occasion concede that through the fault of no one, the situation is hopelessly out of hand (e.g., political forces dictated the decision). A means for termination of the contract then should be used.

Procedures for Termination of the Contract

When both parties agree that the contract should be terminated, they ought to refer to agreements contained in the contract concerning appropriate remuneration and close-out procedures. A brief report identifying the reasons for termination should be prepared and filed. If either party does not wish to terminate the contract or if a dispute exists concerning what would constitute just recompense or concerning some other factor, then it is appropriate to implement the adjudication process agreed upon in the contract.

There is one very natural point at which to consider termination of the contract, namely, at the end of the design phase (unless the design fee or separate contract approach was used). Other points of possible termination need to be built into the contract. For the products, the deadlines constitute points at which one can examine contract fulfillment. Determining whether the evaluation is following the agreed-upon procedures is somewhat more problematic. The use of a "milestone" approach has been used with some success. Within the contract one stipulates a specific point in time by which certain events are to have occurred. At each of these time points the client and contractor can jointly review progress to see whether things are on time and on target. For example, the contract for the evaluation of a science education program may call for the administration of a pretest to students, interviews with each participating teacher, and a cost comparison with four major curriculum competitors to have taken place by December 1. On or shortly after that date, the client and contractor confer to examine delays, overexpenditures, and the like, and the reasons for them. If the problems are serious enough, the possibility of renegotiation or termination might be considered.

Determining which breaches of the contract are serious enough to merit considering termination is dependent on the situation and the individuals. Certain "breaches" are so trivial that termination would be absurd. For example, assume that the last teacher interview was conducted on December 2 instead of November 30 because the evaluator caught the flu and had to reschedule. No one in their right mind would consider dissolution of the contract on that ground. On the other hand, if no one has seen or heard of the evaluator six months into a twelve- month evaluation contract, it is relatively simple to decide that breach of contract has occurred, and to terminate. Usually, however, the situation is not so clear cut. Judgment and intelligent application of experience is required.

Perhaps the best advice one can offer is that the communication of dissatisfaction must be direct and open and documented very carefully. If the contractor feels that work for which the client is responsible is not being performed adequately, and that this failure is adversely affecting the evaluation effort, that should be discussed between the parties. The results of that meeting should be noted in a memorandum or letter. If the client believes that the evaluator is failing to perform his responsibilities, again this situation should be discussed and documented. Almost any unilateral attempt to terminate the contract without some prior expression of dissatisfaction is foolhardy. It is an invitation to a debilitating and protracted dispute.

One great advantage of an agreed-upon adjudication procedure is the fact that one is reminded of what will be required to satisfy the information demands of the arbiter(s). In preparing that information, one is often able to track down the real source of the problem and amicably renegotiate or terminate the contract rather than enter a contentious fray.

Checklist for Use in Monitoring the Contract

The checklist in Figure 7 is proposed for use in assessing how well the evaluation is proceeding.

	Check One for Each Item	
	Yes	No
1. Have the procedures for monitoring the progress of the work been agreed upon, i.e., have milestone review points and product dealines been clearly set?		
2. If circumstances are different than those anticipated in the contracxt, has a renegotiation occurred?		
3. If renegotiation was not possible, has a mutually satisfactory agreement to terminate the contract been reached?		
4. If a dispute exists, have the two parties met to attempt a resolution? Have the results of that meeting been documented?		
5. If the dispute cannot be resolved among the parties to the contract, has the adjudication process been invoked?		
Summary Based on questions 1-5 above, is the conduct of the evaluation proceeding in a mutually satisfactory fashion? (If yes, proceed to completion of the evaluation; if no, modify or terminate contract as necessary.)		

Figure 7: Checklist for Monitoring Evaluation Contracts

EXHIBITS FOR CHAPTER 11

EXHIBIT 11.1: BASIC CONTRACT FOR AN EVALUATION DESIGN

This agreement entered into as of this 1st day of June, 1986 by and between the school district of Metropol, hereinafter referred to as the "district" and

Evaluator's Anonymous, Inc.
119 Bal Fontaine Road
Juneau, Alaska

hereinafter referred to as the "contractor."

Whereas, the school district of Metropol proposes to evaluate the Preschool Concept Development Program which is to be installed in several kindergarten classrooms as of September 7, 1986; and

Whereas, the school district desires to avail itself of the services of a contractor experienced and qualified in this field; and

Whereas, the contractor is willing to undertake this endeavor;

Therefore, the parties do mutually agree as follows:

1. Scope of Services

The contractor agrees to design an evaluation of the Preschool Concept Development Program which will provide answers to the following questions:

A. How is this program being implemented in the classroom in which it is used?

B. Are the children in classrooms in which this program is used mastering its objectives?

C. Do the children in classrooms using this program achieve a higher mean score on an appropriate examination than children in other kindergarten classrooms?

D. Do the teachers using this program view it as a valuable adjunct to their instructional effort?

In order to accomplish this evaluation, the contractor agrees to present to the Board of Education a proposed evaluation design no later than June 15, 1986. The evaluation design is to incorporate the following provisions:

A. No more than 6 of 12 available classrooms are to receive the program.

B. The selection of classrooms for participation must be sensitive to the multiple ethnicity of Metropol and still permit valid comparisons of participating and non-participating classrooms.

C. Any instruments to be created, adapted, or used in this evaluation are to be specified in the design. Moreover, the frequency of use and intended respondents are to be similarly specified.

D. The statistical analyses to be performed in connection with this evaluation are to be specified in the design.

E. Dates are to be specified for the submission of an interim and a final report.

The proposed evaluation design will be reviewed by a committee selected by the School Board of the district and comprised of:

1. One member of the Board of Education
2. The Superintendent of Schools
3. One elementary school principal
4. One kindergarten teacher
5. One parent of an incoming kindergarten student

The review is to take place on or before June 18, 1986. Based upon the review of the proposed design, the committee will make one of three decisions for and in behalf of the district: (1) to accept the design as is and issue a contract to the contractor to proceed with the evaluation in terms specified within the design; (2) to list required modifications in the design to serve as a basis for negotiation of the design with the contractor; or (3) to reject the design and terminate further involvement of the contractor in the evaluation. In the event the second decision is rendered, negotiations are to begin on June 20, 1986 at a meeting to be held in the school district office in Metropol. They are to conclude in an agreement to proceed with the implementation of a negotiated evaluation design specified by contract or to terminate negotiations no later than July 1, 1986.

2. Basis of Payment

Irrespective of the nature of the committee's decision resulting from review of the submitted design, the Board of Education agrees to pay the contractor a sum not to exceed $800.00 for the preparation and submission of the evaluation design proposal. The contractor shall submit to the school district an invoice for services performed and authorized reimbursable expenses. The contractor is authorized to charge 22 percent of all involved costs in and for indirect costs. Each invoice shall show for each employee of the contractor that worked on this project during the invoice period, the name and hours worked directly on the project. Also accompanying the invoice shall be evidence of reimbursable costs paid.

The contractor shall also provide a detailed budget for the proposed evaluation. The names of those individuals who will be primarily responsible for the evaluation shall be provided. The school district will provide keypunching services, computational equipment time on an IBM 360-50, and access to the Bio Med and SPSS statistical packages. Costs for these activities are not to be included in the proposed budget.

School District of Metropol   Evaluator's Anonymous, Inc.

By _____   By_____

Date _____   Date _____

EXHIBIT 11.2: COMPREHENSIVE CONTRACT FOR AN EVALUATION STUDY

This agreement entered into as of this 1st day of July, 1986 by and between the school district of Metropol, hereinafter referred to as the "district," and

Evaluator's Anonymous, Inc.
119 Bal Fontaine Road
Juneau, Alaska

hereinafter referred to as the "contractor."

Whereas, the design submitted by the contractor for the evaluation of the Preschool Concept Development Program (PCDP) has been modified by negotiation; and,

Whereas, the School Board of Metropol approves the recommendation of their negotiation committee to proceed with the evaluation; and,

Whereas, the contractor is willing to undertake this endeavor;

Therefore, the parties do mutually agree as follows:

1. Period of Contract

This contract shall be in force from 1 July, 1986 to 31 August, 1987 at which time the services agreed to are to have been provided and all products delivered as called for in this contract and in accord with the deadlines included herein.

2. Scope of Services

The contractor shall perform those services necessary to accomplish the evaluation of the Preschool Concept Development Program in accord with the agreed-upon design. Specifically, the contractor shall:

Select by use of procedures specified hereafter six kindergarten classrooms to receive the PCDP instructional material and three kindergarten classrooms to serve as comparison classrooms. The classrooms are to be chosen so that they differ with respect to the percent of the children who speak a native language in their home, as shown in Table 1.

TABLE 1
SAMPLING PLAN

Percent of the students who speak a native language	0 - 37%	31 - 65%	66 - 100%
PCDP Classrooms	2	2	2
Comparison Classrooms	1	1	1

During the school year each PCDP classroom is to be observed for one hour per week on the average by two members of the contractor's staff. One half of this observation time will be devoted to the use of the PCDP Implementation Observation Schedule. The remaining half will be non-structured. Monthly progress reports will be provided to each PCDP teacher on the extent to which he or she is in conformity with expected PCDP teaching practice.

On 30 March, 1987 the contractor will submit an interim report on any modification made in the PCDP Implementation Observation Schedule, as well as a report on its characteristics. Included in the latter report will be evidence concerning its objectivity as well as a correlational analysis of the relationship between teacher self-report data and the observation data.

A final report on data collected by use of the schedule will be included in the evaluation report due on 31 August, 1987.

During the months of September and May, each student in the nine participating classrooms will be administered the Saltonstall Developmental Analysis Test by qualified test administrators employed by the contractor. The test is to be individually administered.

The contractor will be responsible for all statistical analysis. The May test data are to be subjected to covariance analysis with the September scores entered as the first covariate. The PCDP classrooms will be contrasted with the comparison classrooms using the classroom means of the May scores adjusted for the pre-scores as the units of analysis. Based on indices of the degree of implementation of the expected teaching practice derived from the observational data, the PCDP classroom are to be contrasted on these same adjusted classroom means.

The contractor will also analyze the PCDP mastery test data provided by the school district for participating classrooms. Among the information to be presented will be the percent of students who have mastered the various PCDP objectives at the defined criterion levels. These data are also to be presented so as to permit comparison among classrooms by implementation indices.

The contractor will develop a teacher questionnaire form which will include a section permitting teachers to rate themselves in terms of their implementation of PCDP. The questionnaire is to be submitted to the school district for review by September 15, 1986 and revised after negotiations concerning changes. These questionnaires are to be administered during November, February and May. Collection of this questionnaire data will be the responsibility of the school district. The contractor will present frequency analyses of the questionnaire data in the final evaluation report. During the course of the evaluation, there will be three types of reports expected. Monthly progress reports to the participating teachers on their implementation of PCDP are to be provided in October, November, December, January, February, March and April. These reports are to be kept confidential, i.e., only the teacher in question is to receive a copy.

A technical report on the PCDP Implementation Observation Schedule is due in March. Ten copies of this report are to be provided to the school district office.

The first draft of the final evaluation report is due on 30 July, 1987. Ten copies are to be provided to the school district office. After review by a school district appointed committee discussed further in section three of this contract, and subsequent negotiations, a final report will be submitted on 31 August, 1987. Fifty copies are to be provided to the school district for distribution to the School Board officials, school district staff, parents and other interested parties.

The final report is to preserve the confidentiality of all teachers and students as stipulated in section four of this contract.

3. Cooperation of the School District

To facilitate the accomplishment of this evaluation, the school district commits itself to undertake and accomplish the following:

The school district will provide the contractor with a schedule of the planned classroom use of the PCDP materials within each participating classroom. This schedule will be updated on a weekly basis to insure adequate observational coverage.

The school district will insure that the contractor has access to the selected classrooms for observational purposes. To promote fidelity of the information obtained, the timing of the contractor's observational visits need not be pre-arranged with the teacher nor the school principal.

The school district will collect and provide to the contractor mastery test data for each student in the PCDP program. These tests, of which there are three, will be administered to the students during November, February and May. All mastery test data to be analyzed will be provided to the contractor by 15 June, 1986, keypunched on IBM compatable floppy disks in a mutually agreed-upon format.

The school district will keypunch the Saltonstall test data on IBM compatable floppy disks according to a mutually agreed-upon format. These disks will be provided to the contractor within 15 calendar days after the delivery of the information to be keypunched to the school district offices.

The school district will establish a review committee comprised of:

1. Dr. Mellisa Frank, the Superintendent of the Metropol School District.
2. Dr. Wilson Boyd, the Director of Elementary Instruction.
3. Ms. Julie Rath, the Principal of the Weathertown School.
4. Ms. Jean Richards, a representative chosen by the district's kindergarten teachers.
5. Dr. Roland Green, Professor of Educational Psychology, University of Alaska.

This committee will review the technical report, the teacher questionnaire and the first draft of the final report and return their comments and criticisms to the contractor, within 15 calendar days of receipt. The committee will also serve as the negotiating body for reaching agreement concerning necessary changes in these documents.

4. Additional Contract Provisions

A. Non-Discrimination

The contractor agrees that in performing this contract there shall be no discrimination against any worker, employee or applicant, or any member of the public, because of race, sex, creed, color or national origin, nor otherwise commit an unfair labor practice. The contractor further agrees that this clause will be incorporated in all contracts entered into with suppliers of materials or services, contractors and subcontractors and all labor organizations, furnishing skilled, unskilled and craft union skilled labor, or who may perform any such labor or services in connection with this contract.

B. Compliance With Laws

The contractor shall at all times observe and comply with all laws, ordinances and regulations of the federal, state, local and city government, which may in any manner affect the performance of the contract.

C. Insurance

The contractor will purchase and maintain during the life of this contract insurance coverage which will satisfactorily insure against claims and liabilities which could arise because of the execution of this contract.

D. Conflict of Interest

No member of the governing body of the City of Metropol or other unit of government and no other officer, employee, or agent of the City or other unit of government who exercises functions or responsibilities in connection with the carrying out of the Project to which this contract pertains, shall have any personal interest, direct or indirect, in this contract. The contractor covenants that he presently has no interest and shall not acquire any interest, direct or indirect, in the project to which this contract pertains which would conflict in any manner or degree with the performance of his services hereunder.   The contractor further covenants that in the performance of this contract no person having any such interest shall be employed.

E. Confidentiality

The contractor agrees to preserve the confidentiality of all subjects participating in this evaluation: no teacher, student or school will be identified or identifiable in the written or oral reports provided to the district or any other party. (The use of fictitious names is permitted in reports to illustrate individual uses if that is deemed a desirable reporting technique).

F. Prior Review

No written report of this evaluation will be released by the contractor to any party without the concurrence of the District Review Committee. The district similarly agrees to secure the approval of the contractor prior to the dissemination of evaluation findings.

G. Other Research Interests

The contractor is free to use the instruments developed for use in this project or the results derived therefrom in other pursuits as long as this use does not violate any other contractual provision.

The contractor is similarly permitted to administer the "Teaching Climate Index" to those participating teachers who volunteer to respond to collect data for use in ongoing research in the area. The administration of this instrument is not to occur during normal school hours.

H. Publication Rights

The contractor is free to publish a report of this evaluation in a professional journal or to present an account at a professional society meeting with the following restrictions:

1. The confidentiality of the district, as well as that of the individuals involved, is preserved.

2. The article or presentation is first submitted to the district for prior review (see section 4.F).

I. Negotiation/Arbitration

In the event of a dispute between the client and the contractor concerning any provision of this contract, that dispute will be submitted to a panel for arbitration. The panel will be comprised of:

1. Dr. Harrison Greeley, Professor of Education, the University of Alaska, Fairbanks.

2. Dr. James Evans, Senior Research Associate, The Northwest Regional Educational Laboratory, Portland, Oregon.

3. Dr. Michelle Williams, Associate Superintendent of Public Instruction, Alaska Department of Education.

The findings of this panel will be binding on both parties.

J. Termination of Contract

This agreement may be terminated by written mutual consent. In the event of termination the contractor shall be reimbursed for its costs incurred to the date of termination.

5. Milestone Dates

The dates of which products must be delivered and/or major activities must be concluded are shown below.

1 July 1986	• Contract Agreement
30 August 1986	• Classrooms (PCDP and comparison) selected
15 September 1986	• District provides client with classroom schedule for use of PCDP -- schedule to be updated by district on a weekly basis
	• Draft of PCDP Implementation Questionnaire delivered to district for review
	• Observation of PCDP classroom begins
30 September 1986	• Saltonstall Developmental Analysis Test (SDAT) administered to PCDP and comparison classrooms
	• Committee review of PCDP Implementation Questionnaire completed and delivered to contractor
15 October 1986	• Monthly Implementation Reports provided to PCDP teachers
	• Data from SDAT provided to district for keypunching
31 October 1986	• Keypunched SDAT data delivered to contractor
	• PCDP Implementation Questionnaire delivered to district
15 November 1986	• Monthly Implementation Reports provided to PCDP teachers

30 November 1986	• PCDP Implementation Questionnaire administered to teachers by district
	• PCDP Mastery Test 1 data collected by district
15 December 1986	• Monthly Implementation Reports provided to PCDP teachers
15 January 1987	• Monthly Implementation Reports provided to PCDP teachers
15 February 1987	• Monthly Implementation Reports provided to PCDP teachers
29 February 1987	• PCDP Implementation Questionnaire administered to teachers by district
	• PCDP Mastery Test 2 data collected by district
15 March 1987	• Monthly Implementation Reports provided to PCDP teachers
30 March 1987	• Draft of Interim Technical Report on the PCDP Implementation Observation Schedule delivered to district
15 April 1987	• Monthly Implementation Reports provided to PCDP teachers
	• Committee review of Interim Report delivered to contractor
15 May 1987	• Monthly Implementation Reports provided to PCDP teachers
	• Final version of Interim Report delivered to district
30 May 1987	• Saltonstall Developmental Analysis Test (SDAT) administered to PCDP and comparison classrooms

	• PCDP Implementation Questionnaire administered to teachers by district
	• PCDP Mastery Test 3 data collected by district
15 June 1987	• Data from SDAT provided to district for keypunching
	• Keypunched data provided by district for all administrations of PCDP Implementation Questionnaire and Mastery Tests
30 June 1987	• Keypunched SDAT data delivered to contractor
30 July 1987	• Draft of Final Report due
15 August 1987	• Committee review of Final Report delivered to contractor
31 August 1987	• Final Report due

6. Basis of Payment

The district agreed to pay the sum of $19,975.00 to the contractor for the conduct of this evaluation. Payment is to be made as follows:

1 July 1986	$7,975.00
1 October 1986	$3,000.00
1 February 1987	$3,000.00
1 May 1987	$3,000.00
Acceptance of Final Report on or about 30 August 1987	$3,000.00

The contractor assures the district that the indirect costs charged against this contract will not exceed 20.5% of the direct costs incurred.

In the event of contract termination, the contractor will be reimbursed for its costs to the date of termination.

School District of Metropol   Evaluator's Anonymous, Inc.

By _____   By _____

Date _____   Date _____

EXHIBIT 11.3: SIMPLIFIED AGREEMENT FOR AN EVALUATION STUDY

Evaluators Anonymous, Inc.
119 Bal Fontaine Road
Juneau, Alaska

Superintendent L. K. Williams
Metropol School District
Metropol, Alaska

Dear Superintendent Williams:

I am pleased to submit an agreement document for evaluating the Pre-school Concept Development Program now in operation in the Metropol School District. Enclosed are two copies of the contract for your signature. Please return one copy to me.

We are looking forward to working with you during the next several months. If I may provide further information, please do not hesitate to call upon me.

Sincerely,

Harriet Brand
President

HB/ph

AGREEMENT

This agreement is made and entered into by and between the School District of Metropol, Alaska, hereinafter called the district, and Evaluator's Anonymous, Inc., hereinafter called the contractor.

1.0   Purpose

The district and the contractor mutually agree to carry out activities that will result in the evaluation of the Pre-school Concept Development Program (PCDP).

2.0   The contractor will:

2.1   Devise a sampling strategy to permit comparison of classrooms in which PCDP is used and other similar classrooms.

2.2:   Devise an observational schedule for use in classrooms using PCDP in order to determine the extent to which the program is implemented as intended.

2.3   Observe each PCDP classroom on a one-hour-per-week basis and provide a monthly report to each participating teacher.

2.4   Administer the Saltonstall Developmental Analysis Test to classrooms using PCDP and comparison classrooms in September, 1986 and May, 1987.

2.5   Develop a questionnaire to elicit information about program use for teachers using PCDP.

2.6   Provide a technical report on the observation schedule in March, 1987.

2.7   Analyze all data, including that provided by the district.

2.8   Prepare a draft copy of the final report by 30 July, 1987.

2.9   Prepare a revised final report by 30 August, 1987.

3.0   The district will:

3.1   Provide the contractor with a schedule of classroom use of PCDP.

3.2   Collect questionnaire data from teachers using PCDP during November, 1986; February, 1987; and May, 1987.

3.3 Collect student data on PCDP mastery tests, according to the following schedule:

Mastery Test 1	November, 1986
Mastery Test 2	February, 1987
Mastery Test 3	May, 1987

3.4 Keypunch all data in a mutually agreed-upon format.

3.5 Provide free access to the district's computer system for data analysis.

3.6 Return all documents submitted for review within 15 days of receipt.

3.7 Provide a sum of $19,975.00 to the contractor for the conduct of this evaluation.

4.0 Conditions

4.1 The period of performance shall be from July, 1986 to 30 August, 1987.

4.2 This shall be a fixed price contract in the amount of $19,975.00 for the performance of work stipulated in paragraphs 2.1 through 2.9. Forty copies of the final report shall be delivered to the district without restriction as to its use. In addition, the contractor shall have unrestricted use of the contents of the products, either in the extant or an adapted form, for its continued use in the field of education, with or without reference to the district as determined by the district.

4.3 The payment schedule to the contractor will be as follows:

1 July, 1986	$7,975.00
1 October, 1986	$3,000.00
1 February, 1987	$3,000.00
1 May, 1987	$3,000.00
Acceptance of Final Report on or about 30 August, 1987	$3,000.00

4.4 This agreement may be terminated by written mutual consent. In the event of termination the contractor shall be reimbursed for its costs incurred to the date of termination.

School District of Metropol	Evaluator's Anonymous, Inc.
By _____	By _____
Date _____	Date _____

REFERENCES

1. Far West Laboratory (1980). Educational programs that work (7th Edition). San Francisco, CA: Author.

2. Moore, M. (1978). Discrimination or favoritism? Sex bias in book reviews. American Psychologist, 33, 936-938.

3. McReynolds, P. (1971). Reliability of ratings of research papers. American Psychologist, 26, 400-401.

4. Scarr, S., & Weber, B. L. R. (1978). The reliability of reviews for the American Psychologist. American Psychologist, 33, 935.

5. Scott, W. A. (1974). Interreferee agreement on some characteristics of manuscripts submitted to the Journal of Personality and Social Psychology. American Psychologist, 29, 698-702.

6. Cicchetti, D. V. (1980). Reliability of reviews for the American Psychologist: A biostatistical assessment of the data. American Psychologist, 35, 300-303.

7. Cole, S., Cole, J. R., & Simon, G. A. (1981). Chance and consensus in peer review. Science, 214, 881-886.

8. Gottfredson, S. D. (1978). Evaluating psychological research reports: Dimensions, reliability, and correlates of quality judgments. American Psychologist, 33, 920-934.

9. Hensler, D. R. (1976). Perceptions of the National Science Foundation peer review process: A report on a survey of NSF reviewers and applicants (Technical Report; NSF Publication No. 77-33). Washington, DC: National Science Foundation.

10. Justiz, M. L., & Moorman, H. N. (1985). New NIE peer review procedures. Educational Researcher, 14(1), 5-11.

11. Klahr, D. (1985). Insiders, outsiders, and efficiency in a national science foundation panel. American Psychologist, 40(2), 148-154.

12. Shulman, L. S. (1985). Peer review: The many sides of virtue. Educational Researcher, 14(1), 12-13.

13. Stake, R. E. (1970). Objectives, priorities, and other judgment data. Review of Educational Research, 40, 181-194+.

14. Stufflebeam, D. L. (Ed.) (1983). Evaluation models: Viewpoints on educational and human services evaluation. Boston, MA: Kluwer-Nijhoff.

15. Kells, H. R., & Robertson, M. P. (1980). Postsecondary accreditation: A current bibliography. North Central Association Quarterly, 54, 411-426.

16. Kirkwood, R. (1982). Accreditation. In H. E. Mitzel (Ed.), Encyclopedia of educational research (vol. 1, 5th ed.). New York: Macmillan.

17. Goodwin, W. L. (1971). Evaluation of the administration of the state Title III, ESEA program. Denver: Colorado Department of Education.

18. Worthen, B. R. (1974). Content specialization and educational evaluation: A necessary marriage? Paper presented at the annual meeting of the American Educational Research Association, Chicago.

19. Wasatch Institute for Research and Evaluation (1982). Evaluation of operation and effects of Title IV expenditures in Utah. Final Report, Salt Lake City, UT: Utah State Office of Education.

20. U. S. Department of Health, Education, and Welfare -- Office of Education (1971). State plan administrator's manual -- Title III ESEA. Washinton, D.C.: Author.

21. Colorado Department of Education (1971). Colorado state plan for the administration of Title III ESEA. Dever: Author.

22. Worthen, B. R. (1981). Journal entries of an eclectic evaluator. In R. S. Brandt, Applied strategies for curriculum evaluation. Alexandria, VA: Association for Supervision and Curriculum Development, p. 58-90.

23. Trohanis, P. L., Woodward, M. P., & Cox, J. O. (1982). Delivering technical assistance. In P. L. Trohanis (Ed.), TADS and technical assistance: Readings on system design, needs assessment, consultation, and evaluation. Chapel Hill, NC: Technical Assistance Development System.

24. Joint Committee on Standards of Educational Evaluation (1981). Standards for evaluations of educational programs, projects, and materials. New York, NY: McGraw Hill.

25. Evaluation Research Society Standards Committee (1982). Evaluation Research Society standards for program evaluation. In R. F. Conner, D. G. Altman, & C. Jackson (Eds.), Standards for evaluation practice. New Directions for Program Evaluation No. 15, San Francisco, CA: Jossey-Bass.

26. Worthen, B. R., & Sanders, J. R. (1987). Educational evaluation: Alternative approaches and practical guidelines. New York: Longman, Inc.

27. Brandt, R. S. (Ed.) (1981). Applied strategies for curriculum evaluation. Alexandria, VA: Association for Supervision and Curriculum Development.

28. Guba, E. G., & Lincoln, Y. S. (1981). Effective evaluation. San Francisco: Jossey-Bass.

29. Anderson, S. B., & Ball, S. B. (1978). The profession and practice of program evaluation. San Francisco: Jossey-Bass.

30. Wright, W. J., & Worthen, B. R. (1975). Standards and procedures for evaluation contracting. Portland, OR: Northwest Regional Educational Laboratory.

31. Brickell, H. M. (1978). The influence of external political factors on the role and methodology of evaluation. In T. D. Cook and others (Eds.), Evaluation studies review annual, vol. 3. Beverly Hills, CA: Sage.

32. Stufflebeam, D. L. (1974). A response to the Michigan Education Department's defense of their accountability system. (Occasional paper No. 1). Kalamazoo, MI: Western Michigan University, School of Education.

33. House, E. R. (1980). Evaluating with validity. Beverly Hills, CA: Sage.

34. Smith, N. L. (1981). Evaluation contracting checklist. Portland, OR: Northwest Regional Educational Laboratory, Research on Evaluation Program.

35. Illinois State Board of Education (1982). Handbook for evaluation of special education effectiveness. Springfield, IL: Author.

36. Stake, R. E. (1976). Evaluating educational programmes. Paris: Centre for Educational Research and Innovation, Organization for Ecomonic Cooperation and Development.

37. Stufflebeam, D. L. (1973). Excerpts from "Evaluation as enlightenment for decision making." In B. R. Worthen & J. R. Sanders (Eds.), Educational evaluation: Theory and practice. Belmont, CA: Wadwsorth.

38. Cronbach, L. J., & others (1980). Toward reform of program evaluation. San Francisco: Jossey-Bass.

SUBJECT AND AUTHOR INDEX